# T
# SECRETARIAL
# HANDBOOK
## FOR THE
# MODERN
# OFFICE

# THE SECRETARIAL HANDBOOK
## FOR THE MODERN OFFICE

### FRED N. GRAYSON

A PERIGEE BOOK

Perigee Books
are published by
The Putnam Publishing Group
200 Madison Avenue
New York, NY 10016

Published simultaneously in Canada by
General Publishing Co. Limited, Toronto

Line art by Howard Grossman

Library of Congress Cataloging-in-Publication Data

Grayson, Fred N.
The secretarial handbook for the modern office.

"A Nautilus Communications project."
1. Office practice—Automation.  2. Office practice.
I. Title.
HF5547.5.G696  1985    621.3′741    85-16889
ISBN 0-399-51138-5

Printed in the United States of America
1  2  3  4  5  6  7  8  9  10

# Acknowledgments

I would like to thank Alan Burton for his expertise and help in writing the section on Ergonomics.

# Contents

# Introduction

The office of tomorrow is already here. Admittedly, not everyone has endorsed the new technology that is available, but undoubtedly, within the next few years, there will be very few offices that have not purchased some of the equipment designed to make your job easier.

The technological office is a combination of people and equipment. One without the other is incomplete. Whether you are a secretary, office manager, executive, or even the president of the company, it is becoming more apparent every day that your life will be radically changed by this new technology. It is important, however, to remember that an automated office will not be successful unless all of the required components are coordinated and integrated.

First, you must be aware of office administration—who is doing what in your office. Many companies are forced to completely reorganize their staffs in order to accommodate automation. Everyone who uses automated equipment must be made aware of how this equipment works and how it affects the user. What new skills will be required? How will these technological advances improve or impede the user's function? What additional training will be necessary in order to cope with these changes? Are new people required and will others be forced to leave or change job functions? These are just some of the factors that come to mind when developing a plan for a technological office.

Second, you must decide what type of equipment is required. Experts in the field of office planning and development divide office automation into two separate areas: data processing/management information services (DP/MIS) and telecommunications. In this book, we will discuss these areas, as well as many of the peripheral items not covered by these main categories—postage machines, copiers, etc. Data processing/management information services involves computers and the various functions and equipment required for the processing of information in the office. Telecommunications concerns communication of information within and outside the office.

Formerly each of these areas represented separate, independent functions served by individuals with knowledge in only one area. But for the true automated environment, it is important to understand the function of both these technical areas in relation to the human needs within the company. Most of the problems that have occurred in attempting to automate offices resulted from underplaying the importance of integrating these various functions. After all, no matter how sophisticated or efficient a new computer may be, without the full cooperation of the individuals responsible for running it, it becomes a useless piece of furniture.

This book introduces the technological office to you and to those who work with you, in an effort to make your transition to automation relatively painless. We will cover the different aspects of office automation in several logical steps to help guide you through the maze of equipment and functions necessary for an efficient office.

In the first two chapters we will introduce equipment and hardware. We will discuss how computers can work for you. A much-used term in computerese is "user friendly," but it is a descriptive phrase. This section will be user and reader friendly. Its step-by-step approach is written in clear English, for if you've never turned on a computer, it is surely counterproductive to struggle through something written for the technologically minded.

Along with what computers can do, it's important to understand how they differ from word processors—"dedicated" machines, designed to perform essentially a single function rather than a multitude of operations. In addition, we will cover data processing, which is computer oriented and necessary for the efficient processing of information.

Another item found in the workplace is the typewriter. Although computers and word processors are used for typing, very few offices don't also have electric typewriters, and more companies are now using electronic typewriters. There are advantages to both, and we will discuss how they are used in today's office, along with computers.

Most of the concepts of telecommunications, mentioned earlier as one of the major areas of office automation, will be covered. Rather than confuse you by presenting all of the equipment available (which could fill several volumes) we will discuss what telecommunications involves, what *types* of equipment are available, and what the various types of services available are, to help you improve your communications capabilities.

Finally, these chapters will cover miscellaneous items, including copiers, calculators, and assorted types of mailroom equipment—those items that improve the quality of your business operations and are now almost completely taken for granted by everyone in business. It's hard to remember when offices didn't have copying machines. And pocket calculators that once cost hundreds of dollars and performed only the basic arithmetic functions can now be purchased for under ten dollars.

Once you have learned to equip your office, other problems must be considered. How do you train people to operate the equipment? Adapting an office to the requirements of the new technology is covered in the third chapter, which is about ergonomics, the study of (and proposed solutions to the problems of) the relationship between people and technology. We will discuss the types of furniture that may be required, how to adjust your current office space, and how to ensure the comfort and convenience of people in the work environment.

With increased automation, the approach to business procedures and systems will seem to change radically. However, these chores will only appear to be different. In essence, they are still the same, but can be accomplished with much more efficiency and speed. Chapter 4 will focus on the individual procedures, and how they are accomplished and enhanced by electronic means.

We will cover the traditional jobs, such as filing, correspondence, duplicating, and accounting, none of which will be performed in traditional ways. In addition, we will discuss electronic networks, which have changed the face of communications in business. Once you understand the functions of different hardware, it is simple to apply the appropriate equipment to these office tasks.

Most books designed for the secretary and others in the office environment include the basic rules of grammar, spelling, punctuation, etc. Of course, it is necessary to know them. However, in the office of the future, the application of many of these rules can be performed automatically. Often it's as simple as inserting a diskette into your computer, answering a question on the screen, pushing a key, and letting the machine find errors and make corrections. We will discuss some of the available programs that can help you improve your basic English skills and increase your effectiveness as a communicator.

In conjunction with the rules, you will now be inundated with a new vocabulary. The Glossary of Technological Terms included here will help you become familiar with the world of the automated office. It's designed to demystify technological terms, and assure you that you will not be overwhelmed by them. This section will also be valuable in improving your correspondence and can be kept on your desk alongside your keyboard (whether it is an electronic typewriter or a desktop computer).

Finally, no reference book designed for the office would be complete without a selection of reference charts and tables. These appendixes will provide you with essential facts and figures about weights and measures, and various signs and symbols, including proofreading marks—another reason to keep this handy book beside you.

It's possible that you have felt intimidated by the prospect of an automated office. Whether you are responsible for developing a plan and purchasing the equipment for your office or you just work in this type of environment, this book is for you. We have tried to make everything as clear as possible and to convey to you just how important this new technology will be for you and your company. Regardless of your level of technological knowledge, most of the concepts are not difficult to grasp. Nor is it difficult to operate equipment in order to improve your effectiveness. The true complexities of technology can best be left to those who design and build the equipment. It is not necessary for you to understand how everything works.

Approach the development of the modern technological office with an open mind. Thousands of people have faced the computer, for example, with apprehension derived from lack of knowledge. Ten minutes of typing with a word processing program or manipulating numbers with an electronic spreadsheet program is enough to convert even the most reluctant individual. We hope you will enjoy this book, and that it becomes a valuable reference guide for you and others in your office.

# 1
# Office Equipment

The selection of equipment available for the technological office can be overwhelming. We will give you a clear and illustrated description of what types of equipment there are that might be expected to appear in youroffice. Like most new experiences, your first encounter with some of these products may be intimidating. However, with a little bit of patience and open-mindedness, anyone can learn the hows and whys of most new technology.

## TYPEWRITERS

There can hardly be an office today that does not have a typewriter. We are all familiar with the standard office typewriter. Since the mid-'60s, most manual office typewriters have been replaced by electric ones. Anything the old manual machine could do, the electric machine can do faster and better.

Essentially, the electric typewriter replaced or automated some steps in the typing process. The electric keyboard responds instantly to the touch and helps a typist increase typing speed. A quick touch of a "return" key sends the carriage back to the beginning of the next line and no longer requires a hand stroke on the carriage return lever. Newer machines (such as the IBM Selectric) offer movable and replaceable typing elements that can be changed for different sizes and styles. In addition, when the return key is hit, the typing element, not the entire carriage, returns to the beginning of the line, further increasing the speed of the machine (as well as lowering the noise level of the office). However, since the development of the *electronic* typewriter in the mid-'70s, the nature of typing in the office has changed considerably.

The electronic typewriter has captured more than 50 percent of the office marketplace in the years since its development in 1978. These machines range in price from $200 for small battery-operated portables to as much as $4000 for machines that are similar to word processors.

The advantages of the electronic typewriters are numerous, but the basic principle of their design is to increase the user's efficiency. Such features as automatic carrier return, for example, speed up the typing process and eliminate much of the attention to the machine normally required by the typist. Other features include automatic keystrokes to provide centering, flush-right margins, automatic letter or line corrections, and even page formatting.

An important feature of most electronics is the memory, which can retain as much as several pages of a typed document. Thus, corrections can be easily made on any document in the memory and reprinted without the entire letter or memo having to be retyped. In addition, most electronic typewriters can be connected (interfaced) with personal computers and high-speed or high-quality printers. In order to further increase their efficiency, many of these machines can be interfaced with video screens (CRTs), data storage modules, and telecommunications equipment, upgrading the typewriter to a fully equipped office computer.

The electronic typewriter requires some education in its use but is comparatively simple to learn to operate. The bulk of material generated in a typical office is letters, memos, or other one-page documents, and the typewriter may still be one of the most efficient ways to produce those documents, the electronic typewriter the most efficient.

Because the electronic typewriter is designed to automate many common typing procedures, tasks are accomplished in much less time, which results in increased productivity. The costs of the typewriters are low, compared with those of computers, and the machines do not require special cables, rewiring, or extensive operator retraining. And even though these machines can be upgraded to reflect many of the features of personal computers, they are actually *faster* for direct typing on a variety of different size documents that require letterhead, forms, multisize envelopes, labels, etc. The printers that accompany personal computers are somewhat limited in the range of paper sizes they can use. Thus, electronic typewriters provide automation and sophistication at comparatively low cost—for both equipment and employee training.

## COMPUTERS

With its fast growth, high level of market acceptance, and successful office penetration, the microcomputer industry has taken the business world by storm. Within the industry is a profusion of different types of businesses, and new companies are opening their doors daily. These companies range from hardware manufacturers to software publishers, distribution operations, data base and communication networks, training services, and peripheral equipment and add-ons manufacturers.

Thousands of businesspeople are purchasing computer equipment and training their staffs to use it. Before we describe many of the benefits of the computer, it is important to make you aware of some of the problems companies face when installing new equipment.

First, there is the problem of training employees to use the machines. Many people are afraid of the new technology and resist the concept of the computer. Large corporations may have management information systems (MIS) departments, which are responsible for training and instituting

procedures But smaller companies do not have these departments, and training is often, at best, informal.

The second problem is the incompatibility of hardware.
Many computers cannot run programs (software) that are
written for other types of machines. In the last few years, the
IBM PC has become one of the standards in the industry,
and dozens of companies have been spawned to produce
computers that are "IBM compatible" in order to take advantage of the large number of programs available for the
IBM.

A third problem that confronts purchasers of computers is
the applicability of the machine's capabilities for the specific
business. Before you purchase a computer or a complete
office system, it's imperative that a complete study be made
of all of the information (data) that is produced by your
company in order to evaluate the ability of a system to manipulate that information. Will everyone who needs this information be able to access it as necessary—and understand
the workings of the hardware? Also, another question has
recently come to light—can this information be protected
from those who should not have access to it?

These problems and considerations require a good deal of
forethought before purchasing decisions are made. But since
hardware manufacturers and software publishers are, of
course, aware of these concerns, they are taking steps to
ensure greater security for purchasers. Despite these concerns, the advantages of using computers in the office environment cannot be touted highly enough. We will describe
some of the highlights of using computers in the office of
today.

Only ten years ago most companies could not afford computers. Computers were large and expensive, and along with
space and financial considerations, they were so technically
complex that most businesses were forced to hire full-time
programmers for them. These were the *mainframe computers* that most of us remember. However, now we have the
personal computer, so named because each person in a business can have one. Although today's computers may be

called *microcomputers* or *minicomputers,* they probably contain as much power as the large mainframes of yesterday. (The newer mainframes, which are considerably smaller than the older machines, are many times' more powerful than microcomputers.) Instead of staff programmers, now there are thousands of different packaged programs you can purchase off the shelf. Business programs cover a wide range of needs, including accounting and financial modeling, word processing, statistical analysis, data base management, and much more. The programs are comparatively easy to use, although they usually require some knowledge of computer operations.

The personal computer is a versatile tool, and it is really not that difficult to understand how it works internally and what its capabilities are. It may be used for many different projects and types of operations. (Shortly we will discuss word processors and differences between "dedicated" equipment and general-use equipment like the personal computer.) Before we examine the functions that a computer can perform, let's take a look at its components and how it works.

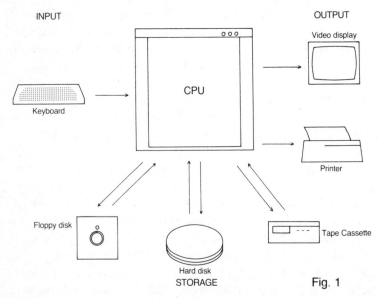

Fig. 1

*The Central Processing Unit (CPU):* This is the cabinet of the machine that contains the operating ability to drive the programs. It is a collection of tiny silicon chips, each containing thousands of electronic circuits. This is the actual brain of the computer.

Information is processed in "bits," which are the smallest pieces of information the computer can process. Eight bits are called a "byte," which is the equivalent of a single character, such as a letter or number. Most computers are 8-bit or 16-bit processors, which means that that computer can process information in bunches of 8 or 16 bits. The 16-bit computer is faster but also more expensive.

The CPU also houses the memory of the computer and stores programs, operating instructions, and other necessary information. This memory is measured by the number of characters it can store and is called "K," which is equal to 1024 characters. Thus, a computer with 128K can store 131,072 characters, or bytes, at one time. When the computer is operating, part of that memory is taken over by the program you are running, the computer's own operating program, and the information you are inputting.

*Storage:* Once a computer is turned off, anything that you have put into its memory (which is a temporary storage memory) is erased. Thus, you need a place to permanently store your documents. Although cassette tape is acceptable for home use, businesses normally need greater storage capability as well as greater accessing speed, so storage disks are used. There are two general types of disks: the floppy disk, which is 3½, 5¼, or 8 inches in diameter and is removable, and the hard disk, which is a fixed disk. The floppy disk is much less expensive than the hard disk, and because it is removable, may afford you greater security. A typical 5¼-inch disk can hold more than eighty pages of information; a double-density disk can hold many times that amount.

The hard disk is better for businesses that require greater storage capacity. It comes in a permanent storage container that hooks directly into the computer. It can store up to one hundred fifty times the amount of information on a floppy disk and accesses the information much faster.

*The Keyboard:* Similar to a typewriter's keyboard, the computer's keyboard is where information is entered into the memory. It contains all of the same keys and characters as a standard typewriter and may also include separate function keys—keys that can be individually programmed to repeat phrases, sentences, or other repetitive information to save you typing time. Some keyboards have a separate numerical pad and you can use those keys like a calculator for entering numbers.

*The Video Display Terminal (VDT):* The terminal, also known as a CRT (cathode-ray tube), is similar to a television video monitor. It is here your keyboard input is visible. You have the ability to see, on the screen, what you are typing as you type.

*The Printer:* There are two general types of printers: the daisy wheel and the dot matrix. The daisy wheel is often called a "letter quality" printer because it employs a typing element much like a print wheel on a typewriter. The characters are hammered onto the paper. Although the daisy wheel produces high-quality printing, it is also noisy.

The dot matrix printer forms characters by pressing wires against the paper in a matrix of tiny dots and produces what is often called "computer type." The more dots in the matrix, the higher the print quality. Although dot matrix printing is not yet acceptable for business correspondence, there are several advantages to the dot matrix machine over the daisy wheel. First, it is usually less expensive, costing from $300 to over $2000, while the daisy wheel may cost from $1000 to over $5000. The dot matrix printer also makes much less noise and is able to print graphics, which most daisy wheel printers can't do. This graphics ability also allows you to control the size and width of the type that can be produced.

In many businesses both printers are employed. The dot matrix printer is used to produce draft documents, and the daisy wheel is used for the final documents.

There is also a third, newer type of printer on the market—the nonimpact printer. Among these machines are printers that write with heat, jet sprays of ink, and lasers. A laser printer is similar to a copier in that images are transferred to a drum, only instead of using ordinary light beams as the copier does, the printer uses laser beams. The laser beam transfers images to a storage drum, which then prints them onto the paper. These printers are part of a new technology that may replace the typewriter-type printers, which require contact with the paper. A major advantage of nonimpact printing is the ability to print in a wide variety of type sizes and styles, as well as to print graphics. And in an office environment, another positive aspect of the nonimpact printer is that it prints much more quietly than machines that strike the paper.

The process of using the computer is very simple. Once it's turned on, you load a program into the CPU by inserting the floppy disk in the disk drive or choosing a program on a hard disk. Your screen lights up, and usually there is a menu from which to choose the operations you desire. Once your choice is made, you use the keyboard to input information which is translated into the appropriate code by the chips and is seen on the screen. When you have finished entering information, you print it out and/or store it on your floppy or hard disk. That's really all there is to it!

As mentioned previously, the computer can be used for everything from accounting and word processing to management training and intracorporate communications. Following is a list of some of the areas where computers can play a major role within businesses. In Chapter 4, "Office Procedures," we will cover these areas in detail.

Word processing
Data processing
Mailing list management
Accounting

Financial modeling and forecasting
Creating business graphics
Telecommunications
Electronic mail
Videotex and information network researching

There are additional uses for a computer in the business environment, which we'll cover in the chapter on telecommunications equipment. It is important, though, to understand the advantages of using computers—how they can help your office.

*Increased Efficiency:* The speed and versatility of the computer enables you to greatly reduce the time it takes to perform many routine office functions. Record keeping on the computer eliminates the need for doing things manually. In accounting, it is no longer necessary to maintain handwritten journals, ledgers, and inventory documents, or even to write checks or issue invoices manually.

*Decreased Costs:* There are two aspects to be considered in decreasing operating costs. The first is the savings of time and effort. Increased speed of operation is a proven cost-saver. The second is the ability of the computer to generate reports instantly to help you keep tighter control on budgets, monitor inventory, control cash flow, etc.

*Improved Quality:* Regardless of how well you or your staff may be trained, it is impossible to eliminate human error. However, by computerizing many of your routine functions, you can eliminate a large percentage of this error. In accounting, the continual accuracy of the computer prevents errors in complex calculations. Word processing programs offer the typist help in producing error-free documents, and the flexibility of revising material until it's 100 percent correct.

*Greater Productivity:* The combination of the attributes of computer use contribute to greater productivity in the office—as a direct result of increased speed and the additional flexibility of business-oriented computer programs.

*Better Customer Relations:* If you are in a business that demands clear lines of communication with your customers, the computer can help you improve your service and business relationships. The speed with which you can generate invoices, check and restock inventory, and customize correspondence is important to both you and your customers.

You can easily see the versatility of the personal computer in the business environment. There are dozens of different machines from which to choose, and it is most important when making a decision that you take into account several different factors, along with the obvious consideration of price. The most important aspect of a computer is the availability of applications programs. No matter how sleek, inexpensive, fast, or large the memory of your computer, without programs to run, it is nothing more than a dumb terminal. It's like having a beautiful car with no gasoline to drive it. Thus, the first step in making a purchasing decision is the creation of a *systems plan.*

1. What are the jobs for which you plan to use the computer? You should look at those areas of your operation in which you appear to be backlogged with paperwork, steeped in red tape, or merely slowed by functions that require long hours of detail work. Other jobs may be repetitive ones that easily lend themselves to automation. In most businesses, the first department to use computers is accounting.

2. What are the functions within each area that can be replaced by the computer? Essentially, this requires preparing job descriptions. It is a complex piece of planning, but it will help direct you toward the correct computer purchasing decision.

After the groundwork has been prepared, you can begin to evaluate software. You can purchase packaged software (existing programs), custom software (programs written for your specific needs), or modified software (packaged software adapted to your requirements). Since there are thousands of packaged programs available, you will probably get started with off-the-shelf programs, and eventually grow into more customized ones. Unless you are part of a very large organization, the expense of creating customized programs may be prohibitive.

Once you have determined that there are programs available that will suit most of your corporate needs and that they are easy to use and understand, you can then find the hardware. Most top-of-the-line programs are produced for a variety of different computers. Whether you use the IBM PC, Apple II, Tandy 2000, Kaypro, Eagle, Epson, or any other business computer, there are usually versions of the programs you need for that machine.

In addition to compatibility with the software, when choosing your hardware there are several important things you should look for:

*Memory Size:* Will there be enough memory to support the different programs you plan to use? Does the machine use floppy or hard disks? Can the computer be expanded to accommodate additional memory, more disks, or can it be connected to other computers?

*Price:* Is the price of the computer and peripheral equipment within your budget?

*Compatibility:* Are there other peripherals in your office that you want to run with this new system? Will you be able to upgrade your equipment at some later date without losing everything you've already developed? Very often when companies upgrade their computers, existing software and the data created on it are no longer able to run on the new machine.

*Service:* Will the manufacturer or supplier give you on-site service, as well as training in the use of the new equipment? Once you're computerized, it is very difficult to be without the use of the computer for any length of time. It's important that the service people come to you and be able to perform repairs right in your office.

As with any piece of machinery you purchase, you should be aware of warranties and reliability of the equipment (just like when you buy a car). It's also important to feel comfortable that the company from which you are buying this equipment will still be in business several years from now.

## WORD PROCESSORS

Despite the reputed versatility of the personal computer in the office, there are some machines that are only capable of performing one task. The predecessor to the personal computer was the dedicated word processor (WP).

Why, you might ask, would companies use a word processor, when they could have all of the capabilities of a computer? Probably the biggest reason is that the "dedicated" nature of the machine offers a wider range of applications for the specific function. This means that when you use a computer for word processing, you are limited by the program you use. Every word processing program is somewhat different, and because the computer must perform many different functions, unless it is powerful enough it probably cannot do everything a dedicated word processor can do. And remember, the more powerful the computer is, the more expensive it will be.

The word processor generally performs one function—processing words. Although many of the newer machines can do other things, such as calculating, that is not their primary function. One of the reasons that companies use these machines is that the dedicated WP is usually less expensive than a computer with comparable features. In an office that primarily processes paper, such as a law firm, the word processor is probably a better piece of equipment. The accounting department in this same office may use a computer to process and maintain the financial records of the firm, but it is more economical to have the one computer and WP terminals for every secretary.

Like the computer, the WP uses a central storage area, which is often a separate piece of equipment that contains hard-disk storage. Individual terminals are connected by cable to this storage area and can access information at will. Each terminal runs the same program, but sends and receives different information. In the chapter on office procedures we will cover in detail the various aspects of word processing.

## DATA PROCESSING

Data processing (DP) is used to describe most computer functions. The computer processes information of various sorts, which is called data. However, data processing is usually used in a more specific sense in an office environment. Separate from the word processing or accounting functions, DP is usually part of a separate division or operation within a company.

In 1812 Charles Babbage, an English mathematician, developed a calculator that was much more sophisticated than any that had preceded it. In fact, Blaise Pascal had developed the first mechanical adding machine in 1642. In 1822, Babbage demonstrated his machine to the public and received government financing to continue his work. He then conceived the idea for an analytical engine, to function beyond the capabilities of calculators then in existence, which would have the following features.

1. Input in the form of punched cards.
2. A memory for arithmetic values.
3. A unit to perform mathematical calculations.
4. A control unit that could execute (and modify) special instructions.
5. Automatic output of answers.

The development of the analytical engine bestowed upon Babbage the title Father of the Computer, since all of his ideas are currently contained in the modern computer.

In the 1890s Herman Hollerith invented a punched card machine in order to mechanize the processing of the U.S.

population census. But until the late 1930s, Babbage's machine was really the only computer around. Then the large electromechanical calculator–computer was developed with ENIAC (the Electronic Numerical Integrator and Calculator). This was the biggest and the fastest computer there was, and it made all others obsolete.

The punched card was the beginning of data processing. The cards were used to start and end programs as well as to carry the data to the machine. The format, though, was limited in the form and amount of data it could handle, as well as in speed, and thus the use of punched cards has decreased over the years. The once popular "Do not fold, spindle, or mutilate" cards were part of this technology. Essentially, a keypunch operator inputs information into a terminal, which converts that information into a series of coded holes on a card, each hole representing a number, letter, or some other symbol. When all of the data is input into the terminal and the cards prepared, it is then time to gather the output in a logical sequence or selection of specific items from that data. A card-sorting machine reads the punched holes and selects and sorts the cards into a specified order. The selected cards are then transferred to the output unit, which now reads the codes and prints out appropriate data.

As technology improved, punched cards began to disappear and were replaced by optical scanning cards and other more advanced methods of inputting and sorting data. The new formats involved the technology of microcircuits and new methods of storage, specifically magnetic tape or disk. Most systems today require intelligent (programmable) terminals from which data is entered, a processing unit that manipulates the data, a storage system to retain the data, and a printer to provide data output. In many companies, these systems can be found in a data processing center.

If your company has a DP center, you may be interested to understand how it functions. The first responsibility of the center is *data control*. It is here where the decisions are made as to how to process the information. The center controls the input and output of all data to be processed. It determines if the material is complete, if it is to be batched (combining similar types of operations), and it coordinates the entire process.

The second part of the DP operation is *data conversion.* All information that comes into the center must be corrected and converted in order for it to be processed, whether on a keypunch machine, key-to-tape, or key-to-disk.

Third, the DP center is responsible for *job control.* It determines the schedules and the assembly of all information. It is also required to maintain all of the equipment, upgrade programs, and handle any problems with hardware and software. Finally, it arranges for the collating, bursting (separating continuous form paper), and resorting of printed data. The DP center should also maintain a library of programs, data, and other documentation necessary for its operation.

You can see that the technological office requires some type of data processing. Obviously, most middle- and small-sized companies may have no need for a data processing department. But the operation is the same, regardless of whether or not you have a formal department. Every business processes information, and the only way to keep on top of information is by developing more efficient methods of ensuring the flow of that data through the company. Computers give you those methods. Later in this book, we will give you an overview of some of the available data base (or data management) programs that you can purchase for use on a personal/business computer.

## COPIERS

Until the development of the computer, one of the most important contributions to office equipment was the copier machine. Xerox Corporation was one of the first and biggest of the copier manufacturers, and today the word *Xerox* has become a part of the English language, much the same way

*Kleenex* or *Band-Aids* has. However, Xerox is no longer the only ball game in town.

Since the early 1950s, dozens of companies have entered the copier field, including Canon, Panasonic, Savin, Ricoh, Kodak, and IBM. Today, there are more than 250 different models of machines available. In fact, it is estimated that more than 90 percent of businesses use copiers. That means there are more than three million machines in use. There is an interesting irony here: despite all of the companies that are manufacturing this equipment, spewing out endless reams of paper, we are making a continual effort to develop "paperless offices" with the computer. And as copier equipment becomes more sophisticated, more paper is processed.

We looked at printers and typewriters earlier in this chapter. This equipment is generally called impact technology. Whether it is the striking of a hammer against a piece of metal or plastic type transferring the image through a ribbon onto paper or a dot matrix printer that hits needles to form the appropriate letter or number pattern, there is some type of contact. Copiers, on the other hand, use a different process.

When a document is placed on the copier, a strong light is shined on it, creating a pattern of electrical charges. These charges are imprinted on a rotating drum. The drum then turns through a tray of black powder (or, in some machines, red, green, or brown powder) that adheres to the charged imprint on the drum. The image created by the powder is then transferred to another piece of paper, creating the copy.

Within the copier industry, several new developments have helped to give you a wider selection of machines. First, most of the new machines use microprocessors, similar to those used in computers. These microprocessors make the copiers easy to use. Signal lights advise you when the machine is ready, when it needs a refill of toner, what type of paper you need, and even tell you when and where there is a malfunction. These conveniences make copiers easy to use and maintain. In addition, copiers can now reproduce in a variety of different sizes, at least as large as $11'' \times 17''$, valuable, for instance, in copying and reducing large pages of financial information.

Second, as technology improves, the cost of components comes down. Today you can purchase small desktop copiers for less than $1000. In addition, there is a full line of conveniences that can be added to your copier. These include items such as sorters, which sort copies of a multiple-page document into separate piles, saving you the trouble of manually separating the copies. There are automatic document feeders, which permit you to leave a large report in the machine and have each sheet automatically fed through, freeing you to do other chores. Large-volume paper bins enable you to load a large number of blank pages into the machine, so you do not have to continually refill it with paper—an especially valuable addition when making many copies. Some machines will also trim paper and staple reports together, all with the touch of a button.

In many of the newer machines, you no longer have to worry about dirty hands when adding toner. The toner is contained in disposable cartridges, and you merely pop them in and out as needed. This gives you the added advantage of being able to add color cartridges in some machines. There are also full color machines that will reproduce any color document in tones close to the original.

Most offices use copiers for a variety of different tasks. Financial departments use them to copy invoices, checks, deposit slips, and budget and cash projects, using the reduction features to make the pages more manageable. Legal departments copy contracts and other documents. The promotion department may use the copier to make copies that look like the original by loading letterhead paper into the paper bin and copying the document directly onto the company stationery. Other departments may use the machine to eliminate messy carbons, duplicate memos for multiple distribution, prepare reports, and create business forms and graphs. It's hard to remember what offices did before the copier.

The overall advantage of the new technology in copiers has been their reduction in size. Machines with the same features today require much less space than they did ten years ago. Furthermore, these advances result in lower prices; machines cost about half of what they cost only a few years ago.

Until most offices are completely electronic, and information is stored and transmitted to everyone by computers, the copier will continue to be one of the most important pieces of office equipment available, despite the amount of paper it generates.

## POSTAL MACHINES

In today's busy office, the transmission of correspondence is as vital to the life of the company's operation as the creation. One method of transmission, which we discuss later, is electronic mail—the sending of information via computer. The other method is the traditional, the U.S. Postal Service. Some sophisticated machines have been developed to make your work easier and the processing and delivery of mail more efficient.

As a business grows, so does the amount of paperwork generated within the office. An efficient mailing system helps process some of this paper. Part of this system is a mailing/addressing machine. With some form of printing, your multiple mailings can be processed quickly. Where once you had to hand-write all of your labels, or type them when you were planning a large mailing, these mailing machines do the work for you. The name, address, and other pertinent information is typed on an addressing or embossing machine. As you type, you're able to spot errors, and make corrections to make sure your work is accurate. The final product is a metal or plastic plate, which is the mailing address card.

That card is then run through an addressing/mailing machine. The cards are loaded into the machine in batches, and then the envelopes or other documents are run through. As in the machines used to imprint credit card charges, the envelope comes in contact with the address plate, and, using a roller and a ribbon, an impression of the address is made. On more sophisticated machines, you can program different information to be imprinted from the cards, such as printing in zip code order, sorting names, or selecting by titles.

The next stage in the process is getting the material— letters or packages—ready for mailing. In a total mailing system, all of the components of the operation are combined in one large machine. This is recommended for businesses with large amounts of mail being processed. It combines a document loader, paper tape dispenser for packages, and an electronic scale that guarantees totally accurate weight. (Unlike the spring scale, which is not always accurate, the electronic machine is able to weigh even fractions of an ounce, permitting you to always be assured of the lowest postage rates.) When postage rates change, it's a matter of switching to a new chip, provided by the manufacturer, and the scale is ready to calculate weight and postage at the new rates. Envelopes, stacked into a document loader, are automatically fed through the scale, automatically weighed, and postage affixed. The mail then travels to the end of a carrier, ready for tying and bagging.

Not long ago, one took the postage meter part of the mailing machine to the post office. Payment was made for the amount of postage you needed, and the postmaster would open the machine and reset it to the new amount. Whenever the postage was low, you had to take the meter in. Today's electronic machines can be reloaded by the operator, and all it takes is a telephone call to the company from which you lease your meter. You are given a series of codes, which are entered into the meter via a number-pad, and the meter automatically advances to the new dollar amount. Your meter is refilled in minutes.

There is another attachment for these sophisticated machines—document printers. All packages and envelopes that are processed are recorded by the machine, and an electronic accounting system provides you with a digital and printed copy of the amount you have spent. In large companies with individual departmental budgets, you will be able to track and record mailings and expenses by department.

Of course, all of the parts that make up a total mailing system are available as individual components so you can select only what you need for your operation. One of the major advantages of using the electronic technology to process your mail is additional efficiency. The machines not only measure the appropriate weights and dollar amounts, but also select the most economical mailing class, print paper tapes for parcels, and can handle a large variety of correspondence. Furthermore, metered mail often gets processed faster by the post office.

Security is also a factor to be considered when sending mail. Using a meter eliminates the use of stamps, which often disappear or are destroyed or stick together. In addition, mail that is imprinted on a meter creates a better business image than mail with stamps. Finally, the use of postage meters, like the use of most automated equipment, usually results in greater productivity.

On the receiving end of the mail, there are also electronic letter openers available. Large batches of mail are stacked into the machine and a belt moves it through the cutting blades. The width of the cut is automatically adjusted to allow for different sizes of envelopes. The opened mail is then stacked for easy handling.

## CALCULATORS

Calculators, like copiers, have become a permanent fixture in the office. It's hard to believe they've been around only for about fifteen years. There is hardly a business today that doesn't use a calculator.

Although there is a wide range of different machines on the market, your real consideration should be the functions that the calculator performs in relation to your needs. The differences in basic products tend to be design differences, which may be important to you. For example, the size of the keys may make a difference. If you have large fingers, it will be very difficult for you to use a small, portable machine with tiny keys. If you perform bookkeeping operations, you may want a large, stable machine to sit on your desk; the portable ones usually slide around.

The most common form of office calculator combines a digital display panel and a printout. You can choose to use the paper printout option only when you need a record. Some of the other features that calculators have, besides the four basic mathematical functions, are:

> Fixed or floating decimals
> Programmed keys for specialized functions
> Multifunction memory keys
> Item counters (to tally the number of entries)
> Date key
> Sub-and grand total keys
> Battery as well as AC operation
> Programmable memory and other specific functions
> Special keys to perform markup, percent of increase of sales, square root, number recall, and negative-number calculation

Calculators for the office that once cost several hundred dollars, now cost less than $100. Hand-held calculators that now sell for under $10, once cost $300. The silicon chip, the same one that makes the personal computer possible, is responsible for the increased capabilities of calculators at reasonable prices. You almost can't afford not to have an electronic calculator—unless you're more comfortable with an abacus.

# 2
# Telecommunications Equipment

If the computer can be considered the key to communication with paper, the telephone, and related telecommunications equipment, is the key to communication with voice and magnetically encoded data.

Once upon a time it was very simple to call your local telephone company and ask for a new telephone number, and the company would send installers to wire your telephone line and install the units you wanted. Since 1874, when it was invented, the telephone has gone from a primitive instrument to a necessity for global communication. When push-button telephones appeared, we knew that it wouldn't be long before that new world would open up to all of us. The giveaway to the telephone's future use was the addition of two extra keys on the push-button phones—" * " and "#." But before we even began to discover what these keys were to be used for, the American Telephone and Telegraph Company (AT&T) underwent major reorganization and suddenly we were in the era of telecommunications. The ability to talk to Paris from San Francisco, once considered a major achievement, was now dwarfed by the ability we had to transmit information by voice or computer to one hundred different locations throughout the world at the same time.

Again, the fabulous microchip is responsible for this new industry. Business communications is now one of the major elements of corporate life, and there is obviously much more involved than making and waiting for telephone calls. Today, there are telex and TWX, private branch exchanges (PBXs), computer networks, electronic networks, videotex, electronic postal service, executive workstations, and facsimile machines. In this chapter we will cover the equipment necessary for telecommunications.

## PRIVATE BRANCH EXCHANGES

In the 1968 *Carterphone* decision it was ruled that other telephone companies could compete with AT&T. Dozens of new companies sprang up, producing telephones and systems. This business is one of the fastest growing and changing technologies.

The development of the Private Branch Exchange (PBX) has helped the growth of telephone systems. Basically, the PBX is a computerized switch that performs electronically what was once done manually by the operator at the switchboard. Instead of having to plug in plugs or switch switches, the PBX makes connections automatically, and carries your company's telephone lines to the outside world.

## TELEPHONES AND EXECUTIVE WORKSTATIONS

Today's telephones can transmit data as well as voice, so that executive workstations, which combine telephone and computer operations, can be hooked together. Rather than discuss specific instruments, we will cover some of the highlights of these systems, as well as what to look for when making purchasing decisions.

In most telephone systems there are certain standard as well as optional capabilities available to you. For example, a telephone system can feature:

1. Light Emitting Diode (LED) indicators for the number of the telephone being used. You can quickly

spot which phone line is in use and which is on hold.

2. Programmable numbers, so you can dial numbers automatically from the built-in memory, a timesaver when your job includes a lot of telephoning.
3. Multiline access, so you can have several telephone lines for incoming and outgoing calls.
4. Speakerphone options, so you don't have to lift the receiver to talk or listen.
5. Liquid crystal display lines, which can give you a multitude of information, including the number you've dialed, the length of your call, and account code numbers.
6. The ability to communicate with other executive workstations automatically.
7. Automatic redialing if you've reached a busy signal.
8. Privacy buttons to assure no one else can pick up on your line.
9. Intercom capabilities.
10. Conference call capability.
11. Background music when a call is put on hold.
12. Do-not-disturb buttons that permit you to shut off the phone when you're busy.
13. Paging, which enables you to locate anyone temporarily away from his or her desk.
14. Mute key, so you can talk to someone else in your office without being heard by the party on the phone.
15. Call forwarding to other numbers.

You may not need any of these additional features in your company, especially if it's a small business, but be aware that these features are available. Studies have shown that one of the biggest problems with installing telephones and related systems is the inability to allow for growth and not installing enough wiring. If you want to add more wiring later on, it often means tearing up walls, floors, or ceilings, or running unsightly wiring around baseboards and from ceilings if you don't want to open up hidden areas.

Executive workstations are somewhat more sophisticated

than telephone systems; they usually range from simple VDT screens that can receive information (dumb terminals) to more sophisticated built-in computers and telephones. For those people who want both a telephone system with all the additional features and a stand-alone data processing device, the complete workstation fits the need. This combination of technology can do everything from standard telephone calls to providing a computer for data transmission to other computers. By hooking the workstation into a personal computer, you can utilize many of the computer's programs and operations. Thus you can communicate with the mainframe computer that may be the brain of your company, as well as talk to other employees directly over the VDT.

These integrated units provide an enormous amount of flexibility in a busy office. Within the memory of the data terminal you can store thousands of addresses and telephone numbers. The touch of a button calls a name to the screen and another button automatically dials the number for you. Or another button will send a message you put in to one or two people, or everyone on your mailing list. While you are talking on the telephone, you can push another button and access a public information data base or a memo you sent three months ago to the individual you have on the phone. No more jumping up to search through a file drawer. You can also send electronic mail to other computer users who are on your network of workstations or who subscribe to any of the electronic message services. We'll discuss those users in Chapter 4.

## MODEMS

The purpose of the modem is to permit the computer to talk to the outside world and to other computers. Of course, computers can be hooked together, either directly or through networks. But in order to talk to other computers in other areas or to communicate with information data bases, you need a method of translating the magnetic information in the computer through the telephone lines to the receiving computer.

Without getting too technical, we will explain briefly how these transmissions work. Computers are designed to transmit digital information, and the telephone lines carry sound. Digital information is transmitted in bits, which are voltage levels. These voltage levels are at two stages. The first is an "off" state, or level 0; the second is the "on" state, or level 1. Bits can only be one or the other—on or off. But sound is made up of curves that rise and fall at a variety of levels. The sound rolls from the top to the bottom of a continuing curve. We are then faced with the problem of translating the computer's on and off states into the curves of the signal that can be carried over the telephone wires, and then back again, into the on and off states. This is the purpose of the modem.

A modem MOdulates and DEModulates the digital signals coming from your computer. It actually converts the computer's on and off bits into sound, and then transmits the sound over the telephone lines. That's modulation. When a signal is transmitted to you—or your modulated signal is sent to a receiving computer—the modem now has to demodulate the sound waves. These sound waves are reconverted into digital pulses, which are sent to the computer.

Modems are capable of either sending or receiving data, but not all machines can do both. The ability to both transmit and receive at the same time is called "full duplex." A "half duplex" capability means that you must stop each time you transmit, wait for the other person to send to you, and then begin transmitting again. It's much the same as communicating with walkie-talkies, where one person speaks, then says, "Over," and the other person then presses the speak button to send a message, then says, "Over," and releases the button to permit the first person to speak again. With a full duplex capability, the only requirement is that you must decide, before transmitting information, which machine will receive and which will send. However, regardless of how the modems are set, they can both originate and answer in the same transmission session. When they are set for full duplex, they can be used like telephones. Although it's polite for each person to wait for the other to finish speaking, you can both speak at the same time. This mode is also much faster than half duplex transmission.

When you decide to purchase modems for your computers, a variety of considerations should be taken into account. First, the type of connection your modems will use will be either a direct telephone line connection or an acoustic coupler. The difference is in the way the connections to the telephone lines are made. A direct connect modem plugs directly into a modular telephone jack. The advantage of the direct connection is the elimination of interference and outside noise intruding upon the transmitted signals.

The acoustic coupler uses a pair of rubber cups that fit around the speaker and earpiece of the handset of the telephone. The acoustic cups are more prone to interference. The advantage of acoustic cups is more apparent when you are using a portable computer. If you are in a hotel room or a telephone booth, it is unlikely that you have access to a jack for a direct connect modem. But wherever you are, you can always hook acoustic cups to the handset of a telephone and transmit or receive information.

Another consideration is the speed of transmission. This speed is measured in baud and is called the "baud rate," indicating the number of bits transmitted per second. The two most popular standards are 300 baud and 1200 baud. Thus 300 baud means 300 bits per second are being sent. Where normally there are 8 bits that make up one character, for technical reasons each character *transmitted* is made up of 10 bits per character. Thus, 300 bits per second, divided by 10 bits per character, means that 30 characters per second are being transmitted at 300 baud. At a 1200-baud rate, 120 characters per second are sent. Some countries are beginning to adopt a 2400-baud rate, but it will probably be some time before there will be enough modems that use that speed to make it a standard in this country.

Some modems are set at a fixed baud rate, and others can

handle a range of speeds. When speed of transmission is important, the 1200-baud rate modem is preferable. If you are communicating with an information network, you will be charged at a proportionately greater rate for the faster transmission speed. However, if you are communicating with other computers and you have a large amount of information to transmit, speed becomes important.

Another consideration when choosing baud rates is that over the next five to ten years, telephone rates will undoubtedly rise. The faster modems will save you money in the long run. Although they're considerably more expensive than the slower modems, you can probably justify the expense with the telephone time savings.

An automatic modem gives you an additional capability. When it is combined with the appropriate software, you can answer and transmit while leaving your computer unattended. You can set your machine on the East Coast to call someone on the West Coast after the late-night drop in telephone rates takes effect. Your computer automatically calls the other computer, which can be programmed to answer the telephone, receive the information, and hang up the phone.

In Chapter 4, we discuss in detail accessing data banks and information networks. Since there is a much higher rate for use during prime time, which is normally traditional work hours, it would be of great benefit to be able to do your research on an information network after the rates have dropped. With an automatic modem and proper software and programming, the computer can dial the network, log on to the appropriate segment, and locate the required information, all without you being there. When you come to work the next morning the information is waiting for you, accessed at the lower evening rates.

There are also two physical types of modems: internal and external. The internal modem is actually a "card" that fits into one of the slots (ports) in your computer. It is somewhat less expensive than the external modem, but it also takes up space in the computer. Computers have a limited number of ports, which are used to add memory, color capability, graphics, etc. If you use the internal modem, you use up some of that space.

The external modem is a stand-alone unit to which the computer connects by cable, and it in turn connects to the telephone jack or acoustic cups. The modem can usually be used with a variety of computers, and may very well outlast your computer. If you upgrade your computer, you can still hold on to an external modem, whereas if you have an internal modem and change equipment, your modem may not work with the new system.

Since communication has become such a vital part of our business world, it is almost a waste of a large part of the capabilities of your computer if you do not use it for telecommunication. The modem, whether internal or external, regardless of baud rate, is your link to the electronic world outside your office.

## FACSIMILE MACHINES

The facsimile machine provides a method of sending exact copies of documents electronically from one location to another. Although the computer can send letters via electronic mail at a speed that may rival that of the facsimile machine, the "fax" unit can transmit a document, letterhead, picture, or photograph. The facsimile machine uses the telephone lines to send material to another facsimile. The document is simply inserted into the machine and the order given for the material to be transmitted.

Some machines can be left unattended for overnight use, and can transmit one hundred or more documents automatically. Load the machine with all of the documents you wish to send, push a button or two, and the machine transmits the material to a machine waiting at the receiving end. In addition, a buzzer or bell can notify you when a message is coming through so you can always be aware that a document is being transmitted. Many of the machines work on both "send" and "receive" modes; once material is transmitted, the fax unit senses if something is being sent to it and switches to receive.

## PAGERS AND CELLULAR TELEPHONES

As technology improves, the microchip becomes more powerful, and communications satellites increase in number and decrease in expense, more communications systems will develop. Two systems that are becoming increasingly important are message pagers and mobile telephones.

New paging networks are being developed on both the local and the national level. A greater number of frequencies are now available, permitting more paging networks. Recent studies show that more than 20 million paging units may be in use by 1990. This translates into a multibillion-dollar industry.

Among the most impressive new advances in pagers are units that beep to notify you that there is a message waiting. The pager then spells out the message that has been sent. Imagine the convenience of not having to run to a telephone each time there's a call for you or an appointment to remember. These messages can be sent directly from your office or transmitted through a central message center.

In addition to pagers, which give you greater mobility, there are also mobile telephones. Not too long ago, using a mobile telephone was more of an inconvenience than a time-saver. Frequencies were limited, as were the systems, and there was often a long wait to get through on free lines. Today, with the development of the cellular mobile services, telephoning from remote areas is considerably faster. The system is called "cellular" because each city area is divided into smaller individual territories—cells. Each of these cells has its own low-power radio station connected to a telephone switching system. This cuts down on waiting and transmission time by permitting multiple use of the same radio frequencies, and makes the mobile telephone truly meaningful.

Prior to this cellular system, radiotelephony was limited to forty-four channels in a service area, and service areas were often the size of an entire city, so circuits were always busy. Now, as a driver leaves one cell, the call is transferred to an adjoining cell, without loss of transmission or telephone signal. Although this part of the telecommunications market is growing slowly, the day will come when many of us will save time by using radio telephones on the way to and from the office and to appointments.

# 3
# The Office Environment

This chapter focuses on people—the people who must work at the machines others have designed and built, the people who must translate their energies and lives and efficiencies into tangible and intangible products that create profit and loss statements for the businesses they work for or own. You are the ones who use this equipment and in whose hands the success or failure of the companies rests. Many corporations today realize that you can embrace automation and make it work, or you can reject it, which drags the whole system along at a pace that is hardly compatible with today's technology. Yet it is the rare company that considers the needs and expectations of its workers when designing and constructing a new or remodeled automated office. Even more rare is reliance on employees to aid in the design and development of such an office. When you are changing your manual or semiautomated office to a more sophisticated environment, problems are often overlooked. It is apparently easier to start from scratch.

One of the most critical factors in the process of automating the modern office is how people adapt to the new technology—the machines. The relationship between people and machines has been described frequently and variously by contemporary psychologists, designers, architects, engineers, authors, and more recently by legislators. As a people–machine interface, this relationship is thought to hinge on how well the machines are designed to accommodate their users. Some people call this discipline the science of ergonomics. Others refer to it as the art of socio-technical design. The pragmatist considers the root to be in human engineering. Each of these concerns is valid, and all taken together may approach what is considered the total office environment.

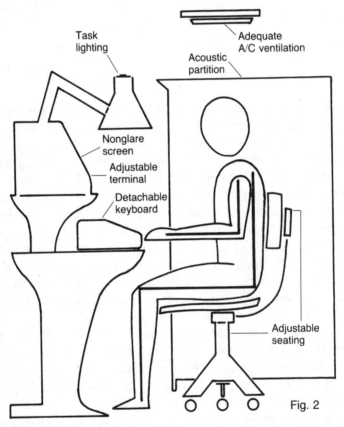

Task lighting

Adequate A/C ventilation

Acoustic partition

Nonglare screen

Adjustable terminal

Detachable keyboard

Adjustable seating

Fig. 2

In this chapter we are also concerned with managers. We very often look only at the workers and how the new technology will affect them, forgetting the degree of impact the changes will have on the managers who must implement them. A manager may have to convert an existing office from traditional to modern, and will be faced with the specific problems that entails. The more fortunate manager may be able to start from scratch and build an entirely new automated office without the pain and anguish of a conversion project. Other managers must plan for the future, because inevitably their offices must join those that have come to rely upon technology and its promises.

The manager must realize that the accuracy and productivity of the video display terminal (VDT) operators are strongly influenced by the comfort and convenience of their work environment. If the ergonomic considerations are disregarded, the manager can also be penalized for losses in accuracy and productivity. We will discuss these issues later on and offer solutions to the problems and answers to the questions.

## ERGONOMICS

Ergonomics is the science of adapting working conditions to suit the worker. Anything that affects the worker is considered an ergonomic concern. Psychology, physiology, anatomy, anthropometry, law, audiology, optics, engineering, and other sciences, disciplines, and studies are involved in ergonomic design. The list of concerns would include elements of the workstation (what we used to call a desk), lighting, acoustics, stress, and the general working environment. A major element in all of this is the VDT. The real and perceived problems caused by the improper design or construction of the workstation and VDT and the interaction with the operator have resulted in tremendous emotional upheaval. Legislation has been proposed to protect the worker in companies with automated functions. Many of the earliest attempts to automate offices did little more than add a computer terminal to an individual's desk, resulting in discomfort, fatigue, and stress due to inadequate or improper design and use of the equipment.

In the past, the large, modern office often had one large room used for data processing. Dozens, perhaps hundreds, of workers sat at their desks typing at their computer terminals. The ceiling was often high, bright light came with fluorescent light fixtures, and one side of the room may have been illuminated by sunlight streaming through the windows. Desks were crowded side by side, and there was virtually no privacy for employees. In addition, noise bounced off the walls and ceilings, and the room was a cacophony.

In smaller offices there were fewer terminals and people. But these environments were just as uncomfortable. The chairs were too low and typists had to put cushions on them to avoid slouching. Desk lamps were usually in the wrong position and cast shadows on the copy and screen. The printer was often beside the worker, and when it was running, the vibrations could be felt throughout the room.

Has this changed? As companies become more adjusted to automation and more sophisticated in dealing with the workers, these "electronic sweatshops" have begun to disappear. Now each employee has a personal working space that can be decorated or arranged to suit individual comforts. The lighting is no longer bright and glaring, but soft and unstressful. Dividers for each area are acoustically treated, and noise is at a much more manageable level.

## CONVERTING THE OLD OFFICE

Once a company decides it is going to automate its business functions, it is a comparatively simple process. Either the corporation is large enough and has enough data processing staff to manage the conversion with in-house people or a professional firm is brought in to handle all the details. In both cases, such matters as room design, decor, workstations, lighting, VDT design, ancillary equipment, and employee hiring and training are all taken care of in one professional swoop. Small companies may assign part of the work to outsiders and develop other parts of the program in-house.

This is not to say that converting your company to a modern, technological showplace is trouble free, but much of the information in this chapter will help you avoid common mistakes in the process. Some of the worst mistakes have been committed by small companies changing from the old to the new. Usually, the biggest mistake has been underestimating the scope of the project. The smaller the company, the less money there is available to correct errors. Another difficulty is that many managers have the mistaken view that a computer is nothing more than a typewriter with a television screen and should be treated as such. Many companies bring in the VDTs, move out the typewriters, and after some training continue business as usual. This goes on until the office is rife with problems, both in personnel and in productivity.

It is important for you, or your manager, to plot a course of action when bringing in computers and other automated devices. This includes bringing together the people who are going to be affected by the changes. The goal, obviously, is a smooth transition from the traditional office to the modern one. In a large corporation it is impossible to bring everyone into the direct discussion, but department supervisors should poll their employees to find out what they need, while advising them what to look for in the future. Some of the areas to be considered are:

Changes in supervision
Wage and classification changes
Project budgets
Safety concerns
Training and retraining of employees
Interruptions of current operations
Internal and external construction
Plumbing and electrical changes
Relocation of departments
Telephone access and dedicated lines

Like the problems and delays encountered when re-decorating one's house, the continual inconveniences caused by changing the office environment can often bring work to a standstill. But the results of this turmoil will be—we hope—greater efficiency and production, as well as higher profits.

## PLANNING FOR THE FUTURE

What about those companies that are still pursuing business the traditional way and are not yet convinced that automation is necessary? Can any company, regardless of its professional thrust or product or service, remain traditional and still be competitive? It's possible, but not likely. It is not unlike the introduction of electricity or automobiles: the first computers were thought of as fads.

The best way for you or others in your company to prepare for the future is to learn everything you can about what technology is here or will be coming. There are dozens of magazines for businesses, covering both design and computers. Professional groups have been formed throughout the country to discuss and explore options in automation. And it is a rare businessperson today who does not receive dozens of brochures advertising training programs in every phase of computer use and operations. In addition, there are computer shows in most major cities, which afford you an opportunity to see what's available for your needs. At a computer show you can touch and feel and see the equipment in operation. Vendors will normally work with you to help develop a complete plan—only, of course, if you purchase their equipment.

It is also important when planning for the future to talk to people who have already implemented technological changes in their offices and to those who will be using the equipment. Continually ask "What would happen if. . . ?" These "what if" questions will help you think through many potential problems. One of the big problems that you or others in your company may face is fear of the unknown.

This book will help you allay some of that fear about technology.

## ACCURACY AND PRODUCTIVITY

One of the keys to improved productivity lies in ergonomics. If the interfacing of people with machines is done in a proper fashion, there is no doubt that improvements will be forthcoming. By the same token, if ergonomic considerations are ignored, there will be a predictable degradation of productivity.

The issue of accuracy is a much easier one to deal with. With a typewriter, one can type just about anything and the machine is too dumb to know whether it makes sense. With a VDT, the computer can be—and usually is—told to check every element of work. If the VDT operator handles outside telephone calls, the computer can prompt questions and even tell the operator that the typed answer is incorrect or impossible. For example, when the operator types in the address "912 Ridgeview Court" the computer's file can tell the operator that "the numbers on Ridgeview Court run from 400 to 600 and 912 is a bad address." When the zip code is typed incorrectly for the name of the city, the computer can ask the operator to check it. In every business environment, the computer's skill at error checking improves accuracy. Most computer systems today will or can force accuracy.

## ELEMENTS OF AN ERGONOMIC OFFICE

### Windows

When architects, planners, managers, and designers meet to determine the allocation of space, several factors are considered. Cost is at the top of everyone's list. The flow of business, product, or process is an important element, as is security. Administrative areas are most often found on the uppermost floors in large companies. Computer centers are most often in the core of the building, surrounded by less sensitive areas. Clerical and general office areas are most often on outside walls and on lower floors. The location of the automated office within the building has a great deal to do with how that room will ultimately be designed.

There was a time when buildings were smaller and architects used a lot of glass to help light their interiors. Today we see modern buildings covering larger areas with more concrete and less exterior glass. In the design of energy efficient buildings, which take advantage of solar resources, glass is often the first thing to be omitted. Because of the physical size of some buildings, offices and work areas can be almost a block away from an outside wall. Designers compensate for this by creating atriums, skylights, wells, or just random glass walls within the structure. What are some of the facts about windows that you should consider when planning your new office?

1. Exterior windows warm a room when it is warm outside and cool a room when it is cold outside, resulting in additional internal heating or cooling requirement. This, in turn, increases operating costs.
2. Unprotected windows (those without blinds) can cause lighting variations that will affect the VDT and cause screen glare.
3. Windows allow distractions for those people who want to watch the world pass by.
4. Those people without windows usually want them.

Each of these concerns has been addressed by various designers and managers. The matter of heat and cold transfer can be mitigated by insulated glass—double panes of glass. The placement of the windows can affect temperature transfer, since west-facing windows receive more sunlight and heat than north-facing windows. Windows can be designed as narrow vertical openings rather than full walls of glass. They should also have blinds to block out the sun and perhaps lined, thermal drapes to block heat and cold transfer. Various coverings can also be used to reduce incoming light sufficiently to prevent VDT screen glare; for example, smoked glass significantly reduces the entry of light. If you are refurbishing (retrofitting) your office, there are reflective or smoked coatings for glass that serve the same purpose.

If you have a windowless inner office other steps should be taken. Without windows, more interior open space is needed to avoid a claustrophobic feeling. Some designers have used large photographic murals with lighting that changes with the time of day. Others have used outside television cameras connected to monitors in the office so employees will know what the weather is like outside.

## Room Security

The security of the workplace is also an ergonomic concern. The feeling of security should begin as you walk into an office and extend through to the workstation. Some companies provide security guards throughout the building. If you are in a business that requires high security, computer operations is just one more location of concern. In this case, entry to the area should be controlled by the person entering, rather than by someone within the office. Often codes punched on numeric, wall-mounted pads or individually coded cards are used to allow entry. The least desirable method is the use of keys, which can be easily duplicated.

In an environment that requires less security, a manager or receptionist can sit at the entrance to the area and screen visitors as they enter.

## Walls, Ceilings, and Floors

In the ergonomic office it is necessary to consider how the design and construction of walls, ceilings, and floors affect you.

Walls should be covered with a material that deadens

sound. Among available choices are fabric wall coverings, acoustical panels, and ruglike materials that are impervious to wear or abuse. Some designers specify the use of hanging drapes. Whatever material is used, it must be fire retardant. You should also be aware that, unless covered, glass walls and windows tend to liven room sounds rather than deaden them.

Ceilings should be acoustically treated, either with blown-on sound deadening material or with nonmetal tiles suspended on metal rails. Lighting fixtures, if ceiling mounted, should be recessed.

Floors should be covered with a good quality carpeting for noise reduction. The pile depth should permit the free use of chairs equipped with carpet casters. Some rooms will necessarily have computer flooring, although most automated offices will not require this. When computer flooring is used, care must be taken to ensure proper alignment of the support mechanisms. If they are improperly aligned, the computer flooring tends to bounce about when walked on.

### Workstations

Probably the heart of the modern automated office is the workstation. The workstation consists of the elements formerly found in a desk, plus more. It contains one or more general work surfaces, below-counter storage, above-counter storage, integral lighting, a chair, and receptacles for power, phone, VDT, and other accessories.

The primary difference between the desk and the workstation is the fact that the workstation is enclosed. That enclosure provides the employee with an individualized unit and the privacy that one needs in the new technological world. The enclosures make more effective use of space through clustering. Any number of workstations can be grouped or clustered in modules.

Workstations come in an unlimited variety of types and styles. Some modules are permanent, while others are intended to be portable or relocatable. Many you can easily assemble yourself. Multiple units share common walls, reducing cost, space, and construction time. Features include variable work surface heights, acoustical wall panels, and convenient overhead and below-counter storage space. The partitions may be fabric covered to reduce noise and serve as handy message boards. They are most often five or six feet high.

The most attractive workstations have translucent or smoked plastic partitions in both straight and curved configurations. These units permit light to pass through in varying degrees, and in some cases can be seen through. These partitions in particular tend to open up the workspace perceptually.

## The Circle of Reach

Your "circle of reach" within the workstation is easily defined and important to your comfort, although it is different for each person. The circle of reach is described by what you can reach while sitting erect in your chair, without bending out of it. Starting with the left arm, the typist should be able to reach to within 18 inches of the floor, directly between the legs. The distance is calculated in a left-swinging arc as the left arm is moved clockwise, ending to the right of the body when the work surface is reached. A similar arc is traced using the right arm in a counterclockwise direction, beginning between the legs and ending at the work surface to the left of the typist. The circle becomes three dimensional when you include cabinets below and above the work surface.

This circle of reach is important when designing your workstation. In some offices, VDT operators are forced to stretch uncomfortably to file and retrieve papers, and this puts an unnecessary strain on them. Some designers have found it advantageous to place a partition or a desk extension (a return) to the side of the operator and to then attach document bins to it or to the wall. The design should allow all elements of work to be easily accessible to the VDT operator, without the worker having to stretch or move from the chair. Everything should be within the circle of reach.

## Work Surface Heights

The work surface is the flat surface that you work on or on which you place equipment. A desktop is a work surface, as is the top of a typewriter table. In automated offices, the ergonomic determination of work surface heights has become a science of its own. Some companies provide for adjustable workstations so that employees (who come in different sizes) may choose their own work surface heights. Most companies provide for a number of fixed workstations and use chairs to adjust the individual to the fixed surface height. An adjustable work surface for VDTs is recommended.

There are four recognized work surfaces, each with its own height. The standard office desk is almost always fixed at 29½ inches above the floor. This height permits the worker to place elbows and forearms on the work surface when writing and reading. Typewriter stands and tables have, for years, been standardized at 26½ inches. This is the same height that is required for the VDT keyboard. Efforts to place the keyboard (or typewriter) on the top of a desk have been the source of great trouble. By the same token, when so-called computer tables (at 26½ inches) have been used for writing and reading, the result has been neck and back strain for the user. Some work surfaces must be accessible to people who are standing, and these surfaces are generally 38 inches above the floor. Many workstations today have printers, and the best height for these is the lower 26½ inches to permit easy access while seated.

Below-counter storage must be considered both for items necessary at the workstation and for small personal items belonging to the employee. Typically such storage is for things that are used infrequently. Many workstations include provision for the operator to insert floppy disks into a disk drive below the counter. Some of these permit access with-

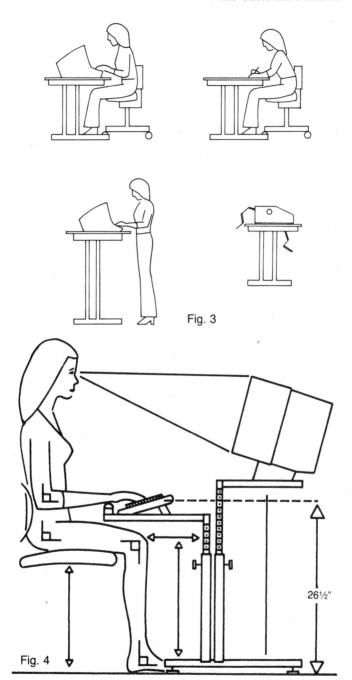

Fig. 3

Fig. 4

26½"

out considerable physical movement by the operator. Others require considerable movement and necessitate bending over and searching for the elusive slot for the disk. If use of disk drives is frequent, the drives should be moved to a location within the circle of reach.

Above-counter storage must be considered for items necessary at that workstation, such as computer disks, reference manuals, and stationery. While such storage can be enclosed, it more typically is not. When the storage is not enclosed, it is important to control what items are stored there and what potential there is for those items to fall if someone should bump against the other side of the workstation (or there is an earthquake).

### The Video Display Terminal (VDT)

The most visible element of the office automation revolution is the VDT. By the end of 1985, it is estimated that there could be more than 14 million VDTs in use in the United States. There is a lot of controversy today about the possible dangers of VDTs, and at the same time a great deal of research has been done to assure users and managers that the equipment is safe. The ergonomic issues that you must be concerned with are:

1. Screen and keyboard position
2. Screen color
3. Eye focus
4. Lighting and glare considerations
5. Equipment maintenance and radiation

*Keyboards:* The VDT keyboard should be adjustable and detachable. The operator should have the ability to adjust the keyboard height to compensate for differences in body physique or stature. People who are more stout may sit farther away from the keyboard than people who are slim; tall people may sit higher in a chair than those who are very short. The operator must be able to adjust the equipment to fit his or her body style. With a detachable keyboard, the operator can move it closer or farther away as the need arises.

Earlier it was stated that the keyboard should be on a work surface 26½ inches above the floor. To be more specific, it is accepted as a standard that the home keys (A-S-D-F-J-K-L-;) be at that height—with the provision that the height can be adjusted by the individual. Although it is important for the VDT operator to be comfortable, the proper keyboard placement for an individual can be calculated by the angle of the arm. When facing the keyboard, the operator's arm should form a 90-degree angle at the elbow. The surface of the keyboard should be at a 10-degree slant. If it is not already slanted, you can place the keyboard on a slanted surface for wrist and arm comfort.

It is beneficial if the home keys are identified for touch. Some keyboard manufacturers indent the F and J keys, while others use raised bumps. Some companies mark the keys themselves. Although most experienced typists have no trouble finding these keys, in subdued lighting it may be difficult to find them quickly.

If you have input into the selection of keyboards, you might bring up a variety of issues. On those machines with separate numeric keypads, you might find it convenient to have a comma as well as the period (decimal point) when writing long numbers. Also, the keyboard on the computer may be somewhat different from the one on your typewriter, and you may have considerable difficulty adapting to it. Try out the feel of the keys also, since some keyboards are smooth to the touch, and on others there is no sensation that you have actually struck the keys. If you will be typing all day, the feel of the keyboard could be very important to you.

*Screens:* Another consideration you should be concerned with is that your adjustable VDT is adjusted properly. If the screen is improperly adjusted you may have to contort your body to see it clearly. This will result in neck, shoulder, and

eye problems. A properly adjusted screen also helps mini-
mize stressful glare.

When you are sitting erect in your chair, the first line of
print on the screen should be 10 degrees below your horizontal vision plane. The bottom line of print should be no more
than 40 degrees below your horizontal vision plane. The
screen itself should be no less than 18 inches, no more than
20 inches from your eyes. It should be angled upward to
match the angle of your face when you are looking down.

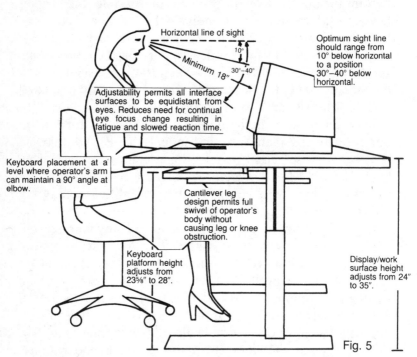

Horizontal line of sight

10°

Minimum 18"   30°–40°

Optimum sight line
should range from
10° below horizontal
to a position
30°–40° below
horizontal.

Adjustability permits all interface
surfaces to be equidistant from
eyes. Reduces need for continual
eye focus change resulting in
fatigue and slowed reaction time.

Keyboard placement at a
level where operator's arm
can maintain a 90° angle at
elbow.

Cantilever leg
design permits full
swivel of operator's
body without
causing leg or knee
obstruction.

Keyboard
platform height
adjusts from
23⅝" to 28".

Display/work
surface height
adjusts from 24"
to 35".

Fig. 5

These angles and distances seem to be accepted as a national standard. However, the computations were based on
seeing letters of standard size and shape, and not all VDTs
display the same size letters. For example, you may have
seen the screen of the original Osborne computer. It had a
miniature (5 inch) screen. If you were placed at the recommended angle and distance from the screen, the result would

certainly be disagreeable. Not all computers generate the same size letters, and not all screens display them the same way. Smaller screens generally show smaller letters, and large screens display larger type.

The color of the screen and the displayed characters does not seem like it should be a problem, but it has become one. Originally all screens were black or dark gray and characters were white or light gray. Today there are many more choices. When the first green letters appeared on black screens, it was a new era. People liked them. When amber letters on black screens arrived, that was the next era. Now some of the more sophisticated systems display characters in multiple colors, with the operator being able to choose from an assortment. On colored screens, the mask (the preprinted information) may be in one color (dark blue) while the data being entered is in another color (bright red). Colors permit operators to pick out relevant information quickly, without having to read an entire document.

There is certainly no agreement among users regarding the best color for the screen. When questioned, most people tend to choose the color that they have become used to, and although they may resist changing colors, once new colors are tried, they become the standard.

*Eye Focus:* The VDT operator normally views or reads from a printed document and translates information from that document onto the screen. The placement of the printed document is critical and affects the focus of the operator's eyes. If the screen is 18 to 20 inches away, an eye focus problem has been created.

Some companies have perceived and dealt with this problem in various ways. The best method seems to be to locate the printed document alongside the screen. This requires a great deal of horizontal eye movement, but it seems a better position for the document than flat on the desk surface. A flat position changes the operator's focal distance between the screen and the document as the operator moves from the document's beginning to its end. Another poor choice of document position is directly above the screen, since it requires the operator to move his or her head up and down, possibly causing neck strain.

*Lighting and Glare:* A room in which VDTs are used should not have too many windows, or if it does, they should be covered with blinds or drapes. When situating a workstation, the rule is that the operator's eyes and the VDT screen should not face an uncovered window. If either do, then a workstation partition should be placed in front of the window to block the view. To assist in controlling problem glare the VDT should be fitted with a nonglare screen in addition to its normal brightness and contrast controls.

The work area should be lighted from indirect and recessed sources with a brilliance not less than 500 lux (50 footcandles) or more than 700 lux (70 footcandles). Ceiling lights should be minimized and used only to provide corridor lighting. Each VDT should have an adjustable light fixture, such as an architect's lamp on a flexible arm, so that the operator can adjust the light directly onto the printed material.

Drapes, shades, or blinds over windows should be closed, especially in direct sunlight. The terminals should be properly positioned with respect to windows and overhead lighting. Screen hoods may be installed. Antiglare filters may be used on the VDT screen. Direct lighting fixtures may need to be recessed. Baffles can be used to cover fluorescent fixtures to prevent them from being a glare source, and special covers on light fixtures may be used to direct the light downward rather than allowing it to diffuse. Properly installed indirect lighting systems will limit the amount of glare, although some reflected glare may still be present. Baffles and filters are especially valuable if you are bringing computers into an existing space not specifically designed for them.

*VDTs and Eyes:* People working with VDTs report discomfort or difficulty with their eyes more often than others with visually demanding jobs. Eye complaints may include irritation, fatigue, and difficulty with focus or accommodation. The April 1983 *Harvard Medical School Health Letter*

speaks of current minimal criteria to assist in meeting basic
requirements:

1. The image on the screen should not flicker.
2. The entire display should be in sharp focus.
3. The contrast between light and dark areas should be at
   least 8 to 1.
4. The characters should be formed in a 5 × 7 matrix of
   dots at the very least.
5. All VDTs should have brightness and contrast controls
   that the operator can find and adjust.

The National Association of Office Workers recommends
regular eye exams for all VDT workers.

### Chairs

It is said that the Egyptians made the first chair in 2687
B.C. Not a lot has changed in the interim. Office managers
undoubtedly spend more time dealing with chairs and chair
problems than with any other single equipment issue. Why?
Because chairs are usually designed by people who rarely
see them in use. Problems also occur because chairs are
subjected to uses that the designers never even dreamed of.
The matter of chairs is an important one.

It is recommended that chairs have an adjustable height
and that backrests be adjustable to the lumbar (midback)
region to provide adequate support. Chairs and work surface heights should also be matched to the individual charac-
teristics of the operator.

Advertisers have attached the ergonomic label to chairs
perhaps more than to any other element of the automated
office. Unfortunately, not all chairs are truly ergonomic. It is
doubtful, in fact, that any chair can completely meet that
claim, even if it has been scientifically designed and engi-
neered.

In some offices, a chair is assigned to an individual; in
other offices chairs are rotated through many shifts. *When*

*chairs are shared, problems invariably arise.* Some people sit in a chair gently, some more heavily. Shared chairs wear out sooner and are more frequently broken or damaged. Unfortunately, sitting in a damaged chair for any length of time may result in progressive discomfort for those who use it.

Assuming that a chair is properly designed and constructed, is there a proper way to sit in it? Most experts agree that if someone sits improperly in a chair, several problems can occur, resulting in back and neck strain, slowed circulation in the legs, and painful muscles and joints, as well as pain or stiffness in the legs, neck, and shoulders. People really need training to sit properly in a chair. Your back should be vertical and pressed gently against a back support. Your back and thighs should be at a 90-degree angle. Your feet should be flat on the floor, with your knees at a 90-degree angle. Your head and neck should be directly in line with your spine.

What makes a chair comfortable—or uncomfortable? A lot has to do with the activity of the person using the chair. In the case of VDT operators, the chair should have casters to permit the operator to easily control access to the workstation and keyboard. Some means must be provided that will permit raising or lowering the seat easily. When at its proper height, the seat should allow both feet to rest flat on the floor with a 90-degree knee angle. The one part of the body that comes into contact with every chair is the ischia— the bones on which the body rests when sitting. When the ischia come into contact with the cushion, they must be comfortable.

Some seat cushions are padded more than others. Some padding quickly compresses, leaving the ischia in contact with either unpadded or uneven surfaces. The contours of a seat cushion can provide comfort to some and discomfort to others. Some seats have more horizontal (front to back) depth than others, and some provide for this depth to be adjusted. Not all VDT operators sit properly in their chairs—some sit tentatively on the forward half of the seat, and others sit fully against the back support. The depth of the seat and where on the seat the person sits determine the amount of support given to the thighs.

Comfort is also governed by the design and position of the seat edge, taking into consideration how deep the person is sitting and the angle of the knees. That sounds complicated, but it is not. If the edge of the seat presses against the underside of the thighs because the feet are not firmly on the floor, the result will be a restriction of circulation.

The backrest and other associated elements also contribute to comfort. It is preferable to keep the spine vertical, and a backrest is provided on most chairs for this purpose (see Fig. 6). The backrest is most commonly designed to enclose or cup the back if the user pushes against the rest, and it most often follows the user for a short distance if the user leans forward. A properly designed backrest will provide support from the lower (lumbar) region of the body through the shoulder blade (thoracic) area.

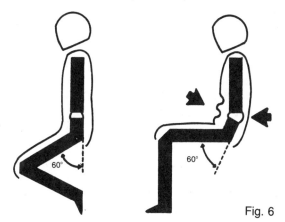

Fig. 6

The ease of adjusting a chair is certainly an ergonomic concern. The method of adjusting most chairs seems to require one to sit first, contemplate the adjustments, then stand up, turn the chair upside down, and make the adjustment. A number of chairs have been developed recently that permit you to make most adjustments while seated.

Some chairs provide armrests, and the Service Employees International Union specifies that "chairs shall also have one-half length armrests." Armrests can be beneficial and increase comfort, but they can also interfere with the chair being drawn close enough to the work surface or the keyboard. If the armrests hold the chair away from the work surface, then the operator will compensate by varying the position of his or her body. The result will be discomfort. If armrests are used, their design and position should be coordinated with the dimensions of the workstation.

One final note of importance: If an operator is too short, despite a properly designed chair, it may be necessary to use a stool to permit the feet to reach the ground.

### Odds and Ends

There are several other ancillary issues that relate to the establishment of an ergonomic office and must be taken into consideration.

*Printers:* Many offices have placed typing printers adjacent to the VDT and the operator. While some printers are very quiet, many more are not, especially daisy wheel printers. Some produce excessive vibration as well. If the printer is placed on a separate printer table, the vibration will not be felt by the operator nor will it interfere with the computer's operation. An acoustical cover will dampen the printer's noise.

*Telephones:* Most workstations have telephones. Small desk sets permit VDT operators to accomplish an almost infinite variety of tasks, which we cover in Chapter 4. They should be situated so that they do not interfere with the operation of the computer.

*Document Holders:* We briefly mentioned document holders earlier in this chapter. There are several kinds of holders available. The most popular seems to be a flexible-arm style that can be positioned where it is convenient for the operator. We mentioned that the holder should be directly alongside and on the same plane as the screen. The placement also depends on right- or left-handedness. Another type of holder is freestanding with a weighted base. This type lacks some flexibility, but it is still superior to copy being placed on the horizontal work surface.

*Air-conditioning:* The indoor temperature at the workstation should normally be kept higher than 65 degrees. During hot weather, adequate ventilation and air-conditioning are generally necessary to provide for reasonable personnel comfort. In some parts of the country, humidity control is also necessary. Because of drafts or inadequate air circulation systems, it is not uncommon for employees to use their own heaters or fans.

*Right-handed vs. Left-handed:* Telephones and other devices must be capable of being situated so as to be comfortable for right- or left-handed people. It is extremely common for right-handed people to place the phone near their left shoulders, and the opposite is true for lefties. Thus the phone should be placed in such a way that the cord does not come between the worker and the keyboard. Similar thought should be given to the placement of floppy disk drives. If movable, they should be situated on the side that is most comfortable for the user. Undoubtedly, there are dozens of other similar situations that will crop up at your workstation, and these should be taken into consideration when the area is designed. This, by the way, is a reason why sharing work areas often does not work.

*Smoking:* Most offices with modular workstations permit smoking, but throughout the country, more companies are banning smoking in those parts of the office that use computers. Smoke can damage the insides of disk drives. If smoking is a necessity, then you should consider an air filter to purify the air at your workstation or in the entire room.

*Food and Drink:* Restrictions are most often placed on food and drink because they can cause damage to the VDT or its components. Obviously, crumbs and liquid (especially those with sugar) are dangerous to the inner workings of most equipment. Care should be exercised if you must eat or drink around your workstation.

*Rest and Stress:* Although these are two separate topics, we will discuss them together, since one leads into the other.

Among the major concerns for computer operators is that of fatigue, as well as visual and psychological problems. Those who spend their days working in front of a VDT can expect fatigue. Studies have shown that data entry operators suffer greater muscular complaints than those who use computers only part of the time. The National Institute for Occupational Safety and Health recommends that VDT operators take a fifteen-minute rest break after two hours of continuous work if they are under moderate visual demands and/or moderate work loads. If you are under higher visual pressure and higher work load or engaged in repetitive work tasks, you should take a fifteen-minute rest break after every one hour of work.

The April 1983 *Harvard Medical School Health Letter* describes the problem of computer use eliminating the need for a body to move around, to reach for a new piece of paper or an eraser, for example. Sitting still too long is known to be bad for people. Long periods of sitting put a strain on the back and neck, slow circulation in the legs, and generally reduce muscle tone. To compensate for the static nature of computer operations, frequent breaks are recommended.

The *Harvard Health Letter* also addresses the issue of job stress. Many of stress-related complaints seem to be the result of the following problems:

1. Users receive inadequate training when computers are introduced.
2. Work load requirements may be unrealistic, set by the capacity of the machine, not that of the operator.
3. Many jobs become monotonous, and employees become isolated from their colleagues.

As a result, many companies have introduced stress management workshops for computer operators. This is just another indication that the ergonomic office has many aspects that should be considered when a business decides to modernize its operations.

As the material we have discussed in this chapter indicates, it is just as important to plan for the interaction of the people and the computers, as it is to purchase the right computers. Requirements in the modern, technological office are different from those in a standard office—created by the new functions of technology. None of these problems is difficult to solve, either. It does, however, take an awareness on your part, and on the part of others in the position of selecting and purchasing equipment and accessories (furniture, lighting, etc.), that these ergonomic concerns are of vital importance.

# 4
# Office Procedures

Recent studies by the US Bureau of Labor Statistics indicate that the need for office workers will grow over the next decade. Figures show, for example, a projected growth in available jobs for secretaries of more than 28 percent over 1980. Office workers will find at least 15 percent more jobs available over the next ten years, and there will be at least 17 percent more jobs available for typists.

These studies also indicate that by the year 2000 there will be almost ten million new jobs dealing, in some way, with computers. The topic of automation is not something that is going to go away. Instead, it will continue to increase in importance, and soon it will be only the very rare office that does not make use of available technology.

With the technological advances that have taken place already, and with those that will follow, approaches to office procedures are changing and will continue to change in order to adapt. The way we function in the office environment will be different. The technological office is automated and provides you with numerous ways to improve your efficiency and the quality of your work.

In this chapter we will examine the impact of technology on the basic office functions we are used to performing. For example, the cornerstone of all business is communications. Correspondence is the basic form of transmitting printed materials. How will computers change the nature of this function? And how will the processes of duplicating and printing alter within the office, to improve efficiency, quality, and speed?

Standard operations such as filing and scheduling are also beginning to change, since most of these jobs can be easily automated. We will look at data processing, the electronic method of filing and scheduling—what it is, how it works, and how you can employ it in your business.

Accounting, too, is changing because of computers. As we mentioned earlier, accounting departments were the first areas of business to become computerized. But, unlike in the early days of computing, even the smallest office can now be automated with the advent of personal computers. The large, powerful mainframes are no longer required to perform accounting procedures. With many of the enhancements for computers that are now available, accounting has become more sophisticated yet more available for every type of business.

We will look at telecommunications also—a world that is light-years away from Alexander Graham Bell's original concept of the telephone. This section will examine how employees talk to each other, how companies communicate, how to gather information, and why it is necessary to be involved in the world of telecommunications.

Finally, we will take a look at another area outside the traditional office—an area called telecommuting. Using all the best aspects of technology, computers, and telecommunications systems, more employees will work at home, not as free-lancers or moonlighters but as regular employees of the company, spending part of their time at home and part in the office. At no time will they have to be out of touch with the day-to-day operations of their company.

Following is an examination of these major areas of office procedures, important to the operation of any business.

## CORRESPONDENCE—WORD PROCESSING

Correspondence is a basic function in most offices. Whether through a memo, letter, report, or publication, the processing of words is the underlying medium. Although typewriters (more specifically, electronic typewriters) can be considered word processors, the true nature of modern word processing can only be found in dedicated word processors or computers.

What is word processing? Essentially, it is the manipulation of words and text by electronic means. Much like electronic calculators, which manipulate and calculate numbers, electronic word processors are fast, accurate, and can be used to produce documents of any length, printed in a variety of different styles.

Word processing on a computer or WP is a comparatively simple process. Using the keyboard like a typewriter, you type (input) your document. As you type, a cursor moves across the video screen. This cursor is a block of light, or an arrow, which can be manipulated from the keyboard. When you type letters or numbers or use directional arrow keys, the cursor follows your command. This cursor moves you throughout the text to perform whatever commands you wish.

Once the document is completed, you can reread it on the screen and make corrections, deletions, or additions. If you wish, you can change the margins or the tabulation. You then command the computer to print out the document, and then store it on the disk for later use. If you wish to make changes in the material, you can easily retrieve it from its electronic file, reopen the document, and make those necessary alterations, then print it again as many times as you want.

These are the essential features of all word processing programs or systems. The ease of information manipulation that they offer, resulting in saved time and increased quality, makes them valuable to almost any office environment.

Let's look at some of the features of word processing programs.

*Automatic Word Wrap:* This is the first and basic time-saver when you are typing correspondence. When using a typewriter, you normally hit the enter or return key when you reach the end of a line to return either the typing element or the entire carriage to the beginning of the next line. With word wrap (sometimes called parsing), when you reach the end of a line the element automatically jumps to the beginning of the next line, thereby saving you the effort of hitting the return key. Although that may only take seconds, if you add up those seconds at the end of a long document, they may have stretched into minutes. With word wrap you can type at a continuous speed, keeping your eye on the original or on the screen.

*Delete and Insert Commands:* Once someone has used a word processing program and explored the possibilities of automatically deleting unwanted material or inserting omitted material into a long document, it is difficult to go back to ordinary typing. Using designated keys, you can command the word processing machine to delete characters, words, lines, and even entire pages from your correspondence. If you wish to add material, for whatever reason, other keys open space and permit you to type those letters, words, or lines directly into the document. No longer is it necessary to retype the entire document to insert or edit material.

*Customized Printing Commands:* Most programs offer a variety of different features to help make your output attractive and more easily readable. For example, you can change the margins at will. If you are typing a promotion letter, you can make some passages wider or narrower than others to call attention to them. You can change line spacing to differentiate between different copy. A letter would probably be single spaced, while a market research report might be triple spaced. All easily accomplished by pushing a few keys. And if you don't like the way it looks, change it in seconds. All of these commands can be stored for future use, so you can create different documents over and over again without worrying about changing commands.

You also have the capability of underlining text as well as printing bold or italic type, if your printer supports those commands. In addition, subscript and superscript are usually part of the program, which is especially valuable if you do any type of technical writing. Furthermore, if you write long reports or manuscripts, the headers and footers are invaluable in presenting the material in an attractive format. You can use these commands to print the title of the work, chapter number, and page number at the bottom or top of each page you specify, much like what is done in a book.

*Global Search:* Here's a valuable timesaver that is especially useful if you type similar documents time after time, with occasional changes. For example, if you type standard form contracts, you may only change names or titles. Using the global search feature, you can instruct the machine to find the previous name on the contract and replace it with the new name. Or the program will pause at each occurrence of a specific letter, word, or phrase, giving you the option to change or delete it. You can ask the machine to find every occurrence of the word *grey* and change it to *gray*. Or change 1984 to 1985 throughout the entire document.

*Form Letter Merge:* One other exciting feature found in only the most sophisticated word-processing programs is the merge ability. This part of the program produces form letters. You type a form letter, inserting simple codes into those spaces you wish personalized, such as name, address, city, state, account number, or anything else. In a separate "variables" document you type in the specifics that will be used to fill in these coded spaces. Then, when you give the merge command, each letter will be printed with the appropriate name, address, etc., to make the letters totally personalized.

*Programmable Keys:* Many programs give you the option of programming many of the keys to perform repetitive typing functions. For example, you could program one key to print out the closing on a letter if you always sign your letters the same way. After programming it, you merely push that key and the "Very truly yours," your name, and title are printed at the end of the letter automatically. If you're typing a legal document, you might wish to program specific keys to insert phrases that may be used frequently throughout the text, to save you the trouble of doing it over and over again.

*Automatic Tabulation:* For anyone who types numbers, automatic tabulation is of enormous benefit. The problem with typing numbers in tabular format is that unless all of the numbers are the same length, you have to continually allow extra spaces in order to make sure numbers align properly beneath one another. With automatic tabulation, the numbers begin at the tab mark, and go backward. If you have a decimal point, once you've hit the period, the numbers then go from left to right. If you were careless about tabulation, you might get the following:

145.00
23.45
1055.63

This is not a clear way to present numbers. However, with automatic tabulation, the numbers would automatically be aligned:

145.00
23.45
1055.63

You don't have to count spaces to be sure they're in correct alignment.

*Centering:* To enhance the attractiveness and readability of most documents, titles and headings should be centered. On a regular typewriter, you must find the approximate middle of the page and then backspace one space for every two characters in the title. After backspacing, you then type the title. In most word processing programs, centering is automatic. You push the appropriate key and the title is automatically centered within the margins of that page. If you readjust the margins, the title is recentered.

*Interactive Programs:* In order to derive the full benefit from your computer, a welcome addition to your word-processing program is the ability to interact with other programs. For example, if you are writing a form letter to your sales staff, you might want to call up their sales records from a data base file (more on that later) and have their sales entered automatically into the letter.

*Windows:* A more recent innovation in this interactive method is a process called "windows." Several of the newer programs give you the option of running parts of several different programs at once and calling up those parts on separate areas (windows or tiles) of the screen. In this way you can type a document and check your appointment schedule at the same time, recall a previous letter you sent to the same person, and in response to an interrupting phone call, bring up last month's sales report on a separate portion of the screen. These programs require larger machine memory and they are more expensive than ordinary word processing programs.

*Spelling Checkers:* Most of the better programs can also interact with spelling programs, dictionaries on a disk that hold as many as one hundred thousand common words. The program checks your document and points out those words it doesn't recognize. If you've written "thier," it will highlight the word and give you the opportunity to correct it. When the dictionary encounters a technical word it does not recognize, you can delete or change the word or keep it the way it is and enter it into the dictionary. The next time the program encounters that word, it will accept it as correct.

There is no question that the use of word processing has improved the efficiency of the office and the correspondence that emanates from it. The speed, flexibility, quality control, and visual appearance of everything from letters to book-

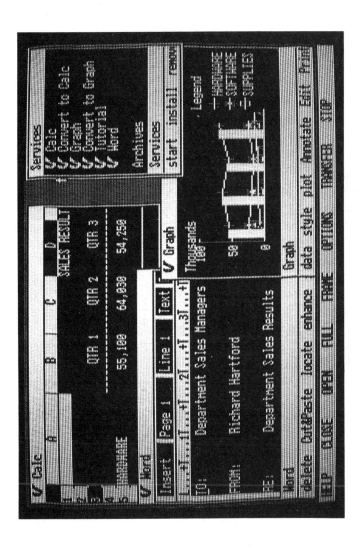

length manuscripts result in a continual saving of time and money for most businesses.

## ELECTRONIC FILING

Most of us understand the procedures for filing. In terms of the technological environment it's not much different. Only the names have been changed. Essentially, filing is the process of organizing and storing your records, whether they are correspondence, personnel records, customer names, or any other paperwork generated by your office. If you are a secretary, office manager, department head, or the president of the company, the work you do and the paperwork you process will be filed somewhere.

In the traditional "paper" office are file cabinets. Each cabinet may be for a different department or a different type of information. And each drawer may be arranged alphabetically. In order to file anything, whether it's an incoming or an outgoing letter, you must locate the proper file cabinet and the appropriate drawer, and then insert the file folder in the right place. If your office is like most standard ones, your file drawers are filled to overflowing, and there is a continual need to locate more space for additional cabinets.

In the technological office, most filing can be done right on the computer. And instead of different file cabinets, you have boxes of computer diskettes. Each box, for 5¼-inch diskettes, would be about 6″ × 8″ × 8″, instead of a file cabinet about 5 feet high by 1½ feet wide and 2 feet deep. Every department would have one or more of these boxes, depending upon the amount of information generated by that department. They fit easily and conveniently on any workstation. Stored inside this box (the file cabinet) would be up to fifty disks. These disks are like the individual drawers and alphabetical dividers in a standard cabinet.

On the disk itself you can hold hundreds of separate records. In normal filing systems, a file folder is labeled with the name of the account or subject. On a computer, after inserting the disk, you "open a record." This merely assigns a title to whatever document you plan to generate. Then, after you use your word processing program to write the letter, it is automatically stored on the disk, whether you print it out or not.

There are a variety of ways to use the disks. An easy method is to have a separate disk for each customer or client. Whatever method you use depends upon the nature of your business. Each disk is then labeled by account name. Whenever you have to write a letter, send a notice, or go into the "file" for reference, you merely select the appropriate disk, read the directory that is automatically generated, and either recall a document for rereading or open a new document. The letters remain filed on the disk. When the disk is full, you are notified by the computer and you can then start a new one.

As with a traditional file cabinet, if you generate a lot of information and deal with many clients, you have to continually add more disks to your file box. However, one look at the size of a disk, and you will quickly realize that it would take thousands of them to fill a traditional standing file cabinet. A standard 5¼-inch disk can store about twenty thousand words, which is about eighty typed pages. Double-density disks can hold as much as ten times that amount, which means almost eight hundred pages.

If you need even greater storage capacity than you can get on a floppy disk, you might consider a hard disk. Hard disks can store as much as 30 to 150 separate floppy disks, as many as twenty million characters. This gives you the ability to file thousands upon thousands of pages of information on one hard disk. Naturally, the standard hard disk is very expensive ($2,000 to $5,000), but since it stores so much information and can be accessed very quickly, it is actually less expensive when measured on a per byte basis.

Often the time saved in using a hard disk alone is worth the price. If you maintain separate diskettes for each client, you have to change disks each time you want to work on a new client's file. With a hard disk, it might be possible to contain all of your clients on that one disk. There's almost no waiting time when calling up another file.

### Data Base Filing

There is another method of filing called data processing, or data base management. With this method, you can store huge amounts of information about everything from sales records to telephone numbers. Shortly we will describe how a data base system would manage a typical telephone file. It is no different than storing complex sales or inventory information. A data base management program may be as simple as maintaining a computerized Rolodex telephone directory or a party invitation list. However, it is one of the most versatile programs for business use.

A data base is a collection of similar information, and the computer is used for electronic filing and record keeping. The programs can be manipulated to create a variety of specific files for the accumulation of information you will need. A data base is used for compiling mailing lists, maintaining salespeople's records, customer files, subscription lists, promotion results, catalog information, employment data, or inventory records.

The easiest way to understand a data base management system is to visualize a box of typical 3″ × 5″ cards. On each card (which appears on the screen) you can enter any kind of information you need. Suppose it's a listing of all of your salespeople. In addition to personal information (name, address, city, zip, telephone number), you might also include territory, product lines, monthly and annual sales, etc. The computer not only stores all of this information and permits you to revise it whenever you wish, but it also gives you the opportunity to manipulate the data.

As you enter information, you can request the program to calculate the monthly sales and give you a running record of total sales. You can ask the computer to then give you a printout of only those salespeople with over $25,000 cumulative sales. Or those with over $25,000 sales in the

West Coast territory whose last names begin with A, R, and V. The computer, following your directions, quickly sorts through all of the records in memory and selects only those names that fit your criteria.

Remember, *data is information.* How do you manipulate that information? Data base management (DBM) is a method of storing, organizing, and recalling information in almost any format you wish. It is a sophisticated, high-speed form of electronic filing.

Before we go into depth on the inner workings of DBM, let's take a look at a fairly common file—an address file. To begin, pick out an address card from your Rolodex file. You will probably find something close to the following on it:

Name
Title
Company
Address
City, State, Zip
Office telephone
Home telephone

There may be other information you normally include, but let's start with this. Usually when you finish writing or typing information onto a card, you then insert the card under the appropriate letter of the alphabet, most often determined by the first letter of the last name. When you wish to recall the name, you look it up alphabetically.

Suppose you have five hundred names in the address book, which have been entered in much the same way. The only way you can find a name is by looking through your file under the appropriate letter of the alphabet.

Take it a step further. Let's put in some real data.

Mr. John J. Adams
Vice President
Empire State Corporation

1234 Western Avenue
Washington, DC 12345
Office phone: 205 555-1234
Home phone: 205 555-0987

This would be a typical entry. If you want Mr. John J. Adams, you could easily find the card quickly. But suppose you wanted Mr. Adams, who is a corporate vice president, as well as all the other vice presidents in your file. You could do it, but you would have to go through every one of your five hundred address cards. If you wanted to find anyone connected with the Empire State Corporation, you would have to go through all of the cards again.

However, if all of those names were filed on a DBM program, after you had entered a few requests into the computer the machine would search through all five hundred names in seconds, select all names with the title vice president, and display them on the screen or print them out. Or, if you wanted everyone who works for the Empire State Corporation, you could specify that you want everyone in that company and the machine would quickly make that selection. It can also find anyone whose last name begins with A, works for Empire, and is a vice president.

This is the very basis of a data base management program. It collects the information (address cards), sorts it (by title, company, or anything else), and can print it out, either on the screen or through the printer. But its capabilities go far beyond the manipulation of an address book. It is a powerful business management tool that can help most businesses organize their information and process it quickly and efficiently.

Data base management systems can be used for any information that your company stores in its files, including:

Address and mailing lists
Sales records
Customer records

Personnel files
Medical records
Inventory records
Supplier lists and records
Job descriptions
Birth, death, marriage, and divorce records

. . . and anything else that you wish to store and retrieve at some later date, the same things that you now store as paper documents in file drawers.

With a fully integrated data base program, you can combine the information on the data base with a form letter in the word processing program and integrate a spreadsheet from your electronic financial modeling program, as well as produce a pie chart of each individual's monthly production.

Basically, information stored in a computerized data base falls into four categories:

1. The *record,* which is a collection of various information about an item, whether that item is a customer, client, employee, published book, sales report, or inventory of airplane parts.
2. The *field,* which is a specific category of information. A field can be a model number, last name, territory, year, or manufacturer's name.
3. The *character,* or combination of characters, within each field. For example, if the field is TERRITORY, the characters might be NE or SW or any other combination of letters. Depending upon how you set up the fields, you are allowed a certain number of characters within each, the purpose of which is to help locate information *by character within a specific field.*
4. Finally, the *file,* which is the collection of all the records in your data base. The nature of your business determines the types of files you maintain. Typical files might include: sales records, personnel records, inventory reports, manufacturing statistics, or expense account records.

When you open a file, you must begin by structuring your data. In our earlier example, the address book is a file. Each address card is a record. Within each record you must specify fields: Each of the pieces of information that make up a complete record is a field. The space for NAME on the address card could be a field, although it's more likely that you would establish both a LAST NAME and a FIRST NAME field. Remember, before you set up your records, you must carefully plan for every bit of information you wish to include—and how you will want to manipulate it. If you will want to pull out all names in zip code order, then ZIP must be a separate field. If you plan to select records of your salespeople by territory, you'll have to set up a field for TERRITORY.

While setting up the fields, you specify the number of characters in each you wish to leave room for. Since you are limited by the size of each record, it's important to be careful when you plan the size of each field. Some programs hold up to one hundred fields, and the total file holds a limited number of characters of information, some programs having over one thousand characters.

Once you've established the various fields you will need for your records, you then get to design your own form. It's easiest to think of a standard index card and how you would put information on it. Instead of typing this information on the card, you design the form right on the video screen and then enter the information into the computer. Once you've done this, you can review the information, edit it, and then store it. Just like you would on a file card. When a collection of records has been stored, you have your electronic file.

Your next step is to design the formats you want to print from your records. Regardless of the number of fields you have in each record, you don't have to print out all of the information. You are limited only by the program's ability to print lines, the amount of information in the file, the width of the page, the number of lines on the page, etc. From the address file, you could print out just the names, just the telephone numbers, or you could print out the entire file of complete records.

Again, the address book is only a very simple example of how to use the computer for filing purposes. You can design almost any kind of file, keep each one on a separate disk, and update the disks whenever necessary.

From our earlier discussion of word processing, you should have some idea of what features to look for in that type of program. In a data base package, you also have many different features to look for. Some of the standard features allow you to:

1. Design and set up your own formats for inputting and editing information.
2. Update selected records. This is normally accomplished via a search routine or global update, which enables you to select all records that match a specific criterium or to locate individual records and update individual items, such as all unit costs in a series of manufactured goods.
3. Change your format even after you have entered information. This need may arise if you wish to add another field perhaps, or expand the length of a field already in your records.
4. Retrieve records, based on your requirements, however you wish and whenever you need to.
5. Calculate total amounts based on formulas you determine. If you want to pull from your files the complete records of all employees in the marketing department, you can also have a total of all salaries paid out in that department in the last year. If you maintain an inventory and cost-control file and wish to alter the formula, all costs and selling prices can be automatically updated.
6. Exchange data with other integrated programs, such as your word processing and spreadsheet programs.
7. Produce records with more than one line, giving you automatic tabulation or column alignment.
8. Choose from a variety of ways to print out your files or reports. You can extract just names and addresses

for a mailing label printout or select only certain fields
to examine. In a personnel record file, for example,
you might wish to look at everyone's name, department, and salary. It may not be important at that time
to see their addresses, taxes withheld, years with the
company, references, etc. This option permits you to
see only what you want to see.

9. Have password protection that, on this type of program, as well as with accounting programs, permits
the files to be opened only by those people with the
correct password, which can be continually changed
for tight security.

10. Sort and arrange your information in alphabetical or
numerical order, which permits you to access information in a number of different ways. You can select
all of the records in numerical order, or you can print
out all of your customer names in alphabetical order.
In a mailing list printout, you might want to sort the
names and addresses in zip code order. Or you can
list your customers in decreasing order of dollar sales,
to see your best customers first.

You can see by now that filing is no longer what it once
was. Not only does the computer permit you increased storage capabilities, but it lends a new dimension to the accumulation and manipulation of your data. Speed and ease of
maintenance are other valuable attributes of electronic filing. Now, instead of being a chore to set up and alphabetize,
filing is more a typing skill.

## SCHEDULING

All businesses run on some type of calendar, usually more
than one. One is normally used to schedule dates and appointments, another to schedule advertising and marketing.
Yet another may be used to target sales-quota dates. Perhaps another is used to schedule production deadlines.

Whatever you use them for, calendars and schedule boards are vital tools in business management.

Once you begin using a computer you will find a variety of different business management software programs available to you, which do everything from project scheduling and decision analysis to tracking information and reminding you of appointments and phone calls. Because of the ability of the computer to sort information instantly and extract *only the information you need at the time,* this type of software is valuable in performing these daily tasks with minimum effort and maximum efficiency.

The easiest way to understand how these computer programs operate is by comparing them with the typical manual systems most of us are familiar with. As an example, let's look at a typical date book, in which you record important meetings and appointments. These books are divided by day, week, month, and year, and by glancing at the appropriate pages, you can find appointments you made, birthdays and anniversaries you don't wish to forget, etc. It's a very simple system.

Next, let's look at a very simple "time management" program, available for most computers. Once you've told the computer prompt (a question asked you by the software) what the year is, it automatically sets all of the dates into the memory, month by month. It can do this for at least twenty years into the future. If you want to see June 16, 1997, you merely type in the date, and the machine will take you there—to tell you the exact day.

Once this is set in the memory of the program, you can then enter specific information. Most programs offer you a list of types of information you can enter. These may include:

Meetings
Conventions
Projects due
Expenses

Dates to remember
Purchases
Medical expenses
Payments due
Travel
Meals
Business or personal appointments
Telephone calls

On most programs you have the ability to set up your own categories. Many of these categories, you'll notice, are similar to those you might use for expense records. There is a reason for that, which we'll touch on later. To use this category list, you will probably have a letter or numerical code to indicate a specific category. When you enter a specific item, it should be accompanied by the appropriate code for that category. The reason for this is to give you the ability to retrieve items by category.

Thus, if you wish to call up all upcoming meetings that you have to attend, you can merely ask the program to select, display, and print out this list of meetings by day, month, or year. In a normal mode, you call up the daily schedule on your screen and then have the option of printing it out for later reference. If you use the computer constantly, you might just call up the schedule on the screen. If you travel a lot or are away from the computer for periods of time, you might want a hard copy—a printout—to take with you. This printout gives you a list of all of the items that you need to know for the day. Generally, the program groups similar items, so you see all of your pending phone calls together (or you can separate calls to be made from calls you're expecting), meetings together, and so on.

You can also sort the categories in different ways to suit your various needs. They can be sorted in chronological order, so you can see what you have to do minute by minute. In some programs you can indicate the status of the item, meaning that when you call up the schedule those items that are the most important to accomplish are listed first, and everything else is listed in descending order of importance. The ability to select the type of printout you need is important, and you could get both a chronological printout and one in order of importance.

One program has a floating "to do" file. You code the items that you must get to but don't have to accomplish within a specific time frame, and those items will follow you from day to day. Once you accomplish the task, you can remove it from the file.

If you have to write a report for the marketing department, prepare the text for an upcoming catalog, and schedule a meeting for the secretarial staff, you may not have specific days on which to accomplish that work. There may, of course, be a due date for each item, but even if those dates are indicated on the calendar, they won't be visible to you unless you turn to those specific days. The floating status category is a constant reminder. Every day, when you turn on the machine, there are those items. If you don't accomplish them by the end of the day, they automatically reappear on the calendar the next day. But you will no longer see any telephone calls or meetings scheduled for the previous day, since the program assumes you've accomplished those items. The only way to get rid of the reminders, however, is to instruct the program to kill them. It's a constant nag, but a valuable one.

We mentioned earlier that many of these categories appear to be similar to expense items. The reason for that is that most time management programs can also provide calculations. You can enter dollars and cents alongside the schedules, and at the end of a day or month can tally up the expenses, either as a total or by category. For the businessperson who keeps track of travel and entertainment expenses (and most businesspeople do), this is an ideal adjunct to the program. At the end of a day, you can enter the expenses incurred for meals, drinks, telephone calls, purchases, entertainment, etc. Whenever you need a tally of your expenses, you can obtain a complete record and a printout to accompany it.

One nicety that many programs provide is a warning bell. If your computer can produce sound, with a built-in or add-on amplifier, the program will automatically buzz or beep you when it is time for an appointment or a necessary telephone call.

These are fairly simple programs that are available for most computers. Although they may seem very sophisticated to the noncomputer person, time management programs are really very elementary. The next level of business management program available is for more complex scheduling. These programs are used for much more in-depth business procedures, especially planning and tracking. They are often called project management programs.

In most business operations, there are a variety of individual tasks that must be accomplished in order for a final product to be produced. Each task has a life of its own, although many tasks are interconnected and must be performed at the same time. Let's look at a commonplace example—throwing a party.

Suppose you are having a party at home for a dozen people. If you've ever done it, you know the anxiety that can accompany the preparations. There are dozens of tasks that must be accomplished, such as:

> Inviting the guests
> Cooking the food
> Ordering the flowers
> Purchasing wine
> Setting the table
> Polishing the silver
> Setting out hors d'oeuvres

These are just a few of the things you must accomplish. Many of us do these things automatically, without thinking.

But many more of us suffer through each stage and often run late in getting things done. Why? Because many of these items overlap, and it's very difficult to accomplish more than one thing—not to mention three or four—at a time.

With a business management program, such as a Program Evaluation and Review Technique (PERT) program, each of the items to be accomplished is entered into the program, along with the approximate amount of time needed to accomplish it. The computer then processes that information, and you can, whenever you need to, update it as you go along. The program would tell you that you could send out invitations well in advance of the party, but in order to begin other tasks (purchasing liquor, food, etc.) you would have to know by a specific date how many people were coming. And, obviously, you could never set the table if you didn't have an accurate count of guests. Once you knew how many people were coming, you could proceed to the next tasks.

You would be able to further break down the preparations by the type of food you were serving. You could know that the salad could be prepared the day before, but if you didn't put in the turkey before 3 P.M., you had very little chance of serving your guests at an appropriate time. Since the flowers take a day to be delivered, you must order them at least the day before. If the wine store only delivers twice a week, you could enter that information and the computer would tell you the latest time you could order the wine and know it'll be delivered in time for your party. Ordering the wine and flowers can be done at the same time, and are then out of your hands. These are examples of parallel tasks, ones that are not dependent upon each other.

Assuming your turkey was put into the oven by 3 P.M., you then have time to whip up the chocolate mousse. The potatoes would go into the oven by 5:30 P.M. (or you would be serving them very underdone). And when would you have time to set the table and polish the silver? In this case, you couldn't set the table until the silver was polished. These are tasks that are dependent upon each other.

Now all of this may seem trivial and easy to accomplish,

but if you are one of those people who never seem to get a job done on time, none of this is trivial—rather, it is overwhelming. The obvious advantage of a computer program that schedules your work is the ability to plan your work well in advance to ensure that you accomplish the objectives of your job on time.

Now let's look at a similar type of situation in the office. Suppose you were responsible for reorganizing your office to make room for the computers. There would be a long list of jobs to accomplish, many of them tied to and so dependent upon others. Some of the items to be accomplished might be:

Design the Office Layout: Before you can bring in a designer you must first evaluate the needs of your office and the individuals who work there. Since designers work on schedules based upon their availability, you must have a cutoff date by which to accomplish your needs evaluation. The scheduling program would give you the outside dates beyond which your schedules would have to change because the designers would not be available for several more months.

Then, of course, there are the times by which the plans for the office must be received and the work started. This is important, especially if work flow in the office is going to be disrupted. If you know, for example, that certain work periods are slower than others, one of those periods would be the ideal time to begin. Obviously, then, all of the planning before beginning must be accomplished by a certain date. The program tracks your progress.

Begin Construction: Now you've moved to the next level. To begin construction you must move people out of the area. Where do they go, and how long will they be there, possibly disrupting the work of others in the office?

Purchase Equipment: Assuming you have completed your design and construction plans, when will the computers be installed? It's not a simple decision. When do you bring in the consultants from the computer company to work with the designers and engineers to plan where the wiring is going? Where are people to be relocated during construction? That has to be worked out when you first design the office. Which means you must have selected the computers before beginning design.

Do you see how various tasks must be considered together in order to accomplish complete office reorganization? We don't have to go into all of the specifics; it is merely an example to demonstrate how tasks are normally tied together or run concurrently with other tasks.

The programs available for task scheduling use all types of sophisticated tracking devices, including Critical Path Method (CPM), Gantt bar charts, Time charts, and PERT charts. They also permit you to change information and update material, give you ongoing information about where you are on any job and flag you when you're running behind.

These are very sophisticated programs, and the better programs are also integrated to work in conjunction with other programs you use. If you use a time management program, a project management program can automatically transfer information on specific tasks to the daily schedule. Thus, when you run your daily schedule in the morning, those tasks relating to the project will appear on your screen, notifying you when you must have accomplished them in order for the entire program to move ahead.

These evaluation programs also let you know when you need more personnel, and so are a perfect way to advise the personnel department that you're going to need more people. Too often notification is given only a day or a week before a department needs additional skilled personnel. It is not always so easy to find the right people on such short notice. However, since the project management program requires that you plan the personnel needs for the accomplishment of each task within the objective as well as the time required, you can be prepared well in advance. As you update your progress, the program automatically recalculates the time remaining and you stay well ahead of your personnel needs.

The use of these different programs definitely can improve

your ability to get work done, usually resulting in more efficient performance. Whether the computer is used for staying on top of your daily needs, as elementary (and vital) as keeping appointments, scheduling meetings, tracking expenses, or for tracking entire corporate projects with sophisticated business management project and scheduling programs, it can take you to higher levels of achievement.

## ACCOUNTING

In most businesses the first department to become computerized is accounting. The computer can improve the effectiveness of the accounting process by the speed and efficiency with which it handles the five major accounting functions:

General ledger
Accounts receivable
Accounts payable
Payroll
Inventory control

Although there are separate programs for each of these functions, the better business programs are totally interactive or integrated and available for most personal computers. This means that entries into one portion of the program are automatically entered into the other appropriate accounting areas. As you post a transaction to the accounts receivable portion of the program, it makes a corresponding entry into the general ledger. The interactive program can even write checks for you.

Basically, the general ledger, which is the center of most accounting operations, is also the center of an accounting package. In a completely integrated operation, entries are made into the general ledger. This portion of the program is able to generate up-to-date reports on the chart of accounts, as well as other transaction journals, ledgers, and trial balances. Some of the programs with greater capabilities can also generate a balance sheet, budget, payroll summary, and cost expenses.

Entries into this portion of the program are processed, and information is transferred into the other relevant modules of the accounting program. As a result, a single entry into the general ledger is available for use in the accounts receivable, accounts payable, payroll, and inventory control portions of the program. Once that information is loaded into the other modules, the data can be manipulated to generate reports relevant to those functions. For instance, the accounts receivable portion of a program can generate any of the following reports:

Invoices
Customer accounts
Cash receipts
Account adjustments
Trial balance
Individual customer statements
Aged receivables
Customer mailing lists
Dunning notices
Transaction summaries
Cash flow

If your business maintains inventory, you will also find the computer invaluable. Although an inventory program can be extremely sophisticated and made to perform the most complex tasks you can conceive, on a more basic level the inventory control program gives you total control of your business. If, for example, one part of your program generates an invoice, the integrated program will, upon a command, automatically transfer appropriate data into the inventory control part of the program, appropriately reduce the inventory on the basis of your invoice, and even advise you when it's time to reorder.

Because each business is somewhat unique, these accounting programs are sufficiently versatile to permit you to design the program around your needs and to generate only those reports that you will find necessary.

## Financial Modeling

In most business, the financial plan is the key to success—or at least to survival. A financial plan created on a computer gives you one major advantage over one done by hand—the ability to ask "What if?" On a personal level, if you were to plan your expenses for the year and balance them against your annual income, you would have a financial plan for the upcoming year. But what if you were to buy a car? Or take a trip to Walt Disney World with the children? How would those items affect your final total? On the computer you can enter and change numbers continuously, and the computer will constantly recalculate the numbers to give you a clear picture of your future. Managers and other executives responsible for corporate planning no longer have to do their calculations by hand.

The financial modeling programs, usually called "electronic spreadsheets," completely replace paper, pencils, and calculators. They give you the ability to test dozens of different assumptions, normally a tedious chore. The first popular spreadsheet program was VisiCalc, and was, by itself, responsible for the sales of hundreds of thousands of computers. There are other programs now available, some with much greater computing power and flexibility. But essentially, they all work on the same principle.

On the video display screen, the program sets up an electronic worksheet at least 60 columns wide by 250 rows deep. Into these columns and rows you can enter numerical data, words or labels, and formulas. The computer manipulates the data according to your instructions, and calculations throughout the entire spreadsheet take seconds, rather than hours. For example, if you were planning a budget for a twelve-month period, you could change one number in the first month on your screen, and all of the numbers throughout the next eleven months would instantly reflect that change.

You can store versions of your budget and keep changing your assumptions in order to compare the results on paper. Store versions of the worksheet and refer to them later or pass them along to another department for input, right on the computer.

### Business Graphics

The use of visual displays as an adjunct to the accounting and financial modeling programs is another effective business tool. In addition, graphics are important in the marketing process. The most common types of graphics are bar, line, and pie charts, and they can be produced in a variety of colors.

Graphics help people understand numbers and assist managers in spotting problems and trends, evaluating sales increases and decreases, as well as in translating the "what if" electronic spreadsheets into a form that may be more easily understood by those who do not work with numbers on a day-to-day basis. Graphics programs may also be used to create marketing presentations, overhead projections, and illustrations that can be used in conjunction with word processing for corporate presentations.

There are certain keys to purchasing programs that will make your life and work easier. Programs should accomplish the job more easily than if it were done manually. Too often, especially in highly specific areas such as accounting, the programs are difficult to use. Also be sure that the language of the package is English, not a programming language, because you, or the person using an accounting-related program, are not a programmer. All of the logical steps and operations of the accounting process must be clearly apparent in the program, and the method by which transactions are normally entered and processed and the way reports are generated should be logical to you, the accountant, book-keeper, or any other businessperson who operates the computer.

If your responsibility is accounting, or any of the financial planning areas of your business, it should be obvious that the power of available programs can enhance this segment of your company's operation.

## TELECOMMUNICATIONS

As more and more offices begin to use computers, it becomes increasingly important to share information. This can be done in a variety of ways. You can move data, or program disks, from machine to machine in order for others to use it. This means that only one person at a time can access the information. When you, or another user, are finished inputting information, you then carry it or mail it to another computer location for use in the other machine.

A second method of sharing information is via the telephone. Through a direct telephone call, one machine can talk to another, uploading (sending) or downloading (receiving) information. There have been many cases of outsiders accessing unauthorized information merely by discovering the password, calling the computer via the telephone, and downloading the information. Not only is that against the law, but vital information can be lost or scrambled. In one illegal entry into a hospital computer, records of patients undergoing chemotherapy were accessed. Fortunately, nothing was changed on the records, which were used to determine the amount of chemotherapy prescribed. It's easy to see the dangers.

To deter electronic intruders, dedicated phone lines can be installed so that only people on that line can call the computer, keeping it comparatively safe from the outside. What does it take to involve your company in telecommunications? First, you need a device to transmit information. In most cases this will be a computer or a computer-phone. If you are using a computer, you will also need a modem to translate the information from the computer to a form that can be transmitted over telephone lines to another computer. The other computer, too, needs a modem, to retranslate the information back into a usable format, as we discussed in Chapter 2.

The topic here is the *use* of telecommunications. And the most obvious and probably most immediate and important aspect of this area is communication between individuals within and outside the company.

Let's examine specific instances in which telecommunicating is important. The first vital area is in the corporation that operates a main office and more than one outside location. It doesn't matter whether the company has one or one hundred separate branches, all of the computers within the company can conceivably talk to each other. A large corporation may operate a mainframe computer within the data processing center. Stored on this computer will be accounting programs, word processing, inventory control, and dozens of other operations vital to the function of the corporation. Throughout the country, other divisions of this company may require the same programs.

With telecommunications, it is not necessary for each division to have its own mainframe. Through the power of the telephone, each employee who requires computer operations can be tapped in directly with the mainframe, and download (load into their own computer) whatever information is necessary. For example, if division A in Wyoming needs 10,000 pounds of grain from the parent company in Atlanta, a few keystrokes can order the grain from the parent and delete that amount from the corporate inventory. Or a vice president can create his or her own financial model in the office and then transmit it instantly to the various branches throughout the country, so everyone is aware of corporate expectations. At the same time, each division head throughout the world can immediately transmit projections to the parent company, and dialogue can take place while the numbers are integrated. Once those numbers have been processed, each of the divisions can see how it compares with the other divisions by recalling them.

Another use for telecommunications in the office environment is electronic mail, a technique that is similar to facsimile and teletype transmissions. Dozens of message network companies have been established to provide this service. Previously, in order to transmit facsimile or teletype documents, the receiver had to have similar equipment to receive the material. Using electronic mail, senders can transmit memos or letters instantaneously either to others within the company on the same computer network (which we'll discuss later in this chapter) or to other computer users throughout the world. And they can send telegramlike letters to any size segment of the population. Many companies use these mail services to send multiple letters for advertising, billing, or even dunning.

These electronic mail services compete with the U.S. Postal Service. Essentially, anyone with a computer, word processor, telex terminal, or electronic typewriter can send a message to anyone else, regardless of whether the recipient has a computer. Services include letters delivered within hours, overnight and next-day delivery, and instant letters, which are delivered electronically to another subscriber to the service.

Information retrieval and gathering is another exciting area of telecommunications. There are over a thousand different electronic data banks that store, compile, and disseminate information in virtually any field. A call via the computer (assuming you subscribe to the data bank's service) can have the files searched electronically, which may uncover information vital to the operation of your business. Although most large companies maintain reference libraries, they cannot keep as current or update as quickly as electronic services can.

Instead of having to search through dozens of books and various indexes, the data base performs the search automatically, based on the parameters you provide. Whatever the field, you provide information in response to the questions from the data source. The computer then searches its files and very quickly responds to your requests, advising you of the amount of material available, where it can be found, what it contains, and if there are any additional charges to retrieve this material. For example, if you are a lawyer researching a case involving airline accidents, there are several specialized legal data bases that you can call by computer. Give the search parameters, and within seconds you will get a response indicating the availability of information in that area.

There are both general and specialized data bases in use today. Companies such as CompuServe, The Source, and Dow Jones News/Retrieval are among the more popular public services. Other specialized data banks are Nexis, Lexis, and Dialog. The specialized data bases can give you access to the Patent Office, Department of Agriculture, Official Airline Guide, stock reports, government regulatory agencies, and the price of corn, frozen orange juice, or pork bellies futures—virtually any information your business may require. Best of all, what you need is available in a fraction of the time it would normally take to search through a library's files.

### Networks

Another method of sharing information is known as a network. This is a form of "hard wiring," which means that various other computers or terminals are connected to one central computer by a cable. It's an ideal format for companies that have several computers and plan eventual growth. In some systems remote terminals can access information from a central computer equipped with a hard disk. While one computer is running a data base program, another can be accessing financial information, and a third may be using the word processing program.

It would be ideal if personal computer users were able to

continually download information from their minicomputer or mainframe. The problem up to now has been a lack of products to help in that interface. Often, the only way to connect these computers is by hiring a programmer to convert information. A small business without a data processing department does not have the capability to create links between different machines.

If these programs are available and you wish to access your mainframe, there are two ways to connect computers. The first is an asynchronous connection, which uses a modem and telephone lines, as we discussed above. It is a fairly simple connection, but its speed of information transmission is comparatively slow.

The second method, synchronous connection, generally use a coaxial cable, and to communicate over any distance you must use specially leased telephone lines. The transmission speed, however, is much greater than that of asynchronous connections.

This type of computer connection is called the Local Area Network (LAN), which is ideal for offices that continually use computers, have no time to waste waiting for free computer access time, and cannot afford a mainframe computer. With interconnecting cables, units can be added as needed. Very simply, by connecting computers and peripherals you can save major costs by using single hard disks, sharing daisy wheel printers, and having expensive programs available for multiple use. Thus the actual cost of each workstation is greatly reduced.

These LANs are available for as few as two or three machines, or for more than dozens of different computers. There are several major methods of interconnecting— twisted pair, coaxial cable, and fiber optical cable—but because there is no accepted standard yet, many people are hesitant about adopting a LAN.

The twisted-pair connection is similar to the wiring used in ordinary telephone lines. It is fairly inexpensive to install, but is also susceptible to outside electrical interference and is somewhat slow in transmission. The coaxial cable is cur-

# Types of Local Area Networks

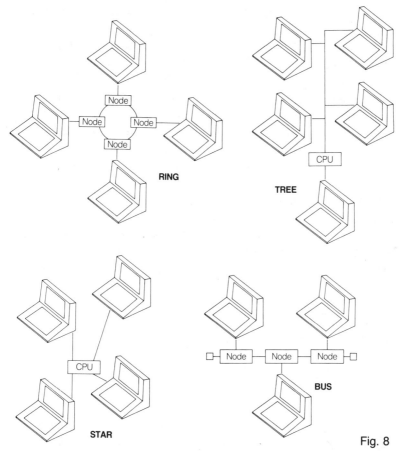

RING

TREE

STAR

BUS

Fig. 8

rently the most popular connection for LANs. There are both "broadband" and "baseband" channels. The broadband cable has room for many different communication channels, while the baseband has only one channel. Each has advantages and disadvantages. Some broadband cables are LocalNet, NetOne, and WangNet. Ethernet and ARCnet are baseband channels.

The fiber-optic cable is not yet so popular as the other cables but may eventually become the preferred medium, since it is shielded from intruding electrical interference and, like the broadband cable, can support many channels.

A major problem with the LAN is that many of the available systems are able to operate only one type of computer system. Since different brands of computers are usually comprised of incompatible operating systems and peripherals, a simple network would have considerable difficulty in communicating between the different systems. This may be somewhat limiting for a company that uses several types of computers. More complex networks are necessary to interface with the different machines, and only then can your TRS-80 Model II talk to your IBM PC, your DEC, Compaq, hard disk drive, as well as an assortment of dot matrix and daisy wheel printers.

Another form of accessing information is the PBX, or Private Branch Exchange. The PBX is an alternative to the LAN; it is used for communications and can transmit both telephone-voice and data information at lightning speeds between terminals. Both voice and data are transmitted as digital bits, requiring the use of modems. The caller uses a telephone handset and computer terminal to transmit to another machine. The information is displayed on the screen and can be stored for later use.

When trying to plan for your needs, it's necessary to determine what equipment you will have to have and how the equipment you may currently have can best be used. How many people will be using the interconnected system? What do you expect to accomplish by networking information? How much power will you need? What data must be protected, and how will your network provide that security? As in computer-purchasing decisions, software is usually the key. Much less software is available for network systems than for individual computers, so you must also be concerned about what software is available for your network.

Because communication is vital to the conduct of business, and as companies both large and small spread their operations throughout the world, the technology is continually upgraded. From simple telephone connections to networks to signals transmitted via satellite, there is hardly a company today doing business the traditional way, using direct-dial telephones, that will not be using some form of electronic telecommunications within the next decade.

## Electronic Mail

The subject of electronic mail covers both electronic mail networks and information services. The former are systems that enable you to communicate with anyone in the world by using your computer or executive workstation telephone system. These systems use both large electronic services and their own networks of computers that communicate with each other. For example, Digital Equipment Corporation, the second-largest computer company in the world, is located in Maynard, Massachusetts. However, it has divisions throughout the world. All of its computers are connected by its own electronic network, which ties together more than thirty thousand computer terminals worldwide.

Information services normally include a data base, from which you can access thousands of different types of information, along with a mail service. Companies that provide these services include CompuServe and The Source, as well as hundreds of informal bulletin-board systems throughout the country.

Electronic mail is designed to be a substitute for traditional paper mail, as well as a replacement for telephone calls. You compose your letter to another person, or group of people, right on your computer. Then, using your computer to do the dialing, you call one of the electronic services. You address the letter to the appropriate recipient, upload (send) the letter to the screen and service, and finally, give the necessary mailing instructions. That's all you do.

At the other end, if the recipient has a computer, he or she turns it on, calls up the mail service using the computer, and is notified that there is mail waiting in the electronic in basket. You can scan all of the messages in your in basket for subject, sender, date, urgency, etc., and download (retrieve) them in any order you wish. The letters can be stored in the computer's memory or printed out on your printer as you download them, to be read later.

Services such as SourceMail on The Source, and Easyplex on CompuServe, require that both the sender and the recipient be members. Both of these information networks offer, along with mail service, other valuable services. In essence they are data banks, available for the use of their members, with hundreds of different types of information. You can, for example, read all the headlines coming off the Associated Press news wire, on an hourly basis. You can gather immediate financial information on thousands of companies. For the busy businessperson or secretary, there is an on-line travel directory, the Official Airline Guide Electronic Edition, that lists thousands of flights and fares at the touch of a few keys.

The charges for sending mail are somewhat different on The Source and CompuServe. Both services charge an hourly rate for access, and the rates vary, depending upon what time of day you use the service. Prime time service, during working hours, is far more expensive than standard service, which usually runs from 6 P.M. to 8 A.M. But your only telephone charge (remember, your computer is calling the data base system to access the service) is for a local telephone call, thanks to many of the telephone network services, such as Telenet and Uninet. Thus, if you use CompuServe, which is located in Ohio, but you live in Key West, Florida, or Anchorage, Alaska, you are only charged for calling a local number.

In addition, then, to your local time charge, you are charged for the time on the computer. In order not to become an expensive proposition, letters are normally first composed on one's word processing program on the computer. After the letter has been edited and is ready to send, it must then be converted to a form that can be sent over telephone lines. The standard code used is ASCII (American Standard Code for Information Exchange), and most good word processing programs will easily convert your letter into ASCII.

Next, using the communications capabilities and program of your computer, you call up one of the services. Most business-oriented computers will have programs able to place the call, log onto the service (by providing identifying numbers and password), and take you directly into the electronic mail section of the data base. Once into this section of the service, you follow the simple directions to send a letter. When asked, you push the appropriate keys on the keyboard, and the letter you have composed is automatically uploaded to the mail service. When uploading is completed, another command then sends the letter to the in box of the intended recipient. That delivery is almost instantaneous.

If you wish to send the letter to more than one person, you must then put in those names and addresses also. The "address" is an electronic ID number, unique to each individual, and it is the only way you can send mail via CompuServe or The Source.

Easyplex and SourceMail are very similar to each other. You are not limited to the number of characters that you can transmit. Thus, you can send long letters, documents, multipage contracts, and even a full report, if time is of the essence. If you plan to use electronic mail to send memos to many people at the same time, you can instruct SourceMail or Easyplex to send the document to a specified distribution list. Suppose you want to notify all of your salespeople of a price change and they must know at once. All of their names and ID numbers can be stored in a separate file, which can be called up by your computer when sending the letter. When the service asks you to whom you wish to send the letter, you instruct it to access this specific file, then upload the letter. Distribution to all on your list will be done immediately. Imagine the speed with which you can contact all of the people who work with you, and the advantages you all share by having immediate access, at low cost, to important information.

Both CompuServe and The Source serve other functions in the exchange of information, which we'll cover soon. There are also other electronic mail services that should be considered. Among them, MCI Mail is the most popular mail service, although there are others, such as Western Union's Easylink, Telemail from GTE Telenet, and On-Tyme II from Tymshare. Every month new electronic mail services become available.

It is not necessary to be connected to a commercial mail service to transmit and receive electronic mail. If, like the Digital Equipment Corporation mentioned earlier, you have a network of computers and telephone terminals in your company, regardless of where they're located you can be hooked into it by software. A single terminal can be designated to receive mail and be left on continuously (like leaving a telex machine unattended). Mail messages are sent directly to this system and the incoming messages removed by the designated recipients. You may establish individual passwords for each person who accesses the mail, so only those for whom the mail is intended can read it.

Electronic bulletin boards are also used to carry messages and mail, but they are somewhat less reliable than the other services. Most of them are run on a volunteer basis and are not for profit. Thus, many come and go. Also, because they are limited in the number of telephone lines that access them, their numbers are more frequently busy than not. Almost anyone with a computer and appropriate software can establish a bulletin board, and there are no controls over them. Most serve as local gossip centers, providing the ability to share public domain programs and permitting users to leave mail. Because they are not regulated, it is not advisable to use bulletin boards as your formal mail service.

If you plan to install some type of electronic mail service in your company, in addition to the computer or executive workstation, it is important to have a program that you can manipulate to serve your needs conveniently. This means that you should have the ability to send *what* you want to mail, *when* you want to mail it, with a minimum of on-line time charges.

Some of the aspects of the software you should look for are:

1. Enough flexibility to encompass several different types of mail services.
2. The ability to compose your documents before you go on-line with the service. This feature saves a considerable amount in time charges with services such as The Source and CompuServe.
3. An address maintenance file, so you can store names, addresses, or ID numbers of regular recipients of your mail and which you can update as necessary.
4. Group addressing, which enables you to send mail to several mailboxes at the same time. In addition, you may want a hidden distribution option, like the "blind carbon copy" often used in business correspondence. Copies of your letters are automatically sent to a specified individual without the knowledge of the original recipient.
5. An automatic dial and retry system, in which the computer dials the number of the mailbox or network system automatically and, if the line is busy, will continue to place the call until there is an answer.
6. Scan and read options in the receive mode. If you receive a large amount of electronic mail, you will want to have the option of looking through the letters before reading them. In this way you can select those letters that are urgent or from certain individuals, without wasting time reading other, less important documents. If, for example, you are expecting a marketing report from your salesperson on the West Coast and a letter concerning a purchasing decision from another location, you might want to find out about the purchase first, without having to read through the entire sales report, which can probably be read later, at your leisure.

7. Display and print-mail utilities, which enable you to view any documents still in the system and, at the same time, make a hard copy printout of a letter if you need one.

8. Forwarding option, a newer feature that allows you to read a document, make comments on it, and forward it to another person. This is a time-saving device, for it eliminates the need to redo an entire letter as a separate and new document.

9. Multiaccessing protocols, which permit others, regardless of where they are located, to retrieve messages and letters from one system. Thus, if you are working at home on your terminal, you can call into the office to download your messages from the computer there. Also, with appropriate passwords, you can permit others access to your specific files in order to leave various messages for them at any time.

As electronic mail systems become more sophisticated as a result of changing technology, many more features will become available. One important addition will be the integration of voice, graphics, and data transmission. You will be able to place a telephone call to the computer and leave your verbal message, and it will be translated by the computer into computer code, so the recipient can download it from the computer as a memo or letter.

The ability to access others instantaneously via the computer adds a new dimension to your business and the functions you perform within your company.

## Information Networks/Research

When we discussed electronic mail, we mentioned information networks, systems that offer electronic mail capabilities as well as a variety of other services. Information networks are actually large data bases of information, accessible by anyone with a computer, modem, appropriate software, and a membership to the network.

Among these networks are general data banks, such as The Source and CompuServe, and other, more specialized data banks, the largest of which is Dow Jones News/Retrieval. There are also other national networks, including BRS After Dark, Delphi, Dialog, NewsNet, Photonet, Lexis, and Nexis.

There are over one thousand other information services (a recent account said there were more than thirteen hundred), most of which are highly specialized. You can retrieve information on subjects such as agriculture, business, stocks and bonds, computers, engineering, patents, medicine, law, news, and even help wanted notices. Although all of this information may be available from other sources, such as newspapers, magazines, journals, radio, and TV, an information network permits you to access this information anytime, almost instantaneously.

Essentially, computerized electronic networks provide you with information when you want it. You don't have to be dependent on newspaper delivery, research trips to the library, or a certain hour to watch the news. It takes little more than a phone call. In addition, there are other services, such as electronic banking transactions, or on-line shopping, where you can order merchandise from selected stores over the computer.

Remember that these networks are actually data bases—collections of information in electronic form that can be accessed by your computer. And, although these data banks may be located in different cities throughout the United States, because of a technology known as packet switched networks, you are able to place a local call to access the data bank, rather than having to make a long-distance call. Thus, if you call CompuServe Information Service, which is located in Columbus, Ohio, you pay only for the local call in your city (or the closest city) to access this computer. Additional charges are incurred by your time on the computer.

Most services charge a variety of fees for their use. There is normally a membership charge to join the service, and in some cases, this fee includes software for your computer. In addition, some services charge a minimum monthly fee, regardless of how often you use the service. And finally, you are charged for your time on the service, those rates varying for prime time (work hours) and standard time (off hours). As you become more adept at using the services, you are able to locate exactly what you need in a minimum amount of time, thus saving yourself connect charges.

Although we discussed it briefly in the section on electronic mail, let's review the mode of getting onto an information network. The first thing is to call the service. Normally, you can do this automatically, with your computer. Once you've answered the required questions, such as ID number and password (also done automatically), you are logged onto the system. You are now "on-line."

Many systems offer you menus, lists of options from which you choose where you want to go within the service. Do you want the electronic encyclopedia? Are you interested in the latest AP news wire? Do you want to send mail? Are you researching patents granted in the last six months? Do you want the latest stock price on your company? Most people using computers for the first time feel intimidated by these services, but actually just minimal typing skills are required, and you need only have some idea as to where in the data base you are going. If you get into trouble and are confused, most of the services have "Help" menus to ease your fears and answer your questions.

Once you have entered the area of the data base you are looking for, you can then narrow your search. Some sections merely run through the latest news or facts on a specific subject. Other sections require you to direct the search. As you locate the information you want, you can read it page by page, print it out on your printer, or store it in the memory of the machine for later use. If you are offered choices, you can select the topic that interests you. In the electronic encyclopedia accessed through several different data bases, you first provide a "search term." Tell the machine what you are looking for. The encyclopedia electronically (and instantly) searches its own index and tells you how many "articles" (entries) on that topic it contains. Next, it advises you of the specifics of those subjects. You can then choose which articles you wish to read and ignore those that are not specific enough for you or not relevant to your needs.

Furthermore, while you are using the encyclopedia, keywords will be highlighted, to indicate that there are other articles available pertaining to those subjects. In this way, you have access to a greater amount of information, without endless research in the library.

Another major advantage of using an electronic information service is the immediacy of the information. Data bases are continually updated in order to provide the user with the most current information.

Following are some of the information services, and a selection of their features that may appeal to you and your company.

*The Source:* This network offers a wide range of consumer and business topics. You can get news, sports, political commentary, science and technological information, and general interest features from newspapers. In addition, there is a business and finance section that provides stock market prices, analysis, news services, computations, personal financial programs, and business and management reference sources. There is also a unique newsletter service that offers a wide range of publications, continually updated. There are conferences, bulletin boards, and, as we described earlier, electronic mail.

*CompuServe:* Many of the services offered here are similar in nature to those of The Source. There is a professional data base that provides information and communication forums for agribusiness, aviation, environmental issues, medical topics, law, and engineering and other technical subjects. Along with the electronic encyclopedia, there are several other valuable reference sections.

*Dow Jones News/Retrieval:* Strong on financial and business topics, this data bank has some unique reference areas.

Along with headlines from the *Wall Street Journal,* you can also research headlines and stories from major financial journals that go back about five years. Using the technique of providing search terms by name or subject, you can locate stories about important business topics. There is a weekly economic update, stock quotations, and forecasts. Furthermore, you can obtain almost any type of in-depth financial information and profiles of more than eight thousand publicly held companies. There are other services, too, that are consumer oriented, such as news and weather, movie reviews, and on-line shopping. You can access MCI Mail through Dow Jones, but there is a charge for using the Dow Jones connection.

*Dialog:* A very fast data bank, Dialog has almost 200 different research areas, including agriculture, books, business information, computer topics, corporate news, education, engineering, government publications, a magazine index data base, medicine, news, and psychology data. You can see by the partial list of topics, that this can prove to be a very valuable information source. Dialog contains more than 55 million records of information.

Dialog, like BRS (a description of which follows), is also known as an encyclopedia data base. It provides much more in-depth material than does a standard information service like CompuServe. These services were once the exclusive province of research librarians in government institutions and large corporations. Now, however, they are available to anyone with a computer. Whatever is not already available on these data bases will surely be on-line in the near future.

*BRS After Dark:* Here is another encyclopedia service with a large selection of business and technical data bases. These include science and medicine, business and finance, reference books, education, social sciences and humanities, energy and environmental topics. Within these areas you have access to journals, abstracts, patent information, government data bases, as well as electronic mail service, a bulletin board system, and personal communications.

*NewsNet:* There are dozens of different topics covered by NewsNet, including environment, research and development, politics, publishing and broadcasting, transportation, manufacturing, law, government and regulatory information, electronics and computers, building and construction, and finance and accounting, among others. In total, there are about 175 different newsletters on-line, within thirty different industry groups. Many of these newsletters are updated daily, especially important when you require pricing trends, current legislation rulings, tax information, or other sensitive and immediate information.

What is described here is just the tip of the iceberg—a few of the more popular data banks, among the more than one thousand available. Where once you would have had to spend a day or more in the local library researching information you might need, today you can call a service, push a few keys, and find the information you want immediately. The ability to do this gives you greater flexibility in your job and allows you to make knowledgeable decisions based on the most current information available and to expand the scope of your business for greater profits.

## PROGRAMS FOR THE OFFICE

There are many different types of computer programs that are useful in everyday office operation. All of these have been written to make your job easier. Some programs, unfortunately, are difficult to use, and the explanations of how to use them (commonly called documentation) are often just as confusing as the operation of the software. Those that are easier to use are called user friendly.

There is no lack of available software. However, because programs are constantly updated, upgraded, replaced, or expanded, the market changes rapidly. Software publishers try to create an entire line of programs to give them greater access to businesses. If a company can get in the door with a data processing program and the customer is happy, the company may then be able to sell the customer an accounting program, for example.

We suggest that if you wish to purchase software, contact a number of the publishers of computer software listed in your Yellow Pages for technical and promotion information. Or ask your computer manufacturer for compatible software. When you do so, be sure to indicate which computer models you use. Unlike books which can be read by everyone, software must be tailored to the particular computer operating system being used. A software publisher normally publishes many versions of programs, more like a publisher of foreign language translations, who publishes different editions of the same book for different countries because those in France read only the French edition, those in Germany read only the German edition, and so on. It is the same with computer programs—the IBM reads only the IBM compatible programs; the DEC reads only the DEC compatible programs, and Apple programs can be read only by the Apple computers.

Very often, software publishers provide demonstration disks, which are a good way to try out programs. You can also ask for suggestions from the company that sells you the hardware or from local computer stores. There are, of course, some programs that are much more popular than others; many software-oriented magazines provide a Top 20 list of the most popular business programs. Although a listing on these charts is often an indication that the programs are good, the bottom line is to make sure the program first fills all of your operating needs.

# 5
# The Language of the Office

Regardless of the type of work you do, there are certain language basics you must know. Communication is the cornerstone to success in both personal and business life, and it is therefore necessary to be aware of the essentials of grammar, punctuation, and other aspects of language that people often find somewhat puzzling. For example, grammar is the key to better letter writing, and what office does not generate dozens of letters a day? Grammar can often make the difference between succeeding and failing, gaining a new client and not. And inability to speak properly may even hold you back in your job. The way you present yourself in your job is just as important as the way you perform that job.

When you move into the technological era, do those skills change? Not really. You are still required to have a good knowledge of grammar and other language skills in order to perform your work properly. Although the computer can do certain tasks for you, it cannot think.

Here is where your skills become more important. We mentioned earlier that there are programs for the computer that can correct your spelling. You insert the dictionary disk, and the computer searches through your letter for those words it does not recognize—misspelled words or words not already stored in the program's memory. You can then decide whether or not to change the spelling and whether to store those words for later use. But the computer still only identifies those words; you must make the decision whether to change them. In order to make that decision, you have to be informed.

We cover here some of the essentials of language, including the basic parts of speech, the rules of word division, and an in-depth guide to compound words. The parts of speech are important because they occur in and structure the meaning of our everyday language. It is necessary to understand the difference between adjectives and adverbs, nouns and prepositions. This knowledge also helps you improve your communication skills.

Word division follows a series of rules, that, once learned, can be recalled whenever you have a problem. When confronted by a particularly perplexing word that must be split, you can always fall back on the dictionary, which provides that information for you. In addition, most good word processing programs provide the ability to hyphenate words. Once the command to hyphenate is given, the computer searches the text for those words that can be hyphenated to make the length of each line more uniform. This is especially important in text that is supposed to be justified (with even lines at both right and left margins). If there is too much space left in a line because a long word has been moved to the next line to avoid a split, that short line will print with an inordinate amount of space between words and will appear out of place in the paragraph. Hyphenation permits you to make the lines more equal in length and the spacing between words more uniform. Again, the computer cannot decide where to put the hyphen. By knowing the rules, you will save time and improve your accuracy—as well as the readability of your letter or report.

Finally, we have included a substantial, but by no means complete, list of compound words. Deciding about the form of the word is a lot more tricky than simple hyphenation. Also, many dictionaries simply do not show all of the compounds of words, especially abridged and paperback dictionaries kept on one's desk. It's important to know when a hyphen is required, when words are combined forms, how to use prefixes and suffixes, and when to merely put space between words. For example, the word *bookcase* should be one word. *Book club* is two words, and *book-lined* is hyphenated. Currently, there are no programs that provide you with the ability to select the appropriate form of the word, and thus we've included the list.

## PARTS OF SPEECH

Some of this material may seen very simple to you, and if so, you are lucky that you are conversant with these basic grammatical forms. If they are somewhat confusing, spend some time reading through this section and then try to practice your knowledge. Read newspapers and magazines, and identify the different parts of speech. Then reread this section and see how much you've learned.

*Noun:* A noun is a word used to name a person, thing, place, or quality. A proper noun is the name of a particular person, place, or thing.

| | |
|---|---|
| person: | Harry, Sally |
| thing: | tree, car, pencil |
| place: | Texas, Bloomingdale's |
| quality: | truth |

*Pronoun:* A pronoun is a word used as a substitute for a noun. There are several classes of pronouns, most of which you'll recognize.

| | |
|---|---|
| personal: | we, you, I, it |
| relative: | who, that |
| interrogative: | who, whom, what |
| demonstrative: | this, that, those |
| indefinite: | some, any, one |
| intensive and reflexive: | herself, himself, myself |
| distributive: | each, everyone |

*Verb:* A verb is a word or group of words expressing action taken by or upon the subject.

fly, run, jump, play, sing

*Adjective:* An adjective is a word that describes or modifies the meaning of a noun or pronoun.

*faster* plane
*slower* horse
*running* brook

*Adverb:* An adverb is a word that modifies a verb, an adjective, or even another adverb. It answers the questions when, where, how, or how much.

*very* happy
calculate *accurately*
*almost* finished

*Preposition:* A preposition is a word used to relate a noun or pronoun to another word in the sentence.

in order *to*
he went *from* here to there.
they stopped *at* the store.

There is a rule for prepositions that is expressed in the sentence: "A preposition is a bad thing to end a sentence on." Sometimes, however, to reconstruct a sentence in order to avoid ending it with a preposition leaves you with a very awkward, unnatural-sounding sentence. For example, "There were things we wanted to talk *about*" is much easier to construct than "There were things *about* which we wanted to talk."

*Conjunction:* A conjunction is a word used to connect words, phrases, clauses, or sentences.

Adrienne *and* I went shopping.
Neither he *nor* I saw the show.
I can't, *but* you can.

*Clause:* A clause is a group of related words which contain a subject and a predicate. An independent clause is a complete statement, or simple sentence. A dependent clause cannot stand alone.

independent clause:     he can jump.
dependent clause:       what the show was about

*Phrase:* A phrase is a group of related words without a subject or predicate, used as a noun, verb, adjective, or adverb.

on the floor
telling the truth

## Sentence Classifications

*Simple Sentence:* A simple sentence contains a single, independent clause.

The house was on fire.

*Compound Sentence:* A compound sentence contains two or more independent clauses.

The house was on fire, but he was not home.

*Complex Sentence:* A complex sentence contains one independent clause and one or more dependent clauses.

While we were going to the game, we saw the solar eclipse.

The parts of speech discussed here are really only the tip of the iceberg. However, these descriptions and examples should be enough to give you an idea of what you should look for in composing business correspondence. When writing, reading, or speaking, you should be aware of how grammar is used. Have you left parts of sentences dangling and incomplete? Have you confused verbs with adverbs? Is what you are saying clear to others? Communicating effectively is the most important aspect of using good grammar.

## RULES OF WORD DIVISION

Word division, or word breaks, is invaluable for anyone who types or writes. It's especially important if you ever prepare material such as reports or documents that must be typeset and printed.

1. You should avoid breaking words on more than two consecutive lines. (You should also avoid ending more than two consecutive lines with the same word, symbol, or group of numbers.)

2. Word division should be avoided in headings.

3. The final word of a paragraph should not be divided.

4. Words should be divided according to pronunciation, and to avoid mispronunciation, they should be divided so that the part of the word left at the end of the line will suggest the entire word: capacity, not capa-city; service-man, not ser-viceman.

5. Words should never be divided on a single letter: usu-ally, not u-sually; imag-inary, not i-maginary.

6. Division of short words (five letters or fewer) should be avoided if possible. Also, two-letter divi-

sion, including the carryover of two-letter end-ings—-ed, -el, -es, -ic, -le, -ly—should be avoided.

7. Words of two syllables are divided at the end of the first syllable: dis-pelled, con-quered.

8. Words of three or more syllables should preferably be divided after the vowel: particu-lar, sepa-rate.

9. In words with short prefixes—ac-, de-, dis-, non-, pre-, un-, etc.—divide after the prefix: non-essen-tial, not nones-sential.

10. If possible, prefixes and combining forms of more than one syllable—anti-, macro-, retro-, etc.—should be kept intact: macro-economics, not mac-roeconomics.

11. Words ending in -er should not be divided unless the division can be made on a prefix, rather than on the -er form.

12. The following word endings are not divided: -ceous, -cial, -cient, -cion, -cious, -geous, -gion, -gious, -sial, -sion, -tial, -tion, and -tious.

13. The suffixes -able and -ible are usually carried over intact to the next line. However, when the stem word loses its original form, these suffixes are divided according to pronunciation: comfort-able, manage-able; but dura-ble, audi-ble.

14. Words ending with -ing, with stress on the primary syllable, are preferably divided on the base word: chang-ing, danc-ing, writ-ing. However, when stress is placed on the second syllable, divide the words between the doubled consonants: forbid-ding, refer-ring.

15. When the addition of -ed, -er, -est, or a similar ending causes the doubling of a final consonant, the added consonant is carried over: pit-ted, glad-dest, control-lable.

16. When the final consonant sound of a word belongs to a syllable ending with a silent vowel, the final consonant (or consonants) becomes part of the added suffix: chuck-ling, han-dling, twin-kled.

17. Words with doubled consonants are usually divided between those consonants: clas-sic, neces-sary, rebel-lion; but call-ing, mass-ing.

18. The following diagraphs (groups of two successive letters that make one sound phonetically) should not be split: ai, ck, dg, gh, gn, ng, oa, ph, sh, and th.

19. Do not divide contractions: doesn't, haven't.

20. Solid compounds are divided between the members: bar-keeper, proof-reader, humming-bird.

21. Try to avoid divisions that add a hyphen to an already hyphenated compound: court-martial, not court-mar-tial. (These words appear in the Compound Word List.)

22. Words of one syllable should not be split: shipped, quenched, through.

23. Two consonants, preceded and followed by a vowel, are divided after the first consonant: abundant, advan-tage.

24. When two adjoining vowels are sounded separately, divide between them: cre-ation, gene-alogy.

25. In breaking homonyms, distinction should be given
to their relative functions and parts of speech:

| | |
|---|---|
| pro-ject (verb) | proj-ect (noun) |
| pro-duce (verb) | prod-uce (noun) |
| rec-ollect (to recall) | re-collect (collect again) |

26. There is a large group of words that end in -meter,
and distinction should be made between metric system terms, and terms indicating a measuring instrument. When dividing metric terms, try not to
divide the -meter suffix or, if you must divide the
suffix, divide after *me*. When dividing measuring
instrument words, divide after the *m*.

| *metric* | *measuring* |
|---|---|
| cen-ti-me-ter | al-tim-e-ter |
| deca-me-ter | mi-crom-e-ter |
| hec-to-me-ter | ba-rom-e-ter |

27. In chemical formulas, the hyphen has an important
function. If a break is unavoidable in a formula,
division is preferably made after an original hyphen
to avoid introducing a misleading one. If it is im-
practical to break on a hyphen, division may be
made after an original comma, and no hyphen is
added.

28. Although there are too many scientific rules to list
here, it is desirable to preserve as a unit chemical
combining forms, prefixes, and suffixes.

29. Abbreviations and symbols should not be broken
at the end of a line: AFL, AT&T, RPM.

30. Figures with fewer than six digits, decimals, and
closely connected combinations of figures and abbreviations should not be broken at the end of a
line: $24,000, 6 P.M., 44.876. If a break in six digits

or more is unavoidable, divide after a comma: 1,244,-099.

31. Closely related abbreviations and initials in proper names and accompanying titles should not be separated, nor should titles—Mr., Esq., Jr., 3rd—be separated from surnames.

32. Wherever possible, avoid dividing proper names.

33. In dates, do not divide the month and day, but the year may be carried over to the next line.

These seem like a lot of rules to remember. However, with this book close at hand, you can quickly locate this section and look up the appropriate rule. As you can see, most of the rules for word division follow common sense and pronunciation. The essence of the word should be retained when making word breaks.

## COMPOUND WORDS

A compound word is a union of two or more words that conveys a single idea. A compound is spelled open (as separate words), with a hyphen, or as one word. A hyphen is often required and is a mark of punctuation that not only unites but separates the component words, and thus makes it easier to read and understand the word, as well as ensuring correct pronunciation. The hyphen used in word division is to aid in breaking the word on two lines while retaining the connection between parts. In compound words, hyphens are used to make words clear.

There are some general rules about compound words, most of which follow common sense, yet preserve the form and meaning of the words.

1. In general, spell open when words appear in regular order and the omission causes no confusion:

banking hours
real estate                                    free enterprise system
interstate commerce law            fellow citizen
piano teacher                              living costs

2. Words are usually combined to express a meaning that would not be so clear if the words were unconnected. These words are often hard to determine without a word list or dictionary.

afterglow            bookkeeping
gentleman            right-of-way

3. A derivative of a compound usually retains the solid or hyphenated form of the original compound.

coldblooded          coldbloodedness
ill-advised          ill-advisedly
X-ray (verb)         X-raying

4. Except after the short prefixes co-, de-, pre-, pro-, and re-, which are generally joined to the word, a hyphen is used to avoid doubling a vowel or tripling a consonant.

cooperation          deemphasis
anti-inflation       semi-intelligent
shell-like           brass-smith

You can imagine how awkward these examples of double vowels and triple consonants might be if not hyphenated: shelllike, antiinflation.

5. Combine two nouns that form a third, especially when the compound has only one primary accent.

airship              cupboard
footnote             workman

6. Combine a noun that consists of a short verb with an adverb as its second element, unless the use of the solid form would interfere with comprehension.

blowout          breakdown
run-in           tie-in

7. Combine as one word compass directions consisting of two points, but use a hyphen after the first point when three points are combined.

northeast               southwest
north-northeast         south-southwest

8. Where two or more hyphenated compounds have a common basic element and this element is omitted in all but the last term, the hyphens are retained.

2-, 4-, 6-, and 8-foot boards
long- and short-term money rates

9. Color terms should be separate words, unless those terms are modifiers.

dark blue            bluish green
iron-gray stove      silver-gray fish

10. Use a hyphen or hyphens to prevent mispronunciation to ensure definite accents on each element of a compound word or to avoid ambiguity.

co-op (which is not the same as *coop)*
un-ionized (which is not the same as *unionized)*
re-cover (which is not the same as *recover)*

11. Use hyphens to join a prefix or combining form to a capitalized word.

anti-American        un-British

12. Use a hyphen between the elements of compound numbers from twenty-one to ninety-nine and in adjective compounds with a numerical first element.

thirty-first              8-hour day
twentieth-century art    two-sided question

13. Hyphens are used between the elements of a fraction, but omitted between the numerator and the denominator when a hyphen appears in either or both.

one-thousandth              two-thirds
twenty-one thirty-seconds    two one-thousandths

14. Use hyphens to connect elements of idiomatic compounds.

blue-pencil                     know-it-all
first-come-first-served basis   hard-and-fast rule

15. Use hyphens in compounds formed of repetitive or conflicting terms and in compounds naming the same thing under two aspects.

boogie-woogie    pitter-patter
young-old        walkie-talkie

16. Use hyphens to join a single capital letter to a noun or a participle.

X-ray      I-beam
T-strap    V-necked

There are many more rules that could be included in this listing. However, many of them are either too obvious or too obscure. As you read through the list that follows, certain consistencies will appear, and the more you consult these words, the more familiar you will become with the appropriate forms, when to use hyphens, and when hyphens are unnecessary.

## COMPOUND WORD LIST

The list in Appendix 1 (page 135) is based on the rules for compounding we just outlined. These codes should be understood:

- Words printed flush left are combined with the indented words to form solid or hyphenated compounds.
- Words preceded by hyphens mean that hyphens should be used to connect the words.
- Words without hyphens are to be combined with the base word as a solid word.
- A spacemark (#) indicates a two-word form, i.e., words divided by a space.
- Abbreviations have been used, as follows:

| | |
|---|---|
| *adv.* | adverb |
| *c.f.* | combining form |
| *conj.* | conjunction |
| *n.* | noun |
| *pref.* | prefix |
| *u.m.* | unit modifier |
| *v.* | verb |

## REFERENCES AND HOW TO USE THEM

There are thousands of different reference books available to you, and as you have already read, much of the information they contain is now available for your computer as well, either as a software program you can use right on your machine or through an information network you can call via your computer. However, there are a few books that will be invaluable for you in your day-to-day work. One, of course, is this book, which will give you a large variety of information about working in the technological office and should be kept on your desk or workstation. Here are some other books that you should have access to.

### Dictionary

Depending upon your needs, you can use either an abridged or an unabridged dictionary. An abridged dictionary is usually sufficient for normal use. There are hundreds of thousands of words in the English language. The abridged dictionary omits the more uncommon forms of words and condenses information. The unabridged dictionary contains a much larger selection of words and goes into more detail in the definitions. In addition, it usually includes obsolete and specialized terms and words. (This book, for example, has its own technological dictionary for your convenience.) You will also be able to locate idiomatic expressions, word derivations, and alternative spellings. Many unabridged dictionaries are also illustrated.

The only major problem you may face when using a dictionary is not knowing how to spell the word you are looking for. If you don't, it puts you in an interesting quandary, since entries are arranged by how they are spelled: How are you going to find the proper spelling if you can't spell the word correctly in the first place? The only solution to finding the proper spelling is to try a variety of different possibilities until you locate the word. If you can spell it and want the definition, that, of course, is much easier.

Following are some of the essential rules for using a dictionary.

1. Dictionaries are arranged in alphabetical order. At the top of each page are reference words to help you find what you are looking for more quickly. These are the first and last words that appear on that page. If the reference words at the top of the page are *primer/*

*printer,* you would know that the first word on the page is *primer* and the last word is *printer.* If your word falls anywhere in between, it appears on that page.

2. For those words that have more than one meaning, there are usually separate listings for each one, or multiple definitions within one listing, each indicated by a number.

3. When there is more than one way to spell a word, each spelling is listed, with the preferred spelling indicated.

4. Dictionaries always list words in their main form. They also show how the word is divided by syllables. When we discussed word division, we mentioned that you can use the dictionary as a guide to splitting words.

5. As well as indicating the main forms of words, the dictionary also gives the part of speech of each word. Common abbreviations are used to indicate those parts: noun—n., verb—v., adjective—adj., adverb—adv., transitive verb—v.t., intransitive verb—v.i. Some dictionaries also give a definition for each form of a word.

6. Prefixes and suffixes are normally indicated, preceded or followed by a hyphen.

7. At the bottom of each page in an unabridged dictionary there is usually a pronunciation guide; in an abridged dictionary several pages at the beginning of the book often serve as the pronunciation guide. This guide lists all of the symbols used in the dictionary to illustrate proper pronunciation. Correct pronunciation is provided for all the words defined, but the symbols used are not necessarily the same for all dictionaries. You should consult the guide before using a new book.

These are just some of the basics of standard dictionaries. There are also dictionaries of specific terms for a large variety of fields, as well as technical dictionaries, literary dictionaries, professional dictionaries, and a vast assortment of others.

### English Usage Books

Hand in hand with the dictionary are books to help you with grammar and English language usage. Perhaps the best-known book is *Roget's Thesaurus,* which is a dictionary of synonyms (two or more words that have the same meaning), antonyms (words with opposite meanings), and homonyms (two or more words that sound the same but have different spellings and meanings). A thesaurus is especially valuable to anyone who writes or speaks publicly, since it provides a key to the richness of the English language and enables you to avoid repetition of words.

There are also style books, which present the proper rules for all areas of writing and editing. Among the best known are *The Chicago Manual of Style* and Strunk and White's *The Elements of Style.* These include everything from handling footnotes, preparing tables, and indicating references to the correct rules of grammar.

### Encyclopedia

An encyclopedia presents short articles about a large variety of subjects. It is excellent for research. There are many different encyclopedia sets, and most run to almost two dozen volumes. There are also one-volume books that may be better for use in an office, especially if you don't require the volume of information provided in a multibook set. Of course, as mentioned earlier in this book, many information services offer on-line computerized encyclopedias, which give you the advantage of instant information, updated at least four times a year.

Obviously, books cannot be updated that frequently. Given the high cost of producing and of buying encyclopedia sets, it is not practical to replace them on a regular basis, and thus the electronic media give you more current information. The printed versions, however, can provide material not normally available on the computer screen, such as maps, diagrams, and other illustrative materials that may help clarify information.

## Atlases and Gazetteers

An atlas is a book of maps covering all parts of the world, normally in a variety of details. For example, if an atlas contains a map of the United States, it might also include separate maps of individual states to provide more information. These maps are usually designed to cover political, physical, and historical facts, as well as to offer geographical information.

A gazetteer is a listing of geographical names and information, rather than the cartographic information provided by an atlas. Although gazetteers may also contain maps, that is not their main function.

## Microfilm, Microfiche, Microcards

We've already covered computerized information data banks, which are becoming more accessible to everyone as the use of computers grows. Also available for printed material are microfilm, microfiche, and Microcards. All are greatly reduced photographic copies of pages from books, magazines, newspapers, research sources, and other periodicals. Because of the small size of each page, which is on film, you use a special projection machine to read the documents. You can scan the pages very quickly, and when you locate something you wish to make a copy of, certain machines have photocopying attachments that enable you to copy that page instantly. The major advantage of this type of information storage is that it takes up very little room in an office, corporate, or public library.

No matter how specialized your business needs, there is a publication that can provide you with in-depth information. In the future, our business environment will be based on the generation and sharing of information, and it is important that all of us understand what is available to us for those purposes and how to make the fullest use of it.

# Appendix 1.
# Compound Word List
# (See key page 130.)

(See key page 130.)

## A

A
BC('s) (n.)
–B–C (u.m.)
-bomb
-day
-flat
-frame
-pole
-sharp
a
borning, etc.
foot
while (adv.)
**abdomino** (c.f.)
*all one word*
**able**
-bodied (u.m.)
-minded (u.m.)
about-face
**above**
-cited (u.m.)
deck
-found (u.m.)
-given (u.m.)
ground (u.m.)
-mentioned (u.m.)
-named (u.m.)
-said (u.m.)
-water (u.m.)
-written (u.m.)
absentminded
ace-high (u.m.)
**acid**
fast
-treat (v.)
works
ack-ack
**acre**
-foot
-inch

**actino** (c.f.)
*all one word*
**addle**
brain
head
pate
add-on (u.m.)
**adeno** (c.f.)
*all one word*
**aero** (c.f.)
-otitis
*rest one word*
**afore**
*all one word*
Afro-American
**after** (c.f.)
*all one word*
agar-agar
**age**
less
long
-old (u.m.)
-stricken (u.m.)
-weary (u.m.)
**ague**
-faced (u.m.)
-plagued (u.m.)
-sore (u.m.)
aide-de-camp
**air**
bag
base
bill
blast
-blasted (u.m.)
blown
brake
brush
burst
cargo
-clear (u.m.)

coach
-condition (all forms)
-cool (v.)
-cooled (u.m.)
course
crew
-dried (u.m.)
-driven (u.m.)
drome
drop
-dry (u.m., v.)
fare
-floated (u.m.)
flow
foil
-formed (u.m.)
frame
freight
gap
glow
hammer
head
hole
hose
lane
lift
#line (line for air)
line (aviation)
liner
link
locked
mail
mark (v.)
marker
mass
minded
park
path
photo

port (all meanings)
scoop
show
sleeve
ship
sick
-slaked (u.m.)
space
speed
stream
strike
strip
#time (radio and TV)
wave
alder-leaved (u.m.)
**ale**
cup
-fed (u.m.)
glass
alkali#land
**all**
-absorbing (u.m.)
-aged (u.m.)
-American
-clear (n., u.m.)
-fired (u.m.)
-flotation (mining)
-inclusive (u.m.)
mark (printing)
-out (u.m.)
-possessed (u.m.)
-round (u.m.)
spice
-star (u.m.)
**acre** (c.f.)
*all one word*
almsgiver

**along**
ship
shore
side
**alpen**
glow
stock
**alpha**
-cellulose
-iron
-naphthol
also-ran (n., u.m.)
**alto**
cumulus
relievo
stratus
**amber**
-clear (u.m.)
-colored (u.m.)
-tipped (u.m.)
**ambi** (c.f.)
*all one word*
amidships
**amino**
#acid
*as prefix, all one word*
**ampere**
-foot
-hour
meter
-minute
-second
**amphi** (pref.)
*all one word*
**amylo** (c.f.)
*all one word*
**anchor**
hold
#light
plate

**angel**
 cake
 -eyed (u.m.)
 -faced (u.m.)
 food
**angio** (c.f.)
 *all one word*
**angle**
 hook
 meter
 wing
**Anglo** (c.f.)
 -American, etc.
 *rest one word*
**anhydr(o)** (c.f.)
 *all one word*
**ankle**
 bone
 -deep (u.m.)
 jack
**ant**
 eater
 hill
**ante** (pref.)
 #bellum, etc.
 -Christian, etc.
 #mortem
 mortem
  (nonliteral)
 *rest one word*
**antero** (c.f.)
 *all one word*
**anthra** (c.f.)
 *all one word*
**anthropo** (c.f.)
 *all one word*
**anti** (pref.)
 -American, etc.
 christ

god
 -hog-cholera
  (u.m.)
 -icer, -imperial,
  -inflation, etc.
 -missile-missile
  (u.m.)
 missile,
  personnel,
  trust, etc.
 -New#Deal, etc.
 *rest one word*
**antro** (c.f.)
 *all one word*
**anvil**
 -faced (u.m.)
 -headed (u.m.)
**any**
 how
 one
 #one (one thing
  or one of a
  group)
 place (adv.)
**aorto** (c.f.)
 *all one word*
**apo** (pref.)
 *all one word*
**apple**
 cart
 jack
 juice
 sauce
 -scented (u.m.)
 April-fool (v.)
**aqua**
 culture
 lung
 marine

meter
 puncture
 tint
 tone
**aquo** (c.f.)
 -ion
 *rest one word*
**arc**
 -over (n., u.m.)
 -weld (v.)
**arch** (pref.)
 band
 bishop
 duke
 enemy
 -Protestant
**archeo** (c.f.)
 *all one word*
**archi** (pref.)
 *all one word*
**archo** (c.f.)
 *all one word*
**areo** (c.f.)
 *all one word*
**aristo** (c.f.)
 *all one word*
**arithmo** (c.f.)
 *all one word*
**arm**
 band
 bone
 chair
 hole
 lift
 pit
 plate
 rack
 rest
 -shaped (u.m.)

**armor**
 -clad (u.m.)
 -piercing (u.m.)
 plate
 -plated (u.m.)
**arm's-length**
  (u.m.)
**arrow**
 head
 -leaved (u.m.)
 plate
 -shaped (u.m.)
 shot
 -toothed (u.m.)
**arseno** (c.f.)
 *all one word*
art-colored (u.m.)
**arterio** (c.f.)
 *all one word*
**arthro** (c.f.)
 *all one word*
**asbestos**
 -covered (u.m.)
 -packed (u.m.)
**ash**
 bin
 can
 -colored (u.m.)
 -free (u.m.)
 -gray (u.m.)
 pan
 pile
 pit
 tray
**assembly**
 #line
 #room
**astro** (c.f.)
 *all one word*

attorney#at#law
**audio**
 frequency
 gram
 meter
 tape
 visual
**auri** (c.f.)
 -iodide
 *rest one word*
authorship
**auto** (c.f.)
 -objective
 -observation
 -omnibus
 -ophthalmoscope
 *rest one word*
**awe**
 -bound (u.m.)
 -filled (u.m.)
 -inspired (u.m.)
 some
**ax**
 -adz
 -grinding (u.m.)
 hammer
 head
 -shaped (u.m.)
axletree
**axo** (c.f.)
 *all one word*
**azo** (c.f.)
 -orange
 -orchil
 -orseilline
 *rest one word*

# B

B-flat
**baby**
 face (n.)
 sit (v.)
**back**
 ache
 band
 bite (v.)
 bone
 breaker
 cap
 chain
 charge
 -country (u.m.)
 cross
 date
 down (n., u.m.)
 drop
 face
 feed
 fill
 fire
 flap
 flash
 flow
 -focus (v.)
 furrow
 ground
 hand
 haul
 -in (n., u.m.)
 lash
 list (v.)
 log
 lotter

packer (n.)
paddle (v.)
pay
payment
pedal (v.)
plate
rest
road
run
saw
scatter
set
shift
slide
space
spin
spread
staff
stage
stairs
stamp
stay
stitch
stop
strap
-streeter
stretch (n.)
string
strip (book)
stroke
-swath (v.)
swept
swing
tack
talk

tender
tenter
-titrate (v.)
track (v.)
trail
up (n., u.m.)
wall
wash
**backer**
 -down
 -off
 -up
**bag**
 -cheeked
  (u.m.)
 pipe
 -shaped (u.m.)
baggage#room
bailout (n., u.m.)
**bake**
 pan
 stove
**bald**
 faced
 head (n.)
 pate
**ball**
 -like
 park
  (nonliteral)
 #park (literal)
 player
 point (n., u.m.)
 stock
ballot#box

**band**
 cutter
 saw
 stand
 string
 -tailed (u.m.)
 wagon
 width
**bandy**
 ball
 -legged (u.m.)
 bangup (n., u.m.)
**bank**
 note
 side (stream)
 bantamweight
**bar**
 post
 tender
 -wound (u.m.)
**bare**
 -armed (u.m.)
 back
 bone
 faced
 foot
 handed
 legged
 necked
 worn
 barge-laden (u.m.)
**bark**
 cutter
 peel
 -tanned (u.m.)

**barley**
 corn
 mow
 #water
 barnstormer
**barrel**
 head
 -roll (v.)
 -shaped (u.m.)
**base**
 ball
 ball#bat
 line
 #line (surveying)
 -minded (u.m.)
**basi** (c.f.)
 *all one word*
 basketball
 bas-relief
**bat**
 blind
 -eyed (u.m.)
 fowl
 wing
**bath**
 mat
 robe
 tub
 batswing (cloth)
 battercake
**battle**
 ax
 dore
 -fallen (u.m.)
 front

**Column 1**

ground
-scarred (u.m.)
ship
stead
wagon
baybolt
**beach**
comber
head
wagon
**bead**
flush
roll
**beak**
head
iron
-shaped (u.m.)
**beam**
filling
-making (u.m.)
**bean**
bag
cod
-fed (u.m.)
pole
pot
setter
-shaped (u.m.)
stalk
**bear**
baiting
herd
hide
hound
off (n., u.m.)
trap
**beater**
-out
-up
**beauty**
-blind (u.m.)
-clad (u.m.)
#shop
beaverpelt
**bed**
chair
chamber
clothes
cord
cover
-fallen (u.m.)
fast
fellow
frame
pad
pan
plate
post
quilt
rail
ridden
rock
sheet
sick
side
sore
space
spread
spring
stand
stead
straw
**bee**
bread
-eater
herd
hive

**Column 2**

beechnut
**beef**
eater
-faced (u.m.)
head
steak
tongue
**bees**
wax
wing
**beetle**
-browed (u.m.)
head
stock
**before**
-cited (u.m.)
hand
-mentioned (u.m.)
-named (u.m.)
behindhand
**bell**
-bottomed (u.m.)
crank
-crowned (u.m.)
hanger
hop
mouthed
ringer
wether
**belly**
ache
band
buster
button
fed (u.m.)
pinch
belowstairs
**belt**
-driven (u.m.)
saw
**bench**
fellow
-hardened (u.m.)
made (u.m.)
mark
   (nonliteral)
#mark
   (surveying)
warmer
bentwing (n., u.m.)
**benzo** (c.f.)
all one word
berry-brown (u.m.)
**best**
man
#man
seller (n.)
**beta**
-glucose
tron
**between**
decks
whiles
**bi** (pref.)
-iliac
rest one word
**big**
-eared (u.m.)
-eyed (u.m.)
head (ego)
horn (sheep)
-horned (u.m.)
-leaguer
mouthed
name (top rank) (n., u.m.)

**Column 3**

**bill**
back
beetle
broker
fold
head
hook
poster
sticker
**billet**
-doux
head
billingsgate
**bio** (c.f.)
-aeration
-osmosis
rest one word
birchbark
**bird**
bath
bander
cage
call
catcher
-eyed (u.m.)
-faced (u.m.)
life
lime
lore
mouthed
seed
shot
watcher
**bird's**
-eye
#nest (literal) (n.)
-nest (n., u.m., v.)
**birth**
bed
day
mark
place
right
biscuit-shaped (u.m.)
**bismuto** (c.f.)
all one word
bitstock
**bitter**
-ender
head
sweet
-tongued (u.m.)
**black**
ball (nonliteral)
-bordered (u.m.)
damp
-eyed (u.m.)
face
fire
guard
jack
leg
list
mail
mark
-market (u.m., v.)
-marketeer
-marketer
mouthed
out (n., u.m.)
plate (printing)
print
-robed (u.m.)
shirted

**Column 4**

snake
strap (n.)
top
**blast**
hole
plate
**blasto** (c.f.)
all one word
**bleach**
ground
works
**blear**
eye
-eyed (u.m.)
-witted (u.m.)
**blepharo** (c.f.)
all one word
blight-resistant (u.m.)
**blind**
-bomb (v.)
-flying (u.m.)
fold
-loaded (u.m.)
#man
spot
stitch
story
blink-eyed (u.m.)
blithe-looking (u.m.)
**blitz**
buggy
krieg
**block**
buster
head
hole (v.)
ship
**blood**
-alcohol (u.m.)
bath
beat
curdling
-drenched (u.m.)
-giving (u.m.)
guilty
-hot (u.m.)
hound
letting
mobile
-red (u.m.)
ripe
shed
shot
spiller
spot
stain
stock
stream
sucker
thirsty
-warm (u.m.)
**bloody**
-nosed (u.m.)
-red (u.m.)
**blossom**
-bordered (u.m.)
-laden (u.m.)
**blow**
back
by (n., u.m.)
cock
down (n., u.m.)
gun
hard (n.)
hole

**Column 5**

iron
lamp
off (n., u.m.)
out (n., u.m.)
pipe
spray
through (u.m.)
torch
tube
up (n., u.m.)
**blue**
-annealed (u.m.)
beard (n.)
blood
bonnet
bottle
coat (n.)
-eyed (u.m.)
grass
-gray (u.m.)
-green (u.m.)
-hot (u.m.)
jack
jacket
nose
-pencil (v.)
point (oyster)
print
stocking
streak (nonliteral)
tongue (n.)
**blunder**
buss
head
**blunt**
-edged (u.m.)
-spoken (u.m.)
**boar**
spear
staff
**board**
rack
walk
**boat**
builder
crew
hook
head
loader
setter
side
swain
wright
**bob**
cat
sled
stay
**bobby**
pin
-soxer
**body**
bearer
bending
builder
-centered (u.m.)
guard
-mind
plate
**bog**
-eyed (u.m.)
trot (v.)
**boil**
down (n., u.m.)
off (n., u.m.)
out (n., u.m.)

**boiler**
-off
-out
plate
works
**boiling # house**
**bold**
face (printing)
-spirited (u.m.)
**bolt**
cutter
head
hole
-shaped (u.m.)
strake
**bomb**
drop
fall
shell
sight
thrower
-throwing (u.m.)
**bondslave**
**bone**
ache
black
breaker
-bred (u.m.)
-dry (u.m.)
-eater
-hard (u.m.)
head
lace
meal
set
shaker
-white (u.m.)
**boobytrap**
**boogie-woogie**
**book**
binder
case
dealer
fair
-fed (u.m.)
fold
-learned (u.m.)
-lined (u.m.)
list
lore
lover
mark
mobile
plate
rack
rest
sale
seller
shelf
stack
stall
stamp
stand
stitch
-stitching (u.m.)
-taught (u.m.)
wright
**boom**
-ended (u.m.)
town
truck
**boondoggling**
**boot**
black
hose
jack
lace

last
leg
lick
strap
**bore**
hole
safe
sight
**bosom**
-deep (u.m.)
-folded (u.m.)
-making (u.m.)
**bottle**
-fed (u.m.)
neck
-nosed (u.m.)
**bottom # land**
**boughpot**
**bow**
back
bent
grace
head
knot
legged
-necked (u.m.)
pin
shot
sprit
stave
string
wow
**box**
car
haul
head (printing)
truck
**boxer**
-off
-up
**brachio** (c.f.)
*all one word*
**brachy** (c.f.)
*all one word*
**brain**
cap
child
-cracked (u.m.)
fag
pan
sick
-spun (u.m.)
storm
-tired (u.m.)
wash
**brake**
drum
head
meter
shoe
**brandnew** (u.m.)
**brandy**
-burnt (u.m.)
wine
**brass**
-armed (u.m.)
-bold (u.m.)
-smith
works
**brave**
-looking (u.m.)
-minded (u.m.)
**brazen**
-browed (u.m.)
face
**bread**
basket

crumb
earner
fruit
liner
plate
seller
stuff
winner
**break**
away (n., u.m.)
ax
back (n., u.m.)
bone (fever)
down (n., u.m.)
-even (u.m.)
fast
fast # room
front
-in (n., u.m.)
neck
off (n., u.m.)
out (n., u.m.)
point
through (n., u.m.)
up (n., u.m.)
wind
**breaker**
-down
-off
-up
**breast**
band
beam
bone
-deep (u.m.)
-fed (u.m.)
-high (u.m.)
hook
mark
pin
plate
plow
rail
rope
**breath**
-blown (u.m.)
-tainted (u.m.)
taking
**breech**
block
cloth
loader
-loading (u.m.)
lock
pin
plug
sight
**breeze**
-borne (u.m.)
-lifted (u.m.)
-swept (u.m.)
**bribe**
-free (u.m.)
giver
taker
**bric-a-brac**
**brick**
bat
-built (u.m.)
-colored (u.m.)
kiln
layer
liner
mason
-red (u.m.)
setter

**bride**
bed
bowl
cake
chamber
cup
groom
knot
lace
maiden
stake
**bridge**
builder
head
pot
tree
**briefcase**
**bright**
-colored (u.m.)
-eyed (u.m.)
**brilliant**
-cut (u.m.)
-green (u.m.)
**brine-soaked** (u.m.)
**bringer-up**
**bristle**
cone (u.m.)
-pointed (u.m.)
**broad**
acre
ax
band (radio) (n., u.m.)
-beamed (u.m.)
brim
cast
cloth
head
leaf (n.)
-leaved (u.m.)
loom
minded
-mouthed (u.m.)
share (n., v.)
sheet (n.)
side
sword
wife
woven
**broken**
-down (u.m.)
-legged (u.m.)
-mouthed (u.m.)
**bromo** (c.f.)
*all one word*
**bronchio** (c.f.)
*all one word*
**broncho** (c.f.)
*all one word*
**broncobuster**
**bronze**
-clad (u.m.)
-covered (u.m.)
-red (u.m.)
**broom**
-leaved (u.m.)
-making (u.m.)
stick
**brother**
-german
hood
-in-law
**brow**
beat
point
post

**brown**
back
-eyed (u.m.)
out (n., u.m.)
print
**brush**
ball
# holder
off (n., u.m.)
-treat (v.)
**brusher**
-off
-up
**buck**
eye
-eyed (u.m.)
horn
hound
passer
plate
pot
saw
shot
skinned
stall
stay
stove
tooth
wagon
wash
**bucket-shaped** (u.m.)
**buff**
-tipped (u.m.)
-yellow (u.m.)
**bug**
bear
bite
-eyed (u.m.)
**buildup** (n., u.m.)
**built**
-in (u.m.)
-up (u.m.)
**bulb-tee** (u.m.)
**bulbo** (c.f.)
*all one word*
**bulk**
head
-pile (v.)
weigh (v.)
**bull**
baiting
dog
doze
-faced (u.m.)
fight
frog
head
-mouthed (u.m.)
neck
nose
pen
ring
toad
-voiced (u.m.)
whack
whip
**bullethead**
**bull's**
-eye
(nonliteral)
-foot
**bumble**
bee
foot
kite

**bung**
  hole
  start
**burn**
  -in (n., u.m.)
  out (n., u.m.)
  up (n., u.m.)
burned-over (u.m.)
burner-off
**burnt**
  -out (u.m.)
  -up (u.m.)
**bus**
  driver

  fare
  #girl
**bush**
  beater
  buck
  fighter
  -grown (u.m.)
  hammer
  -headed (u.m.)
  -leaguer
  ranger
  whacker
  wife
bustup (n., u.m.)

**busy**
  body
  -fingered (u.m.)
  head
**butt**
  -joint (v.)
  saw
  stock
  strap
  -weld (v.)
**butter**
  ball
  -colored (u.m.)
  fat

  fingers
  head
  milk
  mouth
  nut
  print
  -rigged (u.m.)
  scotch
  -smooth (u.m.)
  wife
  -yellow (u.m.)
**button**
  -eared (u.m.)
  -headed (u.m.)

  hold
  hole
  hook
  mold
  buzzerphone
**by**
  -and-by
  -by
  -the-way (n., u.m.)
  -your-leave (n., u.m.)
  *rest one word*

## C

**C**
  -sharp
  -star
  -tube
**cab**
  driver
  fare
  #owner
  stand
cabbagehead
cable-laid (u.m.)
**caco** (c.f.)
  *all one word*
cage#bird
**cake**
  baker
  bread
  -eater
  mixer
  -mixing (u.m.)
  pan
  walk
**calci** (c.f.)
  *all one word*
calk-weld (v.)
**call**
  back (n., u.m.)
  down (n., u.m.)
  -in (n., u.m.)
  note
  -off (n., u.m.)
  out (n., u.m.)
  -over (n., u.m.)
  up (n., u.m.)
camshaft
**camel**
  back (rubber)
  -backed (u.m.)
  driver
  -faced (u.m.)
camel's-hair (u.m.)
**camp**
  fire
  ground
  stool
**can**
  capper
  not
canalside
**candle**
  bomb
  -foot
  -hour
  lighter
  lit
  -meter
  -shaped (u.m.)
  stand
  stick
  wick

  wright
candystick
**cane**
  -backed (u.m.)
  brake
  crusher
  cutter
**canker**
  -eaten (u.m.)
  -mouthed (u.m.)
cannonball
canvas-covered (u.m.)
**cap**
  -flash (v.)
  nut
  screw
  sheaf
  shore
**car**
  barn
  break
  builder
  fare
  goose
  hop
  lot
  -mile
  pool
  port
  sick
  wash
**carbo** (c.f.)
  *all one word*
**carbol** (c.f.)
  *all one word*
**carcino** (c.f.)
  *all one word*
**card**
  case
  -index (u.m., v.)
  player
  sharp
  stock
**cardio** (c.f.)
  -aortic
  *rest one word*
**care**
  free
  -laden (u.m.)
  taker
  -tired (u.m.)
  worn
**carpet**
  bagger
  beater
  -cleaning (u.m.)
  -covered (u.m.)
  fitter
  layer

  -smooth (u.m.)
  -sweeping (u.m.)
  weaver
  -weaving (u.m.)
  web
  woven
**carpo** (c.f.)
  -olecranal
  *rest one word*
carriage-making (u.m.)
**carrot**
  -colored (u.m.)
  head
  (nonliteral)
  juice
  top (nonliteral)
**carry**
  all (n., u.m.)
  around (n., u.m.)
  back (n., u.m.)
  forward (n.)
  -in (n., u.m.)
  out (n., u.m.)
**cart**
  wheel (coin)
  whip
  wright
**case**
  bearer
  finding
  hammer
  harden
  lot
  mated
caser-in
cash-flow
**cast**
  away (n., u.m.)
  back (n., u.m.)
  -by (u.m.)
  off (n., u.m.)
  out (n., u.m.)
  -ridden (u.m.)
  -weld (v.)
caster
  -off
  -out
castlebuilder (nonliteral)
**cat**
  back
  beam
  block
  call
  -eyed (u.m.)
  face (n.)
  fall
  footed

  gut
  head
  hole
  -ion
  nap
  nip
  -o'-nine-tails
  stitch
  walk
**catch**
  all (n., u.m.)
  -as-catch-can (u.m.)
  cry
  penny
  plate
  up (n., u.m.)
  weight
  word
**cater**
  corner
  wauling
**cat's**
  -eye (nonliteral)
  -paw (nonliteral)
**cattle**
  #boat
  feed
  -raising (u.m.)
  yak
**cauliflower**
  -eared (u.m.)
  #ware
**cave**
  dweller
  -dwelling (u.m.)
  #fish
  -in (n., u.m.)
cease-fire (n., u.m.)
cedar-colored (u.m.)
**celi** (c.f.)
  *all one word*
**celio** (c.f.)
  *all one word*
**cement**
  -covered (u.m.)
  mason
  -temper (v.)
census-taking (u.m.)
**center**
  #field (sports)
  head (printing)
  most
  -second
**centi** (c.f.)
  *all one word*
centimeter-gram-second

  **centri** (c.f.)
  *all one word*
**centro** (c.f.)
  *all one word*
**cephalo** (c.f.)
  *all one word*
**cerato** (c.f.)
  *all one word*
**cerebro** (c.f.)
  -ocular
  *rest one word*
**cervico** (c.f.)
  -occipital
  -orbicular
  *rest one word*
**cess**
  pipe
  pit
  pool
chaffcutter
**chain**
  -driven (u.m.)
  stitch
**chair**
  fast
  mender
  person
  -shaped (u.m.)
  warmer
**chalk**
  cutter
  -white (u.m.)
chapfallen
chapelgoing
**char**
  broiler
  coal
  pit
**charge**
  #book
  off (n., u.m.)
  out (n., u.m.)
chattermark
cheapskate
**check**
  bite
  hook
  -in (n., u.m.)
  list
  mark
  nut
  off (n., u.m.)
  out (n., u.m.)
  passer (n.)
  point
  rack
  rail
  rein
  ring
  roll
  rope

row
sheet
strap
string
up (n., u.m.)
washer
weigher
**checker**
-in
-off
-out
-up
**cheek**
bone
strap
cheerleader
**cheese**
burger
cake
cloth
curd
cutter
head
lip
parer
plate
**chemico** (c.f.)
  *all one word*
**chemo** (c.f.)
  *all one word*
**cherry**
-colored (u.m.)
stone
  (nonliteral)
#stone (literal)
**chestnut**
-colored (u.m.)
-red (u.m.)
**chicken**
bill
-billed (u.m.)
#breast
breasted
feed
heart
pox
#yard
**chief**
#justice
-justiceship
#mate
**child**
bearing
bed
birth
crowing
hood
kind
life
-minded (u.m.)
ridden
wife
chill-cast (u.m., v.)
**chin**
band
-bearded (u.m.)
-chin
cloth
cough
-high (u.m.)
rest
strap
**china**
-blue (u.m.)
#shop
Chinatown
chipmunk

**chiro** (c.f.)
  *all one word*
**chisel**
-cut (u.m.)
-edged (u.m.)
#maker
chitchat
chitter-chatter
**chloro** (c.f.)
  *all one word*
**chock**
ablock
-full (u.m.)
**chocolate**
-brown (u.m.)
-coated (u.m.)
#maker
choir#master
**choke**
bore
damp
out (n., u.m.)
point
strap
**chole** (c.f.)
  *all one word*
**chondro** (c.f.)
-osseous
  *rest one word*
**chop**
-chop
stick
chowchow
**Christ**
-given (u.m.)
-inspired (u.m.)
**chromo** (c.f.)
  *all one word*
**chrono** (c.f.)
  *all one word*
**chuck**
hole
plate
wagon
chucklehead
chunkhead
churchgoer
**churn**
-butted (u.m.)
milk
**cigar**
case
cutter
-shaped (u.m.)
**cigarette**
#holder
#maker
-making (u.m.)
**cine** (c.f.)
  *all one word*
**circum** (pref.)
arctic, pacific,
  etc.
-Saturnal, etc.
  *rest one word*
**cirro** (c.f.)
  *all one word*
**cis** (pref.)
alpine
atlantic
-trans (u.m.)
  *rest one word*
**city**
-born (u.m.)
-bred (u.m.)
folk
#man

scape
**clam**
bake
shell
clampdown (n., u.m.)
**clap**
net
trap
clasphook
class-conscious (u.m.)
**claw**
bar
-footed (u.m.)
hammer
hatchet
-tailed (u.m.)
**clay**
bank
-colored (u.m.)
pan
pit
works
**clean**
-cut (u.m.)
handed
out (n., u.m.)
-shaved (u.m.)
-smelling (u.m.)
up (n., u.m.)
**clear**
cole
-cut (u.m.)
cut (forestry) (n., v.)
-eyed (u.m.)
-sighted (u.m.)
up (n., u.m.)
wing
**cleft**
-footed (u.m.)
-graft (v.)
**cliff**
dweller
-dwelling (u.m.)
hanger
side
top
-worn (u.m.)
climbpath
clinch-built (u.m.)
clink-clank
clinker-built (u.m.)
**clip**
-clop
-edged (u.m.)
sheet
clipper-built (u.m.)
cloak-and-dagger (n., u.m.)
**clock**
case
face
-minded (u.m.)
setter
watcher
**clod**
head
hopping
pate
**close**
bred
-connected (u.m.)
cross
-cut (u.m.)

down (n.)
-fertilize (v.)
fisted
handed
-knit
minded
mouthed
out (n., u.m.)
up (n., u.m.)
**closed**
-circuit (u.m.)
#shop
cloth-backed (u.m.)
**clothes**
bag
basket
brush
horse
pin
press
rack
**cloud**
base
burst
cap
-hidden (u.m.)
**clover**
bloom
leaf
seed
sick
**club**
foot
hand
haul
mobile
ridden
root
-shaped (u.m.)
**co** (pref.)
-op
exist, operate, etc.
  *rest one word*
**coach**
-and-four
builder
whip
**coal**
bag
bed
bin
-black (u.m.)
breaker
dealer
digger
-faced (u.m.)
hole
-laden (u.m.)
#loader
pit
rake
sack (astron. only)
shed
ship
coastside
**coat**
hanger
rack
tailed
**cob**
head
meal
shed
web

**cock**
bill
brain
crow
eye
fight
head
pit
spur
sure
-tailed (u.m.)
up (n., u.m.)
cockleshell
cockscomb
**cod**
bank
fishing
head
pitchings
smack
**coffee**
break
cake
-colored (u.m.)
-growing (u.m.)
pot
cofferdam
coffin-headed (u.m.)
cogwheel
coin-operated (u.m.)
**cold**
blooded
-chisel (v.)
cuts
-draw (v.)
finch
-flow (v.)
-forge (v.)
frame
-hammer (v.)
-hammered (u.m.)
pack
-press (v.)
-roll (v.)
-rolled (u.m.)
-short (u.m.)
-shortness
-shoulder (v.)
type (printing)
-work (v.)
**cole**
seed
slaw
**coli** (c.f.)
  *all one word*
**collar**
bag
band
bone
**colo** (c.f.)
  *all one word*
**color**
bearer
blind
#blindness
fast
-free (u.m.)
#line
type (printing) (n.)
-washed (u.m.)
comb-toothed (u.m.)

**come**
-along (tool)
back (n., u.m.)
-between (n.)
down (n.)
-off (n., u.m.)
-on (n., u.m.)
-out (n.)
-outer
uppance
comic # book
commander # in # chief
**common**
place
# sense (n.)
sense (u.m.)
weal
wealth
companionship
**cone**
-shaped (u.m.)
speaker
conference # room
Congressman # at # Large
**contra** (pref.)
-acting
-approach
-ion
*rest one word*
**cook**
off (n., u.m.)
out (n., u.m.)
shack
stove
**cooped**
-in (u.m.)
-up (u.m.)
**cop**
# out (v.)
out (n.)
**copper**
-bottomed (u.m.)
-colored (u.m.)
head
-headed (u.m.)
nose
plate
-plated (u.m.)
works
**copy**
cat
cutter
desk
fitter
holding
reader
right
**coral**
-beaded (u.m.)
-red (u.m.)
**cork**
-lined (u.m.)
screw
**corn**
bin
bread
cake
cob
cracker
crib
crusher
cutter
dodger
-fed (u.m.)

husk
loft
meal
stalk
starch
**corner**
bind
post
corpsmember
**costo** (c.f.)
*all one word*
**cotton**
-clad (u.m.)
-covered (u.m.)
-growing (u.m.)
# mill
mouth (snake)
packer
seed
sick
countdown (n., u.m.)
**counter**
# check (banking)
# septum
-off
act,
propaganda,
etc.
*as combining form, one word*
**country**
-born (u.m.)
-bred (u.m.)
folk
people
side
**court**
bred
-martial
ship
**cousin**
-german
hood
-in-law
**cover**
alls
let
side
up (n., u.m.)
**cow**
barn
bell
catcher
-eyed (u.m.)
gate
hand
herd
hide
hitch
lick
path
pen
pox
puncher
shed
sucker
**crab**
cake
catcher
eater
faced
hole
meat
stick

**crack**
down (n., u.m.)
jaw
pot
-the-whip (n., u.m.)
up (n., u.m.)
**cradle**
side
song
**cranio** (c.f.)
*all one word*
**crank**
case
-driven (u.m.)
pin
pit
shaft
crapehanger
crashdive (v.)
crawlup (n., u.m.)
**crazy**
bone
cat
**cream**
cake
-colored (u.m.)
creditworthiness
**creek**
bed
side
**creep**
hole
mouse
crepe # de # chine
crestfallen
**crew**
cut
member
cribstrap
**crime**
fighter
wave
crisscross
**crook**
*all one word*
**crooked**
-foot (n.)
-legged (u.m.)
-nosed (u.m.)
-toothed (u.m.)
**crop**
-bound (u.m.)
-haired (u.m.)
head
-year
**cross**
-appeal
arm
band
bar
beam
bearer
bedded
belt
bench
-bidding
bill (bird)
# bill (legal)
bind
bolt
bond
bones
bred
breed
-bridge (v.)

-brush (v.)
-carve (v.)
-channel (u.m.)
-check
-claim
-compound (v.)
-connect (v.)
-country (u.m.)
-cultivate (v.)
current
-curve (math.) (n.)
cut
-date (v.)
-drain (v.)
-dye (v.)
-dyeing (n.)
-examine (v.)
-eye (n., u.m.)
-eyed (u.m.)
fall
feed
-fertile (u.m.)
-fertilize (v.)
-fiber (u.m.)
file
fire
flow
foot
-grained (u.m.)
hair
hand
hatch
haul
head
-immunity
-index (u.m.)
-interrogate (v.)
-interrogatory
-invite (v.)
legged
legs
-level (v.)
-license (v.)
lift (v.)
lock
lots
mark
member
patch
path
plow (v.)
-pollinate (v.)
-purpose (n.)
-question
rail
-reaction
-refer (v.)
-reference
road
row
-service
-shaft
-slide
-staff
-sterile
-stitch
-stone
-stratification
-sue (v.)
-surge (v.)
talk
tie
town
track
trail

tree
under (n., u.m.)
-vote
walk
web
wind
word
**crow**
bait
bar
foot
**crow's**
-foot (nonliteral)
-nest (nonliteral)
crownbar
crybaby
**crypto** (c.f.)
-Christian, etc.
*rest one word*
**crystal**
-clear (u.m.)
-girded (u.m.)
-smooth (u.m.)
cubbyhole
**cumulo** (c.f.)
*all one word*
**cup**
bearer
cake
ful
head
**curb**
side
stoner
cure-all (n., u.m.)
**curly**
head
locks (n.)
currycomb
cussword
**custom**
-built (u.m.)
-made (u.m.)
-tailored (u.m.)
**cut**
away (n., u.m.)
back (n., u.m.)
glass
-in (n., u.m.)
off (n., u.m.)
out (n., u.m.)
rate (u.m.)
throat
-toothed (u.m.)
-under (u.m.)
-up (n., u.m.)
**cutter**
-built (u.m.)
-down
head
-off
-out
-rigged (u.m.)
-up
cuttlebone
**cyano** (c.f.)
*all one word*
cyclecar
**cyclo** (c.f.)
-olefin
*rest one word*
**cysto** (c.f.)
*all one word*
**cyto** (c.f.)
*all one word*

# D

**D**
-day
-major
-plus-4-day
**dairy**
-fed (u.m.)
-made (u.m.)
**damp**
proofing
-stained (u.m.)
damping-off (n., u.m.)
dancehall
danger#line
**dare**
-all (n., u.m.)
devil
say
**dark**
-eyed (u.m.)
horse
(nonliteral)
-skinned (u.m.)
**dash**
plate
wheel
**data**
#bank
#base
**date**
lined
mark
daughter-in-law
**dawn**
-gray (u.m.)
streak
**day**
beam
bed
break
-bright (u.m.)
dawn
dream
-fly (aviation) (v.)
-flying (u.m.)
going
lighted
lit
long (u.m.)
mark
side
star
-to-day (u.m.)
**de** (pref.)
-air
icer
-ion
centralize,
energize, etc.
*rest one word*
**dead**
-alive
beat (n.)
born
-burn (v.)
-cold (u.m.)
-dip (v.)
-drunk (u.m.)
-ender
eye (n.)
-eyed (u.m.)
fall
head
-heated (u.m.)
-heater

-heavy (u.m.)
latch
#load
lock
melt
pan
pay
-roast (v.)
weight (n., u.m.)
**deaf**
-mute
-muteness
**death**
bed
blow
day
-divided (u.m.)
-doom (v.)
#house
-struck (u.m.)
trap
watch
-weary (u.m.)
deckhand
**deep**
-affected (u.m.)
-cut (u.m.)
-felt (u.m.)
-freeze (u.m., v.)
-frying (u.m.)
going
-grown (u.m.)
-laid (u.m.)
most
mouthed
-rooted (u.m.)
-seated (u.m.)
-set (u.m.)
-sunk (u.m.)
-voiced (u.m.)
**deer**
drive (n.)
-eyed (u.m.)
food
herd
horn
hound
meat
stalker
stand
**dehydr(o)** (c.f.)
*all one word*
**demi** (pref.)
-Christian, etc.
-incognito
*rest one word*
**dermato** (c.f.)
*all one word*
desert-bred (u.m.)
desk#room
dessertspoon
**deutero** (c.f.)
*all one word*
**devil**
-devil
dog (a marine)
-inspired (u.m.)
-ridden (u.m.)
**dew**
beam
cap
-clad (u.m.)
claw
damp
-drenched (u.m.)

drop
fall
-fed (u.m.)
-laden (u.m.)
lap
point
**dextro** (c.f.)
*all one word*
**di** (pref.)
*all one word*
**dia** (pref.)
*all one word*
**diamond**
back
-backed (u.m.)
-shaped (u.m.)
**diazo** (c.f.)
-oxide
*rest one word*
**dice**
cup
play
**die**
-away (u.m.)
back
case
-cast (u.m., v.)
caster
-cut (u.m., v.)
cutter
hard (n., u.m.)
head
#proof (philately)
(n.)
setter
sinker
-square (u.m.)
stock
**diesel**
-driven (u.m.)
-electric (u.m.)
dillydally
**dim**
-lighted (u.m.)
lit
out (n., u.m.)
diner-out
**ding**
bat
dong
dining#room
**dinitro** (c.f.)
#spray
*rest one word*
**dip**
-dye (v.)
-grained (u.m.)
head
stick
dipper-in
**direct**
-connected
(u.m.)
-indirect
direction-finding
(u.m.)
**dirt**
-cheap (u.m.)
fast
-incrusted (u.m.)
plate
**dirty**
-faced (u.m.)
-minded (u.m.)
#work

**dis** (pref.)
*all one word*
**dish**
cloth
pan
rack
rag
washer
wiper
**disk**
jockey
pack
plow
-shaped (u.m.)
**ditch**
bank
digger
rider
side
dittograph
dive-bomb (v.)
**do**
-all (n., u.m.)
-gooder
-little (n., u.m.)
-nothing (n.,
u.m.)
**dock**
hand
head
side
**dog**
bite
-bitten (u.m.)
breeder
cart
catcher
-drawn (u.m.)
-ear (v.)
-eared (u.m.)
face (soldier)
-faced (u.m.)
fall
fight
food
-headed (u.m.)
hole
leg
#owner
race
shore
sled
-tired (u.m.)
tooth
-toothed (u.m.)
trick
trot
watch
-weary (u.m.)
**doll**
face
-faced (u.m.)
dollyhead
**donkey**
back
-drawn (u.m.)
-eared (u.m.)
doomsday
**door**
bed
bell
case
check
frame
head

jamb
knob
mat
nail
plate
post
-shaped (u.m.)
sill
step
stop
**dope**
passer
pusher
sheet
**dorsi** (c.f.)
*all one word*
**dorso** (c.f.)
-occipital
*rest one word*
**double**
-barrel (n., u.m.)
-barreled (u.m.)
-bitt (v.)
-breasted (u.m.)
-charge (v.)
check (n., v.)
checked (u.m.,
v.)
-chinned (u.m.)
cross
(nonliteral)
deal (v.)
-decker
-distilled (u.m.)
-duty (u.m.)
-dye (v.)
-edged (u.m.)
-ender
-entendre
handed
-headed (u.m.)
header
-jointed
-leaded (u.m.)
-quick (u.m.)
talk
tone (printing)
tree
-trouble
-up (u.m., v.)
#work
**dough**
-colored (u.m.)
face
-faced (u.m.)
head
mixer
nut
**down**
beat
by
cast
check
coast
come
-covered (u.m.)
crier
cry
curved
cut
dale
draft
drag
face
fall

| | | | | |
|---|---|---|---|---|
| feed | **draft** | net | head | foot (tool) |
| filled | age (allowance) | off (n., u.m.) | -in (n., u.m.) | -footed (u.m.) |
| flow | #age | pin | pipe | pin |
| fold | -exempt (u.m.) | plate | screw | pond |
| grade | **drag** | point | **drop** | walk |
| gradient | bar | sheet | away (n., u.m.) | **due** |
| growth | bolt | span | bolt | -in (n., u.m.) |
| hanging | net | stop | -forge (v.) | out (n., u.m.) |
| haul | pipe | string | front | duffelbag |
| hill | rope | tongs | hammer | **dug** |
| lead | saw | tube | head | out (n.) |
| lock (n.) | staff | **drawer** | kick | -up (u.m.) |
| look | wire | -down | leaf (n., u.m.) | **dull** |
| most | **dragger** | -in | leg | -edged (u.m.) |
| payment | -down | -off | off (n., u.m.) | head |
| pour | -in | -out | out (n., u.m.) | -looking (u.m.) |
| rate | -out | **drawing** | sonde | -witted (u.m.) |
| right | -up | #board | stitch | dumdum |
| river | **dragon** | #room | **drug** | **dumb** |
| rush | -eyed (u.m.) | **dream** | -addicted (u.m.) | bell |
| shore | #piece | -haunted (u.m.) | mixer | head |
| side | **drain** | lore | passer | waiter |
| sitting | cleaner | world | pusher | **dump** |
| slip | pipe | dressup (n., u.m.) | seller | car |
| slope | plug | dressing #room | **drum** | cart |
| -soft (u.m.) | tile | **drift** | beat | dunderhead |
| spout | **draw** | #boat | fire | **duo** (c.f.) |
| stage | -arch (n.) | bolt | head | *all one word* |
| stairs | arm | meter | stick | **dust** |
| state | back | -mining (u.m.) | -up (n., u.m.) | bag |
| stream | bar | pin | **dry** | bin |
| street | beam | wind | -burnt (u.m.) | brush |
| stroke | bench | **drill** | clean | cloth |
| sun (adv., u.m.) | bolt | case | -cure (v.) | -covered (u.m.) |
| swing | bore | -like | dock | fall |
| take | bridge | stock | -dye (v.) | -gray (u.m.) |
| throw | cut | **drip** | -farm (v.) | -laden (u.m.) |
| thrust | down (n., u.m.) | cock | farming (n., u.m.) | pan |
| town | file | -drip | lot | storm |
| trampling | gate | -dry (u.m., v.) | -pack (u.m., v.) | duty-free (u.m.) |
| trend | gear | sheet | -rotted (u.m.) | dwelling #house |
| trodden | glove | stick | -salt (v.) | **dye** |
| turn | head | **drive** | wash | mixer |
| valley | horse | away (n., u.m.) | **duck** | stuff |
| weigh | knife | belt | bill | works |
| weight | knot | bolt | -billed (u.m.) | **dys** (pref.) |
| wind | link | cap | blind | *all one word* |
| | loom | | | |

## E

| | | | | |
|---|---|---|---|---|
| **ear** | fall | -spoken (u.m.) | shell | **en** |
| ache | fast | eavesdrop | -white (u.m.) | #banc |
| cap | -fed (u.m.) | ebbtide | **eight** | #gros |
| drop | fill | **edge** | -angled (u.m.) | #route |
| drum | grubber | #plane | fold | **encephalo** (c.f.) |
| flap | #house | shot | penny (nail) | *all one word* |
| guard | kin | ways | -ply (u.m.) | **end** |
| hole | lit | **eel** | score | -all (n., u.m.) |
| lap | mover | cake | -wheeler | bell |
| mark | nut | catcher | elbowchair | brain |
| phone | quake | fare | **elder** | gate |
| -piercing (u.m.) | -shaking (u.m.) | pot | #brother | lap |
| plug | slide | pout | brotherhood | long |
| ring | -stained (u.m.) | spear | brotherly | -match (v.) |
| screw | wall | **egg** | -leaved (u.m.) | matcher |
| shot | **east** | beater (all | **electro** (c.f.) | -measure (v.) |
| sore | -central (u.m.) | meanings) | -optics | most |
| splitting | going | cup | -osmosis | -shrink (v.) |
| tab | -northeast | eater | -ultrafiltration | ways |
| wax | -sider | fruit | *rest one word* | **ender** |
| wig | -southeast | head | **embryo** (c.f.) | -on |
| witness | Eastertide | (nonliteral) | *all one word* | -up |
| **earth** | **easy** | hot (n.) | **empty** | **endo** (c.f.) |
| bank | going | nog | handed | *all one word* |
| born | mark (n.) | plant | -looking | **engine** |
| -bred (u.m.) | -rising (u.m.) | -shaped (u.m.) | (u.m.) | #shop |

-sized (u.m.)
work
#worker
#yard
entero (c.f.)
  *all one word*
entry#book
envelope
#holder
#maker
epi (pref.)
  *all one word*
equi (c.f.)
-gram-molar
  *rest one word*
ere
long
now
erythro (c.f.)
  *all one word*
even
glow
handed
minded
-numbered (u.m.)
song
-tempered (u.m.)

tide
ever
-abiding (u.m.)
bearing
blooming
-constant (u.m.)
-fertile (u.m.)
glade
going
green
lasting
more
-normal (u.m.)
-present (u.m.)
-ready (u.m.)
sporting (biol.)
which
every
day (n., u.m.)
#day (each day)
how
one (all)
#one
  (distributive)
#time
evil
doer

-eyed (u.m.)
-faced (u.m.)
-looking (u.m.)
minded (u.m.)
sayer
speaker
wishing
ex
#cathedra
cathedral
communicate
-Governor
#libris
#officio
#post#facto
#rights
-serviceman
-trader
extra
-alimentary
-American
bold
-Britannic
-condensed
  (u.m.)
curricular
-fine (u.m.)

hazardous
judicial
-large (u.m.)
-long (u.m.)
marginal
mural
ordinary
polar
-strong (u.m.)
territorial
vascular
eye
ball
bank
bar
blink
-blurred (u.m.)
bolt
brow
-conscious (u.m.)
cup
flap
glance
glass
hole
lash
lens

lid
mark
-minded (u.m.)
peep
pit
point
service
shade
shield
shot
sick
sight
sore
spot
-spotted (u.m.)
stalk
strain
string
tooth
wash
#weariness
wink
witness

# F

F
-flat
-horn
-sharp
fable
#book
teller
face
about (n., u.m., v.)
-arbor (v.)
cloth
-harden (v.)
-hardened (u.m.)
lifting
mark
-on (n., u.m.)
plate
up (n., u.m.)
fact
finding
sheet
fade
away (n., u.m.)
-in (n., u.m.)
out (n., u.m.)
fail-safe
faint
heart
-voiced (u.m.)
fair
ground
-lead (n., u.m.)
minded
play
-skinned (u.m.)
fairy
folk
hood
tale
faithbreaker
fall
away (n., u.m.)
back (n., u.m.)
-in (n., u.m.)
out (n., u.m.)
-plow (v.)

-sow (v.)
trap
fallow#land
false
-bottomed (u.m.)
-faced (u.m.)
hood
-tongued (u.m.)
fame
-crowned (u.m.)
-thirsty (u.m.)
fan
back
bearer
fare
fold
foot
-jet
-leaved (u.m.)
marker
-shaped (u.m.)
-tailed (u.m.)
fancy
-free (u.m.)
-loose (u.m.)
-woven (u.m.)
-wrought (u.m.)
far
-aloft (u.m.)
away (n., u.m.)
-borne (u.m.)
-distant (u.m.)
-eastern (u.m.)
-famed (u.m.)
fetched
flung (u.m.)
gone
-off (u.m.)
-reaching (u.m.)
seeing
-seen (u.m.)
-set (u.m.)
sight
farm
-bred (u.m.)
hand
hold

people
place
stead
fashion
-led (u.m.)
#piece (naut.)
-setting (u.m.)
fast
-anchored (u.m.)
back
-dyed (u.m.)
going
hold
-moving (u.m.)
-read (v.)
-reading (u.m.)
#time (daylight saving)
fat
back
-bellied (u.m.)
-free (u.m.)
head
-soluble (u.m.)
father
-confessor
-in-law
fault
finder
slip
faux#pas
fear
-free (u.m.)
nought
-pursued (u.m.)
-shaken (u.m.)
feather
bed (v.)
bone
brain
edge
-footed (u.m.)
head
-leaved (u.m.)
stitch
-stitched (u.m.)
-stitching

-tongue (v.)
weight
wing (moth)
fed-up (u.m.)
feeble
-bodied (u.m.)
minded
feed
back (n., u.m.)
bag
bin
crusher
cutter
head
lot
mixer
pipe
rack
stuff
feeder
-in
-up
fellow
craft
ship
*rest two words*
felt
cutter
-lined (u.m.)
packer
fenbank
fencepost
fern
-clad (u.m.)
leaf
-leaved (u.m.)
ferro (c.f.)
-carbon-titanium
-uranium
*rest one word*
fever
less
-stricken (u.m.)
trap
-warm (u.m.)
fiber
-faced (u.m.)

glass
stitch
Fiberglas
  (copyright)
fibro (c.f.)
-osteoma
  *rest one word*
fickleminded
  (u.m.)
fiddle
back
-faddle
head
-shaped (u.m.)
stick
string
field
ball
glass
goal
-strip
fierce
-eyed (u.m.)
-looking (u.m.)
fiery
-flaming (u.m.)
-hot (u.m.)
-red (u.m.)
-tempered (u.m.)
fig
bar
eater
leaf
shell
figure
head
-of-eight (u.m.)
#work (printing)
file
card
-hard (u.m.)
setter
-soft (u.m.)
fill
-in (n., u.m.)
out (n., u.m.)
-up (n., u.m.)

| | | | | |
|---|---|---|---|---|
| **filler** | **firm** | -eared (u.m.) | lamp | -crested (u.m.) |
| cap | -footed (u.m.) | jack | mat | -white (u.m.) |
| -in | -set (u.m.) | **flare** | mop | **fog** |
| -out | -up (n., u.m.) | back (n., u.m.) | space | born |
| -up | **first** | out (n., u.m.) | stain | bow |
| **film** | -aider | path | walker | dog |
| cutter | -born (u.m.) | up (n., u.m.) | -waxing (u.m.) | eater |
| goer | -class (u.m.) | **flash** | **flour** | -hidden (u.m.) |
| going | comer | back (n., u.m.) | bag | horn |
| slide | hand (u.m.) | bulb | bin | -ridden (u.m.) |
| strip | -made (u.m.) | card | #mill | **fold** |
| -struck (u.m.) | -named (u.m.) | cube | sack | -in |
| **fin** | -nighter | gun | **flow** | up (n., u.m.) |
| back | -rate (u.m.) | lamp | chart | **folk** |
| -shaped (u.m.) | -rater | pan | meter | free (u.m.) |
| **fine** | **fish** | point | off (n., u.m.) | lore |
| -cut (u.m., v.) | back | **flat** | sheet | song |
| -draw (v.) | bed | back | through | **follow** |
| -drawn (u.m.) | -bellied (u.m.) | (bookbinding) | **flower** | -on |
| -featured (u.m.) | bolt | bed (printing) | bed | through (n., u.m.) |
| -looking (u.m.) | bone | -bottomed (u.m.) | bud | up (n., u.m.) |
| -set (u.m.) | bowl | car | -crowned (u.m.) | **follower-up** |
| **finger** | cake | -compound (v.) | #grower | **food** |
| breadth | eater | fold | -hung (u.m.) | packer |
| -cut (u.m.) | eye | foot (n.) | pot | sick |
| hold | -eyed (u.m.) | hat | -scented (u.m.) | stuff |
| hole | fall | head | #shop | **foolhardy** |
| hook | -fed (u.m.) | iron | **flue-cure (v.)** | **foolscap** |
| mark | food | nose | **fluid** | **foot** |
| nail | garth | out (n., u.m.) | -compressed (u.m.) | -and-mouth (u.m.) |
| parted | hook | -rolled (u.m.) | extract (pharm.) (n.) | ball |
| post | -joint (v.) | sawn | glycerate | band |
| print | kill | top | **fluo** (c.f.) | bath |
| shell | meal | -topped (u.m.) | *all one word* | blower |
| spin | mouth | woods | **fluoro** (c.f.) | brake |
| stall | plate | **flax** | *all one word* | breadth |
| tip | pond | drop | **flush** | bridge |
| **fire** | pool | -leaved (u.m.) | -cut (u.m.) | -candle |
| arm | pot | -polled (u.m.) | -decked (u.m.) | fall |
| back (n.) | pound | seed | -decker | -free (u.m.) |
| ball | trap | wife | gate | gear |
| bell | weir | **flea** | **fluvio** (c.f.) | -grain |
| bolt | works | bite | *all one word* | hill |
| bomb | **fisher** | -bitten (u.m.) | **fly** | hold |
| brand | folk | **fleet** | away | lambert |
| brat | people | foot | back | licker |
| break | **fishyback** (n., u.m.) | -footed (u.m.) | ball | lining |
| brick | **fit** | wing | -bitten (u.m.) | locker |
| -burnt (u.m.) | out (n.) | **flesh** | blow | loose |
| -clad (u.m.) | strip | brush | blown | mark |
| coat | **five** | hook | -by-night (n., u.m.) | note |
| cracker | bar | -pink (u.m.) | catcher | pad |
| crest | fold | pot | eater | path |
| -cure (v.) | -ply (u.m.) | **fleur-de-lis** | -fish (v.) | pick |
| damp | -pointed (u.m.) | **flight** | -fisher | plate |
| -eater | -reeler | crew | -fisherman | -pound |
| fall | score | -hour | #fishing | -pound-second |
| fang | -shooter | path | flap | print |
| fighter | **flag** | -test (v.) | -free (u.m.) | race |
| guard | bearer | **flimflam** | leaf | rail |
| -hardened (u.m.) | pole | **flip** | paper | rest |
| hose | post | -flap | sheet | rope |
| lit | -raising (u.m.) | -flop | speck | scald |
| pit | ship | -up (n., u.m.) | -specked (u.m.) | -second |
| place | -signal (v.) | **flood** | tier | slogger |
| plow | staff | cock | trap | sore |
| plug | stick | flow | weight | stalk |
| -polish (v.) | **flame** | gate | wheel | stall |
| -red (u.m.) | -colored (u.m.) | lamp | winch | step |
| -resistant (u.m.) | -cut (v.) | lighting | **flying** | stick |
| safe | out (n.) | mark | #boat | stock |
| side | thrower | tide | #fish | stool |
| spout | **flannelmouth** | wall | **foam** | -ton |
| trap | **flap** | **floor** | bow | walk |
| truck | cake | beam | | wall |
| wall | doodle | cloth | | |
| warden | | head | | |

-weary (u.m.)
worn
**for** (pref.)
  *all one word*
**fore**
-age
-and-aft (n., u.m.)
-and-after (n.)
-edge
-end
-exercise
  *rest one word*
**forest**
-clad (u.m.)
-covered (u.m.)
#land
side
**fork**
head
lift
-pronged (u.m.)
-tailed (u.m.)
**form**
fitting
#work (printing)
**forth**
coming
right
with
fortuneteller
forty-niner
**foul**
#line

-looking (u.m.)
mouthed
-spoken (u.m.)
-tongued (u.m.)
up (n., u.m.)
foundry#proof (printing)
fountainhead
**four**
-bagger
-ball (u.m.)
-eyed (u.m.)
flusher
fold
-footed (u.m.)
-in-hand (n., u.m.)
-masted (u.m.)
-master
penny (nail)
-ply (u.m.)
score
some
square
-wheeler
**fox**
-faced (u.m.)
hole
hound
skinned
tailed
trot
**fracto** (c.f.)
  *all one word*

frameup (n., u.m.)
**free**
booter
born
drop
-for-all (n., u.m.)
-grown (u.m.)
hand (drawing)
handed
hold
lance
loader
-minded
masonry
-spoken (u.m.)
standing (u.m.)
thinker
trader
wheel (u.m., v.)
wheeler (n.)
#will (n.)
will (u.m.)
**freeze**
down (n., u.m.)
out (n., u.m.)
up (n., u.m.)
**freight**
#house
-mile
#room
french-minded (u.m.)
**fresh**
-looking (u.m.)

-painted (u.m.)
**frog**
belly
eater
-eyed (u.m.)
face
mouth
nose
pond
tongue
  (medicine)
**front**
-end (u.m.)
-focused (u.m.)
runner
stall
-wheel (u.m.)
**fronto** (c.f.)
-occipital
-orbital
  *rest one word*
**frost**
bite
bow
-free (u.m.)
-hardy (u.m.)
-heaving (u.m.)
-killed (u.m.)
lamp
**fruit**
cake
#fly
growing
#shop

stalk
frying#pan
**fuel**
#line
#oil
**full**
back
-bellied (u.m.)
blood
-bound (u.m.)
face
-fashioned (u.m.)
-flowering (u.m.)
-grown (u.m.)
-handed (u.m.)
-headed (u.m.)
-lined (u.m.)
#load
mouth
-strength (u.m.)
-time (u.m.)
fundraising
funlover
**funnel**
form
-shaped (u.m.)
**fur**
-clad (u.m.)
coat
-lined (u.m.)
-trimmed (u.m.)
fuseplug

# G

**G**
-major
-man
-minor
-sharp
gabfest
**gad**
about (n., u.m.)
fly
gaff-topsail
**gag**
-check (v.)
root
gaugepin
**gain**
say
-sharing (u.m.)
**galact(o)** (c.f.)
  *all one word*
gallbladder
**galley**
#proof (printing)
-west (u.m.)
**galvano** (c.f.)
  *all one word*
**game**
bag
cock
**gang**
boss
plank
saw
gapeseed
garnet-brown (u.m.)
**gas**
bag
bomb
-driven (u.m.)
-fired (u.m.)

firing
fitter
-heated (u.m.)
-laden (u.m.)
lamp
lighted
line (auto)
#line (people queue)
lock
meter
works
**gastro** (c.f.)
-omental
  *rest one word*
**gate**
leg (u.m.)
pin
post
tender
works
**gay**
cat
-colored (u.m.)
#dog
-looking (u.m.)
**gear**
case
-driven (u.m.)
fitter
-operated (u.m.)
set
shift
wheel
**gelatin**
-coated (u.m.)
-making (u.m.)
**gelatino** (c.f.)
bromide
chloride

**gem**
cutter
-set (u.m.)
#stone
**genito** (c.f.)
  *all one word*
**gentle**
folk
-looking (u.m.)
-mannered (u.m.)
mouthed
-spoken (u.m.)
**geo** (c.f.)
  *all one word*
germ-free (u.m.)
gerrymander
**get**
-at-able
away (n., u.m.)
off (n., u.m.)
-together (n., u.m.)
up (n., u.m.)
**ghost**
-haunted (u.m.)
write (v.)
**giddy**
brain
head
-paced (u.m.)
gilt-edge (u.m.)
gin-run (u.m.)
**ginger**
bread
-colored (u.m.)
snap
spice
**give**
-and-take (n., u.m.)

away (n., u.m.)
**glacio** (c.f.)
  *all one word*
**glad**
-cheered (u.m.)
-sad
**glass**
blower
cutter
-eater
-eyed (u.m.)
-hard (u.m.)
works
**glauco** (c.f.)
  *all one word*
glidepath
globetrotter
**glosso** (c.f.)
  *all one word*
**glow**
lamp
meter
**gluc(o)** (c.f.)
  *all one word*
**glue**
pot
stock
**glycero** (c.f.)
  *all one word*
**glyco** (c.f.)
  *all one word*
**go**
-ahead (n., u.m.)
-around (n., u.m.)
-as-you-please (u.m.)
-back (n., u.m.)
-between (n.)
by (n.)

cart
-devil (n.)
-getter
-getting (n., u.m.)
-off (n., u.m.)
goalpost
**goat**
-bearded (u.m.)
-drunk (u.m.)
-eyed (u.m.)
herd
**goat's**
-hair
-horn
**God**
-conscious (u.m.)
-fearing (u.m.)
-forsaken (u.m.)
-given (u.m.)
head
-man
-ordained (u.m.)
-sent (u.m.)
-sped (u.m.)
speed
-taught (u.m.)
**god**
child
daughter
father
head
hood
less
mother
parent
send
ship
son
sonship
goggle-eyed (u.m.)

goings-on
**gold**
  beater
  brick (swindle)
# brick (of real
    gold)
  -bright (u.m.)
  -brown (u.m.)
  digger
  -filled (u.m.)
  foil
  -inlaid (u.m.)
  leaf
  plate (v.)
  -plated (u.m.)
  -plating (u.m.)
  smithing
  -wrought (u.m.)
**golden**
  -fingered (u.m.)
  -headed (u.m.)
  mouthed
**good**
  bye
  -fellowship
  -for-nothing (n., u.m.)
  -looker
  -looking (u.m.)
  -natured (u.m.)
# will (kindness)
  will (salable asset)
**goose**
  bone
  -cackle
  -eyed (u.m.)
  flesh
  -footed (u.m.)
  herd
  mouth
  neck
  pimples
  rump
  step
  wing

**gospel**
  like
  -true (u.m.)
**gourdhead**
**Government** (U.S. or foreign)
  -in-exile
  -owned (u.m.)
  wide
**governmentwide** (State, city, etc.)
**grab**
  -all (n., u.m.)
  hook
  rope
**grade**
  finder
  mark
**grain**
  -cut (u.m.)
  -laden (u.m.)
  mark
  sick
**gram**
  -fast (u.m.)
  -meter
  -molecular
  -negative (u.m.)
  -positive (u.m.)
**grand**
  aunt
  child, etc.
  stand
**grant-in-aid**
**grape**
  fruit
  juice
  -leaved (u.m.)
  seed
  stalk
  vine
**graphalloy**
**grapho** (c.f)
  *all one word*
**grass**
  -clad (u.m.)

  -covered (u.m.)
  cutter
  flat
  -green (u.m.)
  hop
  nut
  plot
  roots (nonliteral)
# roots (literal)
  widow
**grave**
  clothes
  digger
  side
  stead
  gravel-blind (u.m.)
**gray**
  back (n., u.m.)
  beard (n.)
  -clad (u.m.)
  coat (n.)
  -eyed (u.m.)
  -haired (u.m.)
  head
  -headed (u.m.)
  out (n., u.m.)
**great**
  -aunt
  coat
  -eared (u.m.)
  -grandchild, etc.
  -headed (u.m.)
  heart
  mouthed
**green**
  back (n., u.m.)
  belt (community)
  -clad (u.m.)
  -eyed (u.m.)
  gage (plum)
  gill
  grocer
  horn
  -leaved (u.m.)

  sand (geology)
  sick
  stuff
  sward
  town (community)
# wood (literal)
  wood (forest)
  greyhound
  gridiron
  griddlecake
**grip**
  sack
  wheel
  gross-minded (u.m.)
**ground**
  hog
  mass
  nut
  path
  plot
  -sluicer
  speed
  wave
# water
  group-connect (v.)
  grownup (n., u.m.)
  grubstake
**guard**
  plate
  rail
  guestchamber
  guidepost
  guided-missile (u.m.)
  guider-in
**gum**
  boil
  chewer
  digger
  drop
  -gum
  lac
  -saline (n.)
  shoe

**gun**
  bearer
  blast
  builder
  cotton
  crew
  deck
  fight
  fire
  flint
  lock
  paper
  pit
  play
  point
  powder
  rack
  -rivet (v.)
  runner
  shot
  -shy (u.m.)
  sight
  stock
  wale
**gut**
  less
  string
**gutter**
  blood
  -bred (u.m.)
  snipe
  spout
**gymno** (c.f.)
  *all one word*
**gyneco** (c.f.)
  *all one word*
**gyro**
# horizon
# mechanism
# pelorus
  plane, compass, etc.

# H

**H**
  -bar
  -beam
  -bomb
  -hour
  -piece
**hack**
  barrow
  hammer
  log
  saw
  hailstorm
**hair**
  band
  breadth
  brush
  -check (n.)
  cloth
  cut (n.)
  do
  dresser
  -fibered (u.m.)
  lock
  pin
  space (printing)
  splitting
  spring
  streak

  stroke (printing)
**half**
  -and-half (n., u.m.)
  -afraid
  -alive
  -angry
  back (football)
  -backed (u.m.)
  -baked (u.m.)
  blood (n.)
  -bound (u.m.)
  -bred (u.m.)
  breed
  caste
  -clear
  cock (v.)
  cocked (nonliteral)
  -dark
  deck
  -decked (u.m.)
  -decker
  -feed (v.)
  -hourly (u.m.)
  -life
# load
  -loaded (u.m.)

  -mast
  -miler
  -monthly (u.m.)
  -on (n., u.m.)
  pace
  penny
  -ripe
  -shy
  -sole (v.)
  staff
  stitch
  -strength (u.m.)
  title
  tone (printing)
  track
  -true
  -truth
  -weekly (u.m.)
  wit
  -witted (u.m.)
  -yearly (u.m.)
  hallmark
**ham**
  shackle
  string
**hammer**
  cloth
  dress (v.)

  -hard (u.m.)
  -harden (v.)
  -hardened (u.m.)
  head
  lock
  toe
  -weld (v.)
  -wrought (u.m.)
**hand**
  bag
  ball
  bank (v.)
  barrow
  bill
  -bound (u.m.)
  bow
  brake
  breadth
  brush
  -built (u.m.)
  car
  -carry (v.)
  cart
  -carve (v.)
  clap
  clasp
  -clean (v.)
  crank

  cuff
  -cut (v.)
  -embroidered (u.m.)
  -fed (v.)
  fold
  grasp
  grenade
  grip
  guard
  gun
  -high (u.m.)
  hold
  hole
  -in-hand (u.m.)
  kerchief
  -knit (v.)
  -knitter
  laid
  -letter (v.)
  lift (truck)
  liner
  made
  -me-down (n., u.m.)
  mix (v.)
  mold (n.)
  mower

| | | | | |
|---|---|---|---|---|
| off (n., u.m.) | -working (u.m.) | ledge | **heavy** | **hepta** (c.f.) |
| out (n., u.m.) | wrought | lighting | back | *all one word* |
| pick (v.) | **hare** | liner | -duty (u.m.) | **here** |
| post | brain | lock | -eyed (u.m.) | about |
| press | foot | long | -footed (u.m.) | after |
| print | hound | mold | handed | at |
| rail | lip | most | -looking (u.m.) | by |
| reading | -mad (u.m.) | note | -set (u.m.) | from |
| saw | harness-making | -on (u.m.) | # water | in |
| scrape (v.) | (u.m.) | phone | weight (n., u.m.) | inabove |
| set | harum-scarum | plate | **hecto** (c.f.) | inafter |
| shake | has-been (n.) | post | *all one word* | inbefore |
| spade | hashmark | quarters | **hedge** | into |
| spike | **hat** | rail | born | of |
| splice | band | reach | breaker | on |
| split | brim | rest | hog | to |
| spring | brush | ring | hop | tofore |
| spun | cleaner | rope | pig | under |
| -stamp (v.) | pin | set | row | unto |
| stand | rack | shake | **heel** | upon |
| stitch | rail | sill | ball | with |
| stroke | stand | space | band | herringbone |
| stuff | hatchet-faced | spin | block | **hetero** (c.f.) |
| -tailored (u.m.) | (u.m.) | spring | cap | -ousia, etc. |
| tap | **haul** | stall | fast | *rest one word* |
| tool | about (n., u.m.) | stand | grip | **hexa** (c.f.) |
| -tooled (u.m.) | away (n., u.m.) | start | pad | *all one word* |
| -tooling (u.m.) | back (n.) | stick | path | **hi** |
| truck | have-not (n., u.m.) | stock | plate | -fi |
| weave | haversack | stream | post | jack |
| wheel | **hawk** | strong | print | **hide** |
| worked | bill | wall | ring | -and-seek (n., |
| woven | -billed (u.m.) | waiter | stay | u.m.) |
| write (v.) | -nosed (u.m.) | wind | strap | away (n., u.m.) |
| written | **hawse** | header-up | tap | out (n., u.m.) |
| wrought | hole | heal-all (n., u.m.) | **helio** (c.f.) | **high** |
| handie-talkie | pipe | **heart** | *all one word* | ball |
| handlebar | **hay** | ache | **hell** | binder |
| **hang** | band | aching | bender | born |
| dog | cap | beat | bent | bred |
| nail | cart | block | born | brow |
| net | cock | blood | bred | (nonliteral) |
| out (n., u.m.) | fork | break | cat | -caliber (u.m.) |
| up (n.) | lift | burn | -dark (u.m.) | -class (u.m.) |
| **hanger** | loft | deep | diver | flier (n.) |
| -back | market | felt | dog | flying (u.m.) |
| -on | mow | free (u.m.) | fire | -foreheaded |
| -up | rack | grief | hole | (u.m.) |
| happy-go-lucky | rake | heavy | hound | handed |
| hara-kiri | rick | leaf | -red (u.m.) | -hat (v.) |
| harborside | -scented (u.m.) | -leaved (u.m.) | ship | jinks |
| **hard** | seed | nut | helpmeet | lander |
| -and-fast (u.m.) | stack | quake | helter-skelter | # light (literal) |
| back (beetle) | wire | seed | hemstitch | light (nonlit.) |
| -baked (u.m.) | **hazel** | sick | **hema** (c.f.) | -minded (u.m.) |
| -bitten (u.m) | -eyed (u.m.) | sore | *all one word* | -power (u.m.) |
| -boiled (u.m.) | nut | string | **hemato** (c.f.) | -pressure |
| case | he-man | struck | *ail one word* | (u.m., v.) |
| core | **head** | throb | **hemi** (pref.) | -priced (u.m.) |
| fist (n.) | ache | -throbbing (u.m.) | *all one word* | # proof |
| handed | achy | -weary (u.m.) | **hemo** (c.f.) | -reaching (u.m.) |
| hat (n.) | band | **hearth** | *all one word* | -rigger (n.) |
| head | bander | rug | **hemp** | rise (building) |
| -hit (u.m.) | block | warming | seed | road |
| -looking (u.m.) | cap | **heat** | string | # seas |
| mouthed | chair | drops | **hen** | -speed (u.m.) |
| nose | cheese | -resistant (u.m.) | bill | stepper |
| pan | chute | stroke | coop | -tension (u.m.) |
| -pressed (u.m.) | cloth | treat (v.) | -feathered | -up (u.m.) |
| -set (u.m.) | dress | -treating (u.m.) | (u.m.) | # water |
| ship | -ender | **heaven** | pecked | higher-up (n.) |
| spun | first | -inspired (u.m.) | roost | **hill** |
| stand | frame | -sent (u.m.) | **hence** | billy |
| tack | gate | **heaver** | forth | culture |
| top (auto) | gear | -off | forward | (farming) |
| -won (u.m.) | hunter | -out | **hepato** (c.f.) | side |
| # work | lamp | -over | *all one word* | top |

**hind**
  brain
  cast
  gut (n.)
  head
  leg
  most
  quarter
  saddle
  sight
  wing
**hip**
  bone
  mold
  shot
**hippo** (c.f.)
  *all one word*
**histo** (c.f.)
  *all one word*
**hit**
  -and-miss (u.m.)
  -and-run (u.m.)
  -or-miss (u.m.)
hitchhiker
hoarfrost
hoary-haired
  (u.m.)
**hob**
  goblin
  nail
  nob
hobbyhorse
hocus-pocus
hodgepodge
**hog**
  back
  -backed (u.m.)
  -faced (u.m.)
  fat
  frame
  hide
  nose (machine)
  -nosed (u.m.)
  pen
  sty
  -tie (v.)
  wash
  -wild (u.m.)
hog's-back (geol.)
hogshead
hoistaway (n.)
**hold**
  all (n., u.m.)
  back (n., u.m.)
  -clear (n., u.m.)
  down (n., u.m.)
  fast (n., u.m.)
  off (n., u.m.)
  out (n., u.m.)
  up (n., u.m.)
**holder**
  -forth
  -on
  -up
**hole**
  -high (u.m.)
  through
**hollow**
  back
    (bookbinding)
  -backed (u.m.)
  -eyed (u.m.)
  faced
  -ground (u.m.)
**holo** (c.f.)
  *all one word*
**home**
  -baked (u.m.)
  body
  born
  bred
  brew
  builder
  comer
  -fed (u.m.)
  felt
  folk
  freeze (u.m., v.)
  front
  furnishings (n.)
  grown
  lander
  life
  made
  plate
  seeker
  sick
  spun
  stead
  stretch
  town
  woven
**homeo** (c.f.)
  *all one word*
**homo**
  #legalis
  #sapiens
**homo** (c.f.)
  -ousia, etc.
  *rest one word*
**honey**
  -colored (u.m.)
  comb
  dew
  drop
  eater
  -laden (u.m.)
  lipped
  moon
  mouthed
  pot
  sucker
  sweet
honor#man
**hood**
  cap
  mold
  wink
**hoof**
  beat
  mark
  print
  -printed (u.m.)
**hook**
  ladder
  nose
  -nosed (u.m.)
  pin
  up (n., u.m.)
**hooker**
  -off
  -on
  -out
  -over
  -up
hoopstick
**hop**
  about (n., u.m.)
  off (n., u.m.)
  scotch
  toad
**hopper**
  burn
  dozer
horehound
**hormono** (c.f.)
  *all one word*
**horn**
  bill
  blende
  blower
  -eyed (u.m.)
  pipe
  stay
  tip
hornyhanded
**horse**
  back
  breaker
  car
  cloth
  dealer
  fair
  fight
  flesh
  hair
  head
  herd
  hide
  hoof
  -hour
  jockey
  laugh
  meat
  mint
  play
  pond
  power-hour
  power-year
  pox
  race
  #sense (n.)
  shoe
  thief
  whip
**hot**
  bed
  blood
  -blooded (u.m.)
  brain
  cake
  -cold
  dog
  foot
  head (n.)
  -mix (u.m.)
  pack
  patch
  plate
  -press (v.)
  rod (nonliteral)
  -roll (v.)
  -rolled (u.m.)
  spot
  -work (v.)
houndshark
hourglass
**house**
  breaking
  broken
  builder
  cleaner
  -cleaning (u.m.)
  coat
  dress
  father
  furnishing(s) (n.)
  guest
  hold
  husband
  mother
  parent
  pest
  -raising (u.m.)
  ridden
  top
  trailer
  wares
  warming
  wife
  wright
**how**
  -do-you-do (n.)
  ever
  soever
**hub**
  cap
  -deep (u.m.)
humankind
**humble**
  bee
  -looking (u.m.)
  mouthed
  -spirited (u.m.)
humdrum
**humero** (c.f.)
  -olecranal
  *rest one word*
**hump**
  back
  -shouldered
    (u.m.)
humpty-dumpty
hunchback
**hundred**
  fold
  -legged (u.m.)
  -percenter
  -pounder
  weight
hung-up (u.m.)
**hunger**
  -mad (u.m.)
  -worn (u.m.)
hurly-burly
**hush**
  -hush
  up (n., u.m.)
**hydro** (c.f.)
  electric, plant,
    power, etc.
  #station
  *rest one word*
**hygro** (c.f.)
  *all one word*
**hyper** (pref.)
  -Dorian, etc.
  *rest one word*
**hypo** (c.f.)
  *all one word*
**hystero** (c.f.)
  -oophorectomy
  -salpingo-oopho-
    rectomy
  *rest one word*

## I

**I**
  -bar
  -beam
  -iron
  -rail
**ice**
  berg
  blind
  #blindness
  blink
  block
  bone
  breaker
  cap
  -clad (u.m.)
  -cold (u.m.)
  -cooled (u.m.)
  -covered (u.m.)
  fall
  #fishing
  floe (island)
  flow
    (current)
  -free (u.m.)
  melt
  pack
  plant
  plow
  quake
  #water
**ichthyo** (c.f.)
  *all one word*
**ideo** (c.f.)
  -unit
  *rest one word*
**idle**
  headed
  -looking (u.m.)
  -minded (u.m.)
**ileo** (c.f.)
  *all one word*
**ilio** (c.f.)
  *all one word*
**ill**
  -advised (u.m.)
  -being (n.)
  -born (u.m.)
  -bred (u.m.)
  #breeding (n.)
  -doing (n., u.m.)
  -fated (u.m.)
  -humored (u.m.)
  -looking (u.m.)
  -treat (v.)
  -use (v.)
  -wisher
  -wishing (u.m.)
**in**
  -and-in (u.m.)
  -and-out (u.m.)
  -and-outer
  -being (u.m.)
  -flight (u.m.)
  -house
  -law (n.)
  asmuch, sofar
  #re, #rem,
    #situ, etc.
**in** (pref.)
  active (u.m.)
  depth (u.m.)
  hospital (u.m.)
  migration (u.m.)
  service (u.m.),
    etc.

| | | | | |
|---|---|---|---|---|
| inch | -esophageal | #man | iron | ironer-up |
| -deep (u.m.) | -umbilical | spring | back | island |
| -long (u.m.) | *rest one word* | ino (c.f.) | -braced (u.m.) | -born (u.m.) |
| meal | inguino (c.f.) | *all one word* | clad | -dotted (u.m.) |
| -pound | *all one word* | insect-borne | fisted | iso (c.f.) |
| -ton | ink | (u.m.) | -free (u.m.) | -octane |
| index-digest | -black (u.m.) | inter (pref.) | handed | -oleic |
| indigo | mixer | -American, etc. | hard | -osmosis |
| -blue (u.m.) | pot | *rest one word* | -lined (u.m.) | *rest one word* |
| -carmine (u.m.) | slinger | intra (pref.) | mold | ivory |
| Indo (c.f.) | spot | -atomic, etc. | -red (u.m.) | -tinted (u.m.) |
| chinese | -spotted (u.m) | *rest one word* | shod | type (photog.) |
| -European, etc. | stain | intro (pref.) | shot (mineral) | -white (u.m.) |
| infra (pref.) | stand | *all one word* | (u.m.) | ivy |
| -anal | well | Irish | #shot (golf) | -clad (u.m.) |
| -auricular | inner | -American (u.m.) | side | -covered (u.m.) |
| -axillary | -city (u.m.) | -born (u.m.) | works | |

## J

| | | | | |
|---|---|---|---|---|
| J-bolt | jam | -built (u.m.) | jig | rock |
| jack | nut | jet | -a-jig | jungle |
| ass | packed | black (u.m.) | back | -clad (u.m.) |
| hammer | jaw | liner | -drill (v.) | -covered (u.m.) |
| head | bone | port | saw | side |
| -in-the-box | breaker | -powered (u.m.) | job | junkpile |
| knife | foot | prop | seeker | jury |
| -of-all-trades | -locked (u.m.) | -propelled (u.m.) | #shop | #box |
| -o'-lantern | twister | stream | joggle#piece | -fixing (u.m.) |
| -plane (v.) | jay | wash | joint#owner | -rigged (u.m.) |
| pot | hawk | jewel | joulemeter | juxta (c.f.) |
| rabbit | walk | -bright (u.m.) | joy | -ampullar |
| screw | jelly | -studded (u.m.) | hop | -articular |
| shaft | bean | jew's-harp | killer | *rest one word* |
| snipe | roll | jib | ride | |
| stay | jerry | head | stick | |
| straw | -build (v.) | -o-jib | jump | |
| tar | builder | stay | off (n., u.m.) | |

## K

| | | | | |
|---|---|---|---|---|
| K | stop | king | strap | knocker |
| -ration | word | bolt | knick | -off |
| -term | kick | head | knack | -up |
| keel | about (n., u.m.) | hood | point | knot |
| block | back (n., u.m.) | hunter | knight | hole |
| fat | -in (n., u.m.) | pin | -errant | horn |
| haul | off (n., u.m.) | kins | head | know |
| -laying (u.m.) | out (n., u.m.) | folk | hood | -all (n., u.m.) |
| #line | up (n., u.m.) | people | knitback | -how (n., u.m.) |
| keepsake | killjoy | kiss-off (n., u.m.) | knob | -it-all (n., u.m.) |
| kerato (c.f.) | kiln | kite | kerrie | -little (n., u.m.) |
| *all one word* | -dry (u.m., v.) | flier | stick | -nothing (n., u.m.) |
| kettle | eye | flying | knock | knuckle |
| drum | hole | knapsack | about (n., u.m.) | bone |
| stitch | rib | knee | away (n., u.m.) | -deep (u.m.) |
| key | stick | -braced (u.m.) | down (n., u.m.) | -kneed (u.m.) |
| bolt | tree | brush | -knee (n.) | Ku#Klux#Klan |
| hole | kilo (pref.) | cap | -kneed (u.m.) | |
| lock | gram-meter | -deep (u.m.) | off (n., u.m.) | |
| note | voltampere | -high (u.m.) | -on (n., u.m.) | |
| punch | watthour | hole | out (n., u.m.) | |
| ring | *rest one word* | pad | up (n., u.m.) | |
| seat | kindheart | pan | | |

## L

| | | | | |
|---|---|---|---|---|
| L | lace | lady | shore | hole |
| -bar | -edged (u.m.) | beetle | side | -hour |
| -beam | #edging | finger | lameduck | #house |
| -block | wing (insect) | killer | (nonliteral) | lighter |
| -shaped | -winged (u.m.) | ship | (n., u.m.) | lit |
| -square | worked | lake | lamp | post |
| labio (c.f.) | lackluster | bed | black | shade |
| *all one word* | ladder-backed | front | -blown (u.m.) | stand |
| laborsaving | (u.m.) | lander | -foot | wick |

**land**
#base
-based (u.m.)
#bird
fall
fast
fill
flood
form
grabber
-grant (u.m.)
holding
lady
locked
look
lord
lubber
mark
mass
mine
-poor (u.m.)
right
scape
sick
side
slide
slip
spout
storm
wash
wire
wrack
lantern-jawed
   (u.m.)
**lap**
belt
-lap
robe
streak
weld (v.)
-welded (u.m.)
-welding (u.m.)
**large**
-eyed
-handed (u.m.)
-minded (u.m.)
mouthed
-scale (u.m.)
**lark**
-colored (u.m.)
spur
**laryngo** (c.f.)
   all one word
**last**
-born (u.m.)
-cited (u.m.)
-ditcher
-named (u.m.)
**latch**
bolt
key
string
**late**
-born (u.m.)
comer
-lamented (u.m.)
-maturing (u.m.)
**latero** (c.f.)
   all one word
lath-backed
   (u.m.)
lathe-bore (v.)
**latter**
-day (u.m.)
most
laughingstock
laundry #room

**law**
-abiding (u.m.)
breaker
-fettered (u.m.)
giver
suit
lawnmower
**lay**
away (n., u.m.)
back (n., u.m.)
-by (n.)
down (n., u.m.)
-minded (u.m.)
off (n., u.m.)
on (n., u.m.)
out (n., u.m.)
up (n., u.m.)
**layer**
-on
-out
-over
-up
**lazy**
bones
boots
legs
**lead**
-alpha
-burn (v.)
-filled (u.m.)
-gray (u.m.)
-in (n., u.m.)
line
#line (medical,
   naut. only)
off (n., u.m.)
out (n., u.m.)
**leaden**
-eyed (u.m.)
pated
-souled (u.m.)
leader #line
**leaf**
bud
-clad (u.m.)
-eating (u.m.)
-red (u.m.)
-shaped (u.m.)
stalk
**lean**
-faced (u.m.)
-looking (u.m.)
-to (n., u.m.)
leapfrog
**lease**
back (n., u.m.)
hold
**leather**
back
-backed (u.m.)
-bound (u.m.)
-brown (u.m.)
-covered (u.m.)
head
neck
side
leavetaking
lee-bow (v.)
**leech**
eater
#rope
**left**
-bank (v.)
#field (sports)
-hand (u.m.)
-handed (u.m.)
-hander

**most**
-sided (u.m.)
wing (political)
**leg**
band
puller
rope (v.)
lend-lease
**lepto** (c.f.)
   all one word
**let**
down (n., u.m.)
off (n., u.m.)
up (n., u.m.)
**letter**
drop
gram
head
-perfect (u.m.)
press
space
**leuc(o)** (c.f.)
   all one word
liberal-minded
   (u.m.)
**lieutenant**
#colonel
-colonelcy
#governor
-governorship
**life**
belt
blood
drop
float
giver
guard
hold
jacket
long
raft
ring
saver
-size (u.m.)
-sized (u.m.)
span
spring
stream
style
tide
vest
weary (u.m.)
lift-off (n., u.m.)
**light**
-armed (u.m.)
-clad (u.m.)
-colored (u.m.)
-drab (u.m.)
-draft (u.m.)
face (printing)
-footed (u.m.)
handed
house #keeping
   (nautical)
#housekeeping
   (domestic)
mouthed
-producing (u.m.)
ship
-struck (u.m.)
weight (n., u.m.)
-year
lighter-than-air
   (u.m.)
**like**
-looking (u.m.)
-minded (u.m.)

**lily**
handed
-shaped (u.m.)
-white (u.m.)
**lime**
juice
kiln
lighter
pit
quat
wash
**linch**
bolt
pin
**line**
-bred (u.m.)
-breed (v.)
casting
crew
cut (printing)
finder
up (n., u.m.)
walker
**link**
up (n., u.m.)
#up (v.)
**lion**
-bold (u.m.)
-headed (u.m.)
-maned (u.m.)
**lip**
read
service
stick
listener-in
**litho** (c.f.)
-offset
   rest one word
**little**
-known (u.m.)
neck (clam)
-used (u.m.)
**live**
#load
long
stock
#wire
wire
   (nonliteral)
**liver**
-brown (u.m.)
-colored (u.m.)
wurst
living #room
loadmeter
loanword
**lob**
fig
lolly
lobster-tailed
   (u.m.)
**lock**
fast
hole
jaw
nut
out (n., u.m.)
pin
ring
step
stitch
up (n., u.m.)
washer
locker #room
**lode**
star
stuff

**log**
jam
roll
sheet
loggerhead
**logo** (c.f.)
   all one word
**long**
-awaited (u.m.)
beard (n.)
-bearded (u.m.)
-billed (u.m.)
bow
cloth
-distance (u.m.)
-drawn (u.m.)
felt
hair (n.)
-haired (u.m.)
hand (nonlit.)
-handed (u.m.)
-handled (u.m.)
head (n.)
horn (cattle)
-horned (u.m.)
leaf
-leaved (u.m.)
-legged (u.m.)
legs (n.)
-lived (u.m.)
mouthed
-necked (u.m.)
nose (n.)
-nosed (u.m.)
-past (u.m.)
play (records)
playing (u.m.)
run (u.m.)
spun
standing (u.m.)
stitch
wave (radio)
ways
wool (sheep)
**look**
down (n., u.m.)
-in (n., u.m.)
out (n., u.m.)
through (n.,
   u.m.)
looker-on
**loop**
hole
stitch
**loose**
leaf (u.m.)
mouthed
-tongued (u.m.)
**lop**
-eared (u.m.)
sided
**loud**
mouthed
speaker (radio)
-voiced (u.m.)
**love**
born
-inspired (u.m.)
lorn
seat
sick
**low**
born
bred
brow (nonlit.)
browed
   (nonliteral)

-built (u.m.)
down (n., u.m.)
-downer
-lander
-lived (u.m.)
-lying (u.m.)

-power (u.m.)
-pressure
  (u.m.)
#water
lower
  case (printing)

most
lug
  bolt
  mark
  sail
lukewarm

lumber
  jack
#room
lumbo (c.f.)
  -ovarian
  *rest one word*

lumen-hour
lung
  -grown (u.m.)
  motor
lying-in (n., u.m.)

# M

M-day
macebearer
machine
  -finished (u.m.)
  gun
  -hour
  -made (u.m.)
#shop
#work
macro (c.f.)
  *all one word*
mad
  brain
  cap
made
  -over (u.m.)
  -up (u.m.)
magnetite
  -basalt
  -olivinite
  -spinellite
magneto (c.f.)
  -optics
  *rest one word*
mahjong
maid
#of#honor
  servant
maiden
  hair
  head
  hood
mail
  bag
  clad
  clerk
  guard
  -order (u.m.)
  pouch
  truck
main
  frame
  mast
  pin
  sail
  sheet
  spring
  stay
  stream
    (nonliteral)
  top
  topmost
#yard
major
  -domo
  -leaguer
  -minor
make
  -believe (n., u.m.)
  fast (n.)
  ready (printing)
  shift
  up (n., u.m.)
  weight
maker
  -off
  -up
making#up

mal (c.f.)
  *all one word*
man
  back
  -child
  -created (u.m.)
  -day
  eater
  -fashion (u.m.)
  -grown (u.m.)
  handle
  hater
  -high (u.m.)
  hole
  hood
  -hour
  killer
  kind
  made (u.m.)
  -minute
  -of-war (ship)
  rope
  servant
  -size (u.m.)
  slaughter
  slayer
  stealer
  stopper
  trap
  -woman
  -year
manic-depressive
manifold
mantel
  shelf
  tree
many
  -colored (u.m.)
  -folded (u.m.)
  plies
  -sided (u.m.)
map
  reader
  tack
marble
  head
  -looking (u.m.)
  -topped (u.m.)
  -white (u.m.)
mare's
  -nest
  -tail
mark
  down (n., u.m.)
  off (n., u.m.)
  shot
  up (n., u.m.)
marker
  -down
  -off
  -up
marketplace
marrowbone
marsh
  buck
  mallow
    (confection)
#mallow (plant)

mass
  -minded (u.m.)
  -produce (v.)
mast
  -brown (u.m.)
  head
master
  #at#arms
  mind
  #of#ceremonies
  ship
  #workman
mat-covered (u.m.)
match
  head
  -lined (u.m.)
  mark
  safe
  stick
maxi (n.)
maxi (pref.)
  *all one word*
May
  #Day
  -day (u.m.)
  pole
  tide
may
  be (adv.)
  beetle
  day (distress
    call)
  hap
mealymouth
mean
  -acting (u.m.)
  -spirited (u.m.)
  time
    (meanwhile)
  #time
    (astronomical)
  tone (u.m.)
  while
meat
  ball
  cutter
  -eater
  -fed (u.m.)
  hook
  -hungry (u.m.)
  packer
  works
  wrapper
mechanico (c.f.)
  *all one word*
medico (c.f.)
  *all one word*
medio (c.f.)
  *all one word*
medium
  -brown (u.m.)
  -size(d) (u.m.)
  weight (n., u.m.)
meek
  -eyed (u.m.)
  -spirited (u.m.)
meetingplace
megalo (c.f.)
  *all one word*

melon
  -laden (u.m.)
  -shaped (u.m.)
melt
  down (n., u.m.)
  water
men
  folk
  kind
meningo (c.f.)
  *all one word*
merry
  -go-round
  meeting
  -minded (u.m.)
meshbag
meso (c.f.)
  *all one word*
mess
  hall
  kit
  tin
  -up (n., u.m.)
meta (pref.)
  *all one word*
metal
  ammonium
  -clad (u.m.)
  -coated (u.m.)
  -lined (u.m.)
  works
meter
  -amperes
  gram
  -kilogram
  -kilogram-second
  -millimeter
metro (c.f.)
  *all one word*
mezzo
  graph
  relievo
  soprano
  tint
micro (c.f.)
  -organism
  *rest one word*
mid (c.f.)
  -American, etc.
  -April
  day
  -decade
  -dish
  -ice
  -1958
  -Pacific, etc.
  -Victorian, etc.
  *rest one word*
middle
  -aged (u.m.)
  breaker
  brow (nonlit.)
  -burst (v.)
  buster
  most
  -of-the-roader
  -sized (u.m.)

splitter
weight
midi (n.)
midi (pref.)
  *all one word*
mighty-handed
  (u.m.)
mil-foot
mild
  -cured (u.m.)
  -spoken (u.m.)
mile
  -long (u.m.)
  -ohm
  post
  -pound
  -ton
  -wide (u.m.)
milk
  -fed (u.m.)
  head
  shake
  shed
  sick
  sop
  -white (u.m.)
mill
  cake
  course
  dam
  feed
  hand
  -headed (u.m.)
  pond
  post
  race
  ring
  stock
  stream
  wright
milli (c.f.)
  gram-hour
  *rest one word*
mincemeat
mind
  -healing (u.m.)
  reader
  set (n.)
  sight
mine
  layer
  ship
  sweeper
  thrower
  works
mini (n.)
mini (pref.)
  *all one word*
minor-leaguer
minute#book
mirror
  -faced (u.m.)
  scope
mis (pref.)
  *all one word*
mist
  bow
  -clad (u.m.)

-covered (u.m.)
fall
**miter**
#box
-lock (v.)
**mix**
blood
up (n.)
mixing#room
mizzenmast
**mock**
-heroic (u.m.)
up (n., u.m.)
mocker-up
**mocking**
stock
-up (u.m.)
**mold**
made (u.m.)
#shop
**mole**
catcher
-eyed (u.m.)
head
heap
hill
**money**
bag
changer
getter
grubber
lender
-mad (u.m.)
saver
**monkey**
-faced (u.m.)
nut
pod

pot
shine
**mono** (c.f.)
-ideistic
-iodo
-iodohydrin
-ion
-ousian
*rest one word*
**month**
end
long (u.m.)
**moon**
beam
bill
blind
#blindness
blink
born
-bright (u.m.)
calf
down
eye
face
gazing
glow
head
lighter
lit
-mad (u.m.)
path
rise
sail
set
shade
shine
shot
sick

struck
tide
walker
-white (u.m.)
moosecall
**mop**
head
stick
up (n., u.m.)
mopper-up
mopping-up (u.m.)
morningtide
**mosquito**
#boat
-free (u.m.)
**moss**
back
-clad (u.m.)
-green (u.m.)
-grown (u.m.)
head
-lined (u.m.)
most-favored-
    nation (u.m.)
**moth**
ball
-eaten (u.m.)
hole
**mother**
hood
-in-law
-of-pearl
**moto** (c.f.)
*all one word*
**motor**
bike
bus
cab

cade
car
coach
cycle
-driven (u.m.)
drome
jet
-minded (u.m.)
ship
truck
van
moundbuilder
**mountain**
-high (u.m.)
side
top
-walled (u.m.)
**mouse**
-brown (u.m.)
-eared (u.m.)
-eaten (u.m.)
hole
trap
**mouth**
-filling (u.m.)
-made (u.m.)
wash
**muck**
rake (v.)
sweat
**muco** (c.f.)
*all one word*
**mud**
bank
bath
cap
-colored (u.m.)
flat

flow
guard
head
hole
lark
sill
slinger
-splashed (u.m.)
stain
sucker
track
muddlehead
**mule**
back
skinner
**multi** (c.f.)
*all one word*
multiple-purpose
    (u.m.)
**music**
lover
-mad (u.m.)
**musico** (c.f.)
*all one word*
**musk**
melon
rat
**mutton**
#chop (meat)
chop (shape)
fist
head
**myria** (c.f.)
*all one word*
**mytho** (c.f.)
*all one word*
**myxo** (c.f.)
*all one word*

# N

**nail**
bin
brush
head
-headed (u.m.)
print
puller
rod
-shaped (u.m.)
-studded (u.m.)
**name**
-calling (u.m.)
-dropping (u.m.)
plate
sake
**narco** (c.f.)
*all one word*
**narrow**
heartedness
-mouthed (u.m.)
minded
**naso** (c.f.)
-occipital
-orbital
*rest one word*
native-born
    (u.m.)
navy-blue (u.m.)
**near**
-acquainted
    (u.m.)
-bordering (u.m.)
by
-miss
sighted
neat's-foot (u.m.)

**neck**
band
bone
-breaking
    (u.m.)
cloth
-deep (u.m.)
fast
guard
-high (u.m.)
hole
lace
mold
tie
**necro** (c.f.)
*all one word*
**needle**
bill
case
-made (u.m.)
point
-shaped (u.m.)
-sharp (u.m.)
worked
ne'er-do-well
**neo** (c.f.)
-Greek, etc.
*rest one word*
**nephro** (c.f.)
*all one word*
**nerve**
ache
-celled (u.m.)
-racked (u.m.)
**net**
ball

braider
-veined (u.m.)
**nettle**
fire
foot
some
**neuro** (c.f.)
*all one word*
**never**
-ending (u.m.)
more
theless
**new**
born
-car (u.m.)
comer
-created (u.m.)
fangled
-fashioned (u.m.)
-front (v.)
-made (u.m.)
-mown (u.m.)
-rich (u.m.)
newlywed
**news**
case
cast
clip
dealer
-greedy (u.m.)
letter
paper
paper#work
paper#worker
photo
print

reader
reel
sheet
stand
story
teller
**nick**
-eared (u.m.)
name
**nickel**
plate (v.)
-plated (u.m.)
-plating (u.m.)
type
**night**
-black (u.m.)
cap
-clad (u.m.)
clothes
club
dress
fall
-fly (aviation)
    (v.)
-flying (u.m.)
gown
-grown (u.m.)
hawk
long (u.m.)
mare
shade
shirt
side
tide
-veiled (u.m.)
walker

**nimble**
-fingered (u.m.)
footed
nimbostratus
    (clouds)
**nine**
fold
holes
-lived (u.m.)
penny (nail)
pin
score
**nitro** (c.f.)
-hydro-carbon
*rest one word*
**no**
-account (n.,
    u.m.)
-fault
-good (n., u.m.)
-hitter (n.)
how
#man's land
-par (u.m.)
-par-value (u.m.)
-show (n., u.m.)
-thoroughfare
    (n.)
whit
**noble**
-born (u.m.)
-featured (u.m.)
heartedness
-looking (u.m.)
-minded (u.m.)
nol-pros (v.)

| non | noon | nose | ring | nut |
|---|---|---|---|---|
| -civil-service | day | bag | -thumbing (u.m.) | breaker |
| (u.m.) | tide | bleed | up (n., u.m.) | -brown (u.m.) |
| -European, etc. | **north** | bone | wheel | cake |
| -pros (v.) | -central | dive | notehead | cracker |
| #sequitur, etc. | (u.m.) | down (n., u.m.) | notwithstanding | hatch |
| -tumor-bearing | east | gay | **novel** | hook |
| (u.m.) | going | guard | -reading (u.m.) | pecker |
| *as prefix, one* | most | -high (u.m.) | #writer | pick |
| *word* | -northeast | hole | -writing (u.m.) | -shaped (u.m.) |
| **none** | -sider | -led (u.m.) | **nucleo** (c.f.) | shell |
| such | | pipe | *all one word* | sweet |
| theless | | | | |

## O

| oak | -lying (u.m.) | -growing (u.m.) | -two-three | **outer** |
|---|---|---|---|---|
| -beamed (u.m.) | peak | -looking (u.m.) | -way (u.m.) | -city (u.m.) |
| -clad (u.m.) | print | #maid | onion peel | #man |
| -green (u.m.) | put | -maidish (u.m.) | **open** | most |
| -leaved (u.m.) | -reckoning (n.) | #man | -air (u.m.) | **outward** |
| **oar** | saddle | -new | -armed (u.m.) | -bound (u.m.) |
| -footed (u.m.) | scape | style (printing) | -back (u.m.) | -bounder |
| lock | scour | timer | -backed (u.m.) | **ovate** |
| **oat** | scum | #woman | band (yarn) | -acuminate |
| bin | -season | -young | cast | (u.m.) |
| cake | set | **oleo** | cut (mining) | -oblong (u.m.) |
| -fed (u.m.) | shoot | #butter | -faced (u.m.) | **ovato** (c.f.) |
| meal | shore | #gear | handed | -oblong |
| seed | side | #oil | #house | -orbicular |
| oathbreaker | -sorts (n.) | #strut | minded | *rest one word* |
| **oblong** | spring | *as combining* | mouthed | **oven** |
| -elliptic (u.m.) | stage | *form, one* | #shop | baked |
| -leaved (u.m.) | street | *word* | side (u.m.) | dried |
| -linear (u.m.) | take | **olive** | -sided (u.m.) | peel |
| -ovate (u.m.) | -the-record (u.m.) | -brown (u.m.) | worked | **over** |
| -shaped (u.m.) | type | -clad (u.m.) | **opera** | age (surplus) |
| -triangular | -wheel (n.) | -drab (u.m.) | goer | age (older) (n., |
| (u.m.) | -wheeler (n.) | -growing (u.m.) | going | u.m.) |
| **occipito** (c.f.) | -white (u.m.) | -skinned (u.m.) | #house | all (all |
| -otic | **office** | wood | **ophthalmo** (c.f.) | meanings) |
| *rest one word* | #boy | #wood (color) | *all one word* | -the-counter |
| **ocean** | seeker | **omni** (c.f.) | **orange** | (u.m.) |
| -born (u.m.) | -seeking (u.m.) | -ignorant | ade | *as combining* |
| -girdled (u.m.) | oftentimes | *rest one word* | colored (u.m.) | *form, one* |
| going | ofttimes | **on** | peel | *word* |
| side | **ohm** | -and-off (n., u.m.) | -red (u.m.) | owl-eyed (u.m.) |
| -spanning (u.m.) | -ammeter | -go (n.) | stick | **ox** |
| **octo** (c.f.) | meter | going | orchard #house | biter |
| *all one word* | -mile | noun, adjective, | orderly #room | blood (color) |
| **odd** | **oil** | *one word* | **organo** (c.f.) | bow |
| -jobber | cake | **once** | *all one word* | brake |
| -job man | can | -over (n.) | **ornitho** (c.f.) | cart |
| -looking (u.m.) | cloth | -run (u.m.) | *all one word* | cheek |
| -numbered (u.m.) | coat | **one** | orrisroot | eye |
| **off** | cup | -acter | **ortho** (c.f.) | -eyed (u.m.) |
| -and on (u.m.) | -driven (u.m.) | -armed (u.m.) | *all one word* | gall |
| beat | -fed (u.m.) | -decker | **osteo** (c.f.) | harrow |
| cast | -forming (u.m.) | -eyed (u.m.) | *all one word* | hide |
| center (u.m.) | -harden (v.) | fold | **oto** (c.f.) | horn |
| color (u.m.) | hole | -half | *all one word* | shoe |
| -colored (u.m.) | meal | -handed (u.m.) | **out** | **oxy** (c.f.) |
| cut (printing) | paper | ness | -and-out (u.m.) | *all one word* |
| day | proofing | -piece (u.m.) | -and-outer (n.) | **oyster** |
| -fall (v.) | seed | self | -loud (u.m.) | bed |
| -flavor (n., u.m.) | skinned | -sided (u.m.) | -Machiavelli, etc. | root |
| -flow | -soaked (u.m.) | -sidedness | migration | seed |
| -go (n.) | spill | signed (u.m.) | -of-date (u.m.) | shell |
| going | stove | -step (dance) | -of-door(s) (u.m.) | -white (u.m.) |
| grade | -temper (v.) | -striper | -of-State (u.m.) | |
| hand | tightness | time (formerly) | -of-the-way | |
| -hours | **old** | (u.m.) | (u.m.) | |
| loading | -fashioned (u.m.) | -time (one | -to-out (u.m.) | |
| look | -fogy (u.m.) | action) (u.m.) | *as prefix, one* | |
| | | | *word* | |

# P

pace-setting
(u.m.)
**pachy** (c.f.)
  *all one word*
**pack**
  builder
  cloth
  horse
  -laden (u.m.)
  sack
  saddle
  staff
  thread
  up (n., u.m.)
packing # box
**pad**
  cloth
  lock
  tree
paddlefoot
**page**
  -for-page (u.m.)
  # proof (printing)
painkiller
painstaking
**paint**
  brush
  mixer
  pot
  stained (u.m.)
**pale**
  belly
  -blue (u.m.)
  buck
  -cheeked (u.m.)
  face (n.)
  -faced (u.m.)
  -looking (u.m.)
  -reddish (u.m.)
**paleo** (c.f.)
  -Christian, etc.
  *rest one word*
pallbearer
**palm**
  -green (u.m.)
  -shaded (u.m.)
**palmi** (c.f.)
  *all one word*
**pan**
  -American, etc.
  -broil (v.)
  # ice
  *rest one word*
**Pan**
  # American
    Union
    (official name)
  hellenic
panel-lined
  (u.m.)
panic-stricken
  (u.m.)
**panto** (c.f.)
  *all one word*
panty hose
**paper**
  back (n.)
  # box
  cutter
  hanger
  shell (n., u.m.)
  -shelled (u.m.)
  -thin (u.m.)
  weight
  -white (u.m.)

papier # mache
**para** (c.f. or pref.)
  -aminobenzoic
  -analgesia
  -anesthesia
  # red
  *rest one word*
parcel-plate (v.)
**parchment**
  -covered (u.m.)
  # maker
  -making (u.m.)
**parieto** (c.f.)
  -occipital
  *rest one word*
parimutuel
**part**
  -finished (u.m.)
  # owner
  -time (u.m.)
  -timer (n.)
  # way
**parti** (c.f.)
  *all one word*
party # line
**parvi** (c.f.)
  *all one word*
**pass**
  back (n.)
  key
  out (n., u.m.)
  port
  through
  word
passenger-mile
passer(s)-by
**passion**
  -driven (u.m.)
  -feeding (u.m.)
  -filled (u.m.)
**paste**
  down (n., u.m.)
  pot
  up (n., u.m.)
patent-in-fee
**path**
  breaker
  finder
**patho** (c.f.)
  *all one word*
**patri** (c.f.)
  *all one word*
pattycake
pawnbroker
**pay**
  back (n., u.m.)
  check
  day
  dirt
  off (n., u.m.)
  out (n., u.m.)
  roll
  sheet
  -TV
**pea**
  coat
  cod
  -green (u.m.)
  jacket
  nut
  shooter
  -sized (u.m.)
  stick
**peace**
  -blessed (u.m.)

breaker
-loving (u.m.)
**peach**
  bloom
  blow (color)
  -colored (u.m.)
pear-shaped
  (u.m.)
**pearl**
  -eyed (u.m.)
  fishing
  -pure (u.m.)
  -set (u.m.)
  -studded (u.m.)
  -white (u.m.)
**peat**
  -roofed (u.m.)
  stack
**pebble**
  -paved (u.m.)
  -strewn (u.m.)
peeloff (n., u.m.)
**peep**
  eye
  hole
  show
  sight
pegleg
pellmell
**pen**
  -cancel (v.)
  head
  knife
  manship
  point
  pusher
  rack
  script
  -shaped (u.m.)
  stock
  trough
**pencil**
  # box
  -mark (v.)
**penny**
  -a-liner
  pincher
  weight
  winkle
  worth
pent-up (u.m.)
**penta** (c.f.)
  -acetate
  *rest one word*
peptalk
**pepper**
  corn
  mint
  pot
  -red (u.m.)
**per**
  cent
  # centum
    compound
    (chemical)
  current
    (botanical)
  # diem
  salt (chemical)
  # se
  sulfide
**peri** (pref.)
  -insular
  *rest one word*
permafrost

|pest
  hole
  -ridden (u.m.)
petcock
peternet
**petro** (c.f.)
  -occipital
  *rest one word*
**pharmaco** (c.f.)
  -oryctology
  *rest one word*
**pharyngo** (c.f.)
  -esophageal
  -oral
  *rest one word*
**phase**
  meter
  out (n., u.m.)
  -wound (u.m.)
**pheno** (c.f.)
  *all one word*
**philo** (c.f.)
  -French, etc.
  *rest one word*
**phlebo** (c.f.)
  *all one word*
**phono** (c.f.)
  *all one word*
**phospho** (c.f.)
  *all one word*
**photo** (c.f.)
  -offset
  -oxidation
  -oxidative
  *rest one word*
**phreno** (c.f.)
  *all one word*
phrasemark
  (music)
**phyllo** (c.f.)
  *all one word*
**phylo** (c.f.)
  *all one word*
**physico** (c.f.)
  *all one word*
**physio** (c.f.)
  *all one word*
**phyto** (c.f.)
  *all one word*
**piano**
  forte
  graph
  player
**pick**
  aback
  ax
  lock
  -me-up (n., u.m.)
  off (n., u.m.)
  over (n., u.m.)
  # over (v.)
  pocket
  pole
  shaft
  up (n., u.m.)
picker-up
picket # line
pickle-cured (u.m.)
**picture**
  # book
  # writing
**pie**
  bald
  crust
  -eater

-eyed
  marker
  pan
  plant
  -stuffed (u.m.)
**piece**
  -dye (v.)
  meal
  mold
**piezo** (c.f.)
  -oscillator
  *rest one word*
**pig**
  -back (v.)
  -backed (u.m.)
  -bellied (u.m.)
  belly
  -eyed (u.m.)
  face
  -faced (u.m.)
  foot
  -footed (u.m.)
  headed
  herd
  out
  pen
  root
  stick
  sty
  tailed
  wash
**pigeon**
  gram
  hole
  -toed (u.m.)
  wing
piggyback
**pike**
  -eyed (u.m.)
  staff
**pile**
  driver
  -driving (u.m.)
  hammer
  up (n., u.m.)
  woven
**pill**
  pusher
  rolling
  taker
**pillow**
  case
  made
  slip
**pilot**
  # boat
  # light
**pin**
  ball
  block
  bone
  case
  cushion
  -eyed (u.m.)
  fall
  feather
  fire
  fold
  head
  hold
  hole
  hook
  lock
  paper
  point

**prick**
rail
setter
spot
stripe
-tailed (u.m.)
up (n., u.m.)
wheel
**pinch**
back
bar
beck
cock
fist
-hit (v.)
-hitter
penny
**pine**
apple
-bearing (u.m.)
-clad (u.m.)
-fringed (u.m.)
-shaded (u.m.)
**pink**
-blossomed (u.m.)
eye (n.)
-eyed (u.m.)
**pipe**
-drawn (u.m.)
dream
fitter
layer
lined
-shaped (u.m.)
stem
walker
welder
**pisci** (c.f.)
*all one word*
pistol-whipped (v.)
pistonhead
**pit**
-eyed (u.m.)
fall
head
-headed (u.m.)
hole
mark
-marked (u.m.)
-rotted (u.m.)
saw
side
**pitch**
-black (u.m.)
blende
#box
-colored (u.m.)
-dark (u.m.)
fork
hole
-lined (u.m.)
-marked (u.m.)
out (n., u.m.)
up (n., u.m.)
**place**
card
kick
plague-infested
(u.m.)
**plain**
back (fabric)
-bodied (u.m.)
clothes (u.m.)
-headed (u.m.)
-looking (u.m.)
-spoken (u.m.)
woven (u.m.)

**plane**
-mile
-parallel (u.m.)
table
(surveying)
**plani** (c.f.)
*all one word*
**plano** (c.f.)
*all one word*
plantlife
**plate**
-incased (u.m.)
layer
mark
#proof (printing)
-roll (v.)
-rolled (u.m.)
**platy** (c.f.)
*all one word*
**play**
-act (v.)
back (n., u.m.)
bill
broker
day
down (n., u.m.)
fellow
goer
going
ground
off (n., u.m.)
pen
reader
script
suit
thing
wright
#yard
**pleasure**
-bent (u.m.)
#boat
-seeking (u.m.)
-tired (u.m.)
-weary (u.m.)
**pleo** (c.f.)
*all one word*
**pleuro** (c.f.)
*all one word*
**plow**
back (n., u.m.)
-bred (u.m.)
hand
horse
pan
point
-shaped (u.m.)
share
shoe
sole
staff
#tail
wright
**plug**
hole
-in (n., u.m.)
tray
-ugly (n., u.m.)
plume-crowned
(u.m.)
**pluri** (c.f.)
*all one word*
**pluto** (c.f.)
*all one word*
**pneumato** (c.f.)
-hydato-genetic
(u.m.)
*rest one word*

**pneumo** (c.f.)
*all one word*
**pock**
mark
-marked (u.m.)
-pit (v.)
**pocket**
book (purse)
#book (book)
-eyed (u.m.)
knife
-sized (u.m.)
-veto (v.)
**poet**
-artist
-painter
pointblank
poison-dipped
(u.m.)
**pole**
arm
-armed (u.m.)
ax
burn
cat
-dried (u.m.)
horse
-pile (v.)
setter
-shaped (u.m.)
sitter
-stack (v.)
star
timber
trap
-vault (v.)
**politico** (c.f.)
-orthodox
*rest one word*
**poly** (c.f.)
*all one word*
**poor**
-blooded (u.m.)
farm
-spirited (u.m.)
**pop**
corn
eye
gun
up (n., u.m.)
**poppy**
-bordered (u.m.)
cock
-red (u.m.)
seed
**port**
fire
folio
hole
hook
manteau
-mouthed (u.m.)
side
**post**
#bellum
#boat
card
-Christian, etc.
#diem
-free (u.m.)
haste
#hospital
(military)
#meridiem
#mortem (literal)
mortem (non-
literal)

#partum
#school (military)
audit, graduate,
etc.
*as prefix, one
word*
**pot**
ash
bellied
boil
eye
hanger
head
herb
hole
hook
hunter
latch
lid
luck
pie
pourri
rack
shot
whiskey
potato #field
**poultry**
#house
#keeper
-keeping (u.m.)
#raiser
-raising (u.m.)
#yard
**pound**
cake
-foolish (u.m.)
-foot
worth
**powder**
-blue (u.m.)
#house
#mill
#room
-scorched (u.m.)
**power**
-driven (u.m.)
-operated (u.m.)
pack
plant
**praise**
-deserving (u.m.)
-spoiled (u.m.)
worthiness
**pre** (pref.)
-Incan, etc.
**president**
-elect
#pro#tempore
**press**
#agent
-agentry
feeder
-forge (v.)
-made (u.m.)
mark
pack (v.)
plate
#proof (printing)
**preter** (pref.)
*all one word*
**price**
#cutter
-cutting (u.m.)
#fixer
-fixing (u.m.)
list
-support (u.m.)

**prick**
-eared (u.m.)
mark
seam
**priest**
hood
-prince
**prime**
#minister
-ministerial
(u.m.)
-ministership
-ministry
**prince**
hood
-priest
**print**
cloth
out
script
**printing**
-in (n., u.m.)
-out (n., u.m.)
**prison**
-free (u.m.)
-made (u.m.)
prisoner-of-war
(u.m.)
**prize**
fighter
taker
winner
-winning (u.m.)
**pro**
-Ally, etc.
#forma
#rata
#tem
#tempore
*as prefix, one
word*
**procto** (c.f.)
*all one word*
**profit**
-and-loss (u.m.)
-sharing (u.m.)
**prong**
buck
-hoe (v.)
horn
-horned (u.m.)
**proof**
read
sheet
**prop**
jet
wash
**proso** (c.f.)
*all one word*
**proto** (c.f.)
-Egyptian, etc.
*rest one word*
**proud**
-looking (u.m.)
-minded (u.m.)
**pseudo** (c.f.)
-Messiah, etc.
-occidental
-official
-orientalism
-orthorhombic
-osteomalacia
-owner
*rest one word*
**psycho** (c.f.)
-organic
*rest one word*

**ptero** (c.f.)
  *all one word*
**public**
  -minded (u.m.)
  -spirited (u.m.)
**pug**
  nose
  -pile (v.)
**pull**
  back (n., u.m.)
  #box
  down (n., u.m.)
  -in (n., u.m.)
  off (n., u.m.)

-on (n., u.m.)
out (n., u.m.)
-push (u.m.)
through
  (n., u.m.)
up (n., u.m.)
**puller**
  -in
  -out
**punch**
  bowl
  card
  -drunk (u.m.)
  mark

-marked (u.m.)
out (n.)
**pure**
  blood
  bred
  #line (biological)
**purple**
  -blue (u.m.)
  -clad (u.m.)
  -colored (u.m.)
  heart (wood)
**push**
  button
  card

cart
  off (n., u.m.)
  -pull (u.m.)
  up (n., u.m.)
**pussy**
  cat
  foot
**put**
  back (n., u.m.)
  off (n., u.m.)
  -on (n., u.m.)
  out (n., u.m.)
  -put (n.)
  -up (n., u.m.)

**putter**
  -forth
  -in
  -off
  -on
  -out
  -through
  -up
**pyo** (c.f.)
  *all one word*
**pyro** (c.f.)
  *all one word*

# Q

**Q**
-boat
-fever
**quadri** (c.f.)
  -invariant
  *rest one word*
**quarter**
  -angled (u.m.)
  back

-bloom (u.m.)
-bound (u.m.)
-breed (u.m.)
-cast (u.m.)
-cut (u.m.)
deck
-miler
pace
-phase (u.m.)

saw (v.)
staff
stretch
**quartermaster**
  #general
  -generalship
**quasi**
  *all hyphened*
queen #bee

**quick**
-change (u.m., v.)
-drawn (u.m., v.)
freeze (u.m., v.)
lime
sand
set
silver
step

#time
-witted (u.m.)
**quin** (c.f.)
  *all one word*
**quit**
  claim
  rent

# R

**rabbit**
-backed (u.m.)
-eared (u.m.)
mouth
-mouthed (u.m.)
**race**
about (n., u.m.)
course
goer
horse
track
**radarscope**
**radio**
  *generally two*
  *words except*
  *the following*
  *forms*
frequency
isotope
telegraph
telephone
radiumtherapy
**rag**
bolt
-made (u.m.)
sorter
tag
**rail**
car
guard
head
-ridden (u.m.)
road
setter
splitter
way #maker
**rain**
band
-beaten (u.m.)
bow
check
coat
drop
fall
-soft (u.m.)
spout
storm

wash
rakeoff (n., u.m.)
**ram**
jet
rod
shackle
ranch #hand
**range**
finder
#light
rider
**rash**
-brain (u.m.)
-headed (u.m.)
-hearted (u.m.)
-minded (u.m.)
**rat**
bite
catcher
hole
-infested (u.m.)
-tailed (u.m.)
-tight (u.m.)
trap
**rate**
-cutting (u.m.)
-fixing (u.m.)
payer
-raising (u.m.)
setting
**rattle**
brain
snake
trap
**raw**
boned
-edged (u.m.)
hide
-looking (u.m.)
**razor**
back
-billed (u.m.)
edge
-keen (u.m.)
-sharp (u.m.)
strop
razzle-dazzle

**re** (pref.)
-cover (cover
  again), -create
  (create again),
  etc.
-cross-
  examination
-ice
-ink
-redirect
  *rest one word*
reading #room
readout (n.)
**ready**
-built (u.m.)
-handed (u.m.)
made (u.m.)
-mix (u.m.)
-witted (u.m.)
**rear**
guard
most
view (u.m.)
reception #room
recordbreaker
**recti** (c.f.)
  *all one word*
**recto** (c.f.)
  *all one word*
**red**
bait (v.)
-billed (u.m.)
-blooded (u.m.)
bone
buck
cap (porter)
coat (n.)
eye (n.)
-eyed (u.m.)
-faced (u.m.)
-haired (u.m.)
handed
head (n.)
-hot (u.m.)
-legged (u.m.)
#line (literal)
#man

out (n., u.m.)
-skinned (u.m.)
tape (nonliteral)
#tape (literal)
-throated (u.m.)
-yellow (u.m.)
**religio** (c.f.)
  *all one word*
repair #shop
**representative**
#at #large
-elect
research #worker
**resino** (c.f.)
  *all one word*
**retro** (c.f.)
-ocular
-omental
-operative
-oral
  *rest one word*
**rheo** (c.f.)
  *all one word*
**rhino** (c.f.)
  *all one word*
**rhizo** (c.f.)
  *all one word*
**rhod(o)** (c.f.)
  *all one word*
**rhomb(o)** (c.f.)
  *all one word*
**rice**
growing
#water
**rich**
-bound (u.m.)
-clad (u.m.)
-looking (u.m.)
**ridge**
band
pole
top
riffraff
rifleshot
**rig**
out (n., u.m.)
-up (n., u.m.)

**right**
about
about-face
-angle (u.m., v.)
-angled (u.m.)
#field (sports)
-handed (u.m.)
-hander
-headed (u.m.)
most
-of-way
wing
  (political)
**rim**
-deep (u.m.)
fire
lock
rock
**ring**
-adorned (u.m.)
-banded (u.m.)
-billed (u.m.)
bolt
giver
head
-in (n., u.m.)
lead (v.)
-necked (u.m.)
-off (n., u.m.)
pin
-porous (u.m.)
-shaped (u.m.)
side
sight
stand
stick
-tailed (u.m.)
-up (n., u.m.)
**rip**
cord
rap
roaring
sack
saw
snorter
tide
-up (n., u.m.)

**river**
  bank
  bed
  flow
  -formed (u.m.)
  front
  head
  scape
  side
  wash
  -worn (u.m.)
**road**
  bank
  bed
  block
  builder
  head
  hog
  map
  side
  -test (v.)
  -weary (u.m.)
**rock**
  abye
  bottom (nonlit.)
  -climbing (u.m.)
  fall (n.)
  -fallen (u.m.)
  fill
  firm
  pile
  -ribbed (u.m.)
  shaft
  slide
**rod-shaped (u.m.)**
**roebuck**
**roentgeno (c.f.)**
  *all one word*

**roll**
  about (n., u.m.)
  back (n., u.m.)
  call
  -fed (v.)
  film
  off (n., u.m.)
  -on (n., u.m.)
  out (n., u.m.)
  top
  up (n., u.m.)
**roller**
  -made (u.m.)
  -milled (u.m.)
**Romano (c.f.)**
  -canonical, etc.
  -Gallic, etc.
**roof**
  garden
  top
  tree
**root**
  cap
  -cutting (u.m.)
  fast
  hold
  stalk
  stock
**rope**
  dance
  layer
  stitch
  walk
**rose**
  -bright (u.m.)
  bud
  head
  -headed (u.m.)

-scented (u.m.)
-sweet (u.m.)
# water
rotorship
**rotten**
  -dry (u.m.)
  -minded (u.m.)
**rough**
  -and-ready (u.m.)
  -and-tumble
    (n., u.m.)
  cast (u.m., v.)
  -coat (v.)
  -cut (u.m.)
  draw (v.)
  dress (v.)
  dry (u.m., v.)
  -face (v.)
  -faced (u.m.)
  hew
  -legged (u.m.)
  -looking (u.m.)
  neck
  rider
  setter
  shod
  -sketch (v.)
  stuff
  tailed
  #work (n.)
  work (v.)
  wrought
**rougher**
  -down
  -out
  -up
roughing-in (u.m.)

**round**
  about (n., u.m.)
  about-face
  -faced (u.m.)
  head
  -made (u.m.)
  mouthed
  nose (tool)
  out (n., u.m.)
  robin (petition)
  seam
  table (panel)
  -tailed (u.m.)
  -topped (u.m.)
  -tripper
  up (n., u.m.)
**rub**
  -a-dub
  down (n., u.m.)
**rubber**
  band
  -down
  -lined (u.m.)
  neck
  -off
  -set (u.m.)
  stamp
    (nonliteral)
    (n., u.m., v.)
  #stamp (n.)
  -stamped (u.m.)
**ruby**
  -hued (u.m.)
  -red (u.m.)
  -set (u.m.)
  -throated (u.m.)
**rudder**
  head

hole
post
stock
rule # of # thumb
**rum**
  -crazed (u.m.)
  runner
  seller
rumpus # room
**run**
  about (n., u.m.)
  around
    (n., u.m.)
  away (n., u.m.)
  back (n., u.m.)
  by (n.)
  down (n., u.m.)
  -in (n., u.m.)
  off (n., u.m.)
  -on (n., u.m.)
  out (n., u.m.)
  through
    (n., u.m.)
  up (n., u.m.)
runner-up
rush-bottomed
  (u.m.)
**Russo (c.f.)**
  -Chinese, etc.
  *rest one word*
**rust**
  -brown (u.m.)
  -eaten (u.m.)
  proofing
  -resistant (u.m.)
  -stained (u.m.)
rye # field

## S

**S**
  -bend
  -brake
  -iron
  -ray
  -shaped
  -trap
  -wrench
**saber**
  -legged (u.m.)
  tooth
  -toothed (u.m.)
**sable-cloaked**
  (u.m.)
**Sabrejet**
**saccharo (c.f.)**
  *all one word*
**sack**
  bearer
  cloth
  #coat
  -coated (u.m.)
  -making (u.m.)
  -shaped (u.m.)
**sacro (c.f.)**
  *all one word*
**sad**
  -eyed (u.m.)
  iron
  -voiced (u.m.)
**saddle**
  back
  -backed (u.m.)
  bag
  bow
  cloth

-graft (v.)
-making (u.m.)
nose
-nosed (u.m.)
sore
-stitched (u.m.)
tree
-wire (u.m.)
**safe**
  blower
  cracker
  -deposit (u.m.)
  guard
  hold
**sage**
  brush
  leaf
  -leaved (u.m.)
**sail**
  cloth
  -dotted (u.m.)
  flying
**sales**
  clerk
  manship
  people
  person
**salmon**
  -colored (u.m.)
  -red (u.m.)
**salpingo (c.f.)**
  -oophorectomy
  -oophoritis
  -ovariotomy
  -ovaritis
  *rest one word*

**salt**
  cellar
  -cured (u.m.)
  mouth
  pack
  pan
  peter
  pit
  pond
  shaker
  spoon
  sprinkler
  works
**salver**
  form
  -shaped (u.m.)
**sample**
  #book
  #box
  -making (u.m.)
**sand**
  bag
  bank
  bar
  bath
  bin
  blast
  blown
  -built (u.m.)
  -buried (u.m.)
  -cast (u.m., v.)
  culture
  fill
  flea
  glass
  heat

hill
-hiller
hog
hole
lapper
lot
paper
pile
pipe
pit
-pump (u.m., v.)
shoe
spit
storm
table
weld (v.)
-welded (u.m.)
-welding (u.m.)
sandy-bottomed
  (u.m.)
sangfroid
**sans**
  #serif
  #souci
**sapphire**
  -blue (u.m.)
  -colored (u.m.)
**sarco (c.f.)**
  *all one word*
sashcord
**satin**
  -lined (u.m.)
  -smooth (u.m.)
**sauce**
  dish
  pan

**sauer**
  braten
  kraut
save-all (n., u.m.)
**saw**
  back
  belly
  -billed (u.m.)
  bones (n.)
  buck
  dust
  -edged (u.m.)
  setter
  timber
  tooth
  -toothed (u.m.)
**sax**
  cornet
  horn
  tuba
**say**
  -nothing
    (n., u.m.)
  -so (n.)
**scale**
  bark
  down (n., u.m.)
  pan
  -reading (u.m.)
scapegoat
**scapulo (c.f.)**
  *all one word*
**scar**
  -clad (u.m.)
  face
  -faced (u.m.)

**scare**
crow
head
**scarfpin**
**scarlet**
-breasted (u.m.)
-red (u.m.)
**scatter**
brain
good
**scene**
shifter
wright
**schisto** (c.f.)
*all one word*
**schizo** (c.f.)
*all one word*
**school**
bag
#board
bookish
bus
children
day
-made (u.m.)
ship
teacher
-trained (u.m.)
**scientifico** (c.f.)
*all one word*
**scissor**
bill
-tailed (u.m.)
-winged (u.m.)
**scissors**
hold
-shaped (u.m.)
#smith
**sclero** (c.f.)
-oophoritis
-optic
*rest one word*
**score**
card
sheet
scot-free
**Scoto** (c.f.)
-Britannic, etc.
scouthood
**scrap**
basket
works
**scratch**
brush
-brusher
-coated (u.m.)
**screen**
out (n., u.m.)
play
**screw**
ball
bolt
cap
down (u.m.)
-driven (u.m.)
driver
head
hook
jack
-lifted (u.m.)
nut
ship
-threaded (u.m.)
-turned (u.m.)
scrollhead
scuttlebutt
scythe-shaped
(u.m.)

**sea**
#base
-based (u.m.)
-bathed (u.m.)
beach
-beaten (u.m.)
bed
#bird
-blue (u.m.)
#boat
-born (u.m.)
-bred (u.m.)
coast
-deep (u.m.)
dog
-driven (u.m.)
drome
-encircled (u.m.)
fare (food)
fighter
folk
food
front
goer
going
hound
lane
lift
mark
port
quake
#room
scape
#scout
scouting
shell
shine
shore
sick
side
stroke
#time (clock)
wall
wing
worn
worthiness
-wrecked (u.m.)
**seam**
blasting
rend (v.)
stitch
weld (v.)
-welded (u.m.)
**seat**
belt
-mile
**second**
-class (u.m.)
-degree (u.m.)
-foot
-guess (v.)
hand
(adv., u.m.)
-rate (u.m.)
**secretary**
#general
-generalcy
-generalship
section #man
seesaw
**seed**
bed
cake
case
coat
kin
stalk

**seer**
band
hand
sucker
**seismo** (c.f.)
*all one word*
**self**
dom
hood
less
ness
same
*reflexive prefix,*
*use hyphen*
**sell**
off (n., u.m.)
out (n., u.m.)
**semi** (pref.)
annual, arid,
etc.
-armor-piercing
(u.m.)
-Christian, etc.
-idleness,
-indirect, etc.
**send**
off (n., u.m.)
out (n., u.m.)
**senso** (c.f.)
*all one word*
**septi** (c.f.)
*all one word*
**septo** (c.f.)
*all one word*
**serio** (c.f.)
*all one word*
**sero** (c.f.)
*all one word*
**serrate**
-ciliate (u.m.)
-dentate (u.m.)
**service**
-connected (u.m.)
**servo**
accelerometer
amplifier
control
mechanism
motor
system
**sesqui** (c.f.)
*all one word*
**set**
-aside (n., u.m.)
back (n., u.m.)
bolt
down (n., u.m.)
-fair (n.)
head
-in (n., u.m.)
off (n., u.m.)
-on (n., u.m.)
out (n., u.m.)
pin
screw
-stitched (u.m.)
-to (n., u.m.)
up (n., u.m.)
**setter**
-forth
-in
-on
-out
-to
-up
**seven**
-branched (u.m.)

fold
penny (nail)
score
-shooter
-up (n.)
severalfold
**shade**
-giving (u.m.)
-grown (u.m.)
**shadow**
boxing
gram
graph
#line
**shag**
bark
-haired (u.m.)
**shake**
down (n., u.m.)
out (n., u.m.)
up (n., u.m.)
**shallow**
-draft (u.m.)
-headed (u.m.)
**shame**
-crushed (u.m.)
faced
**shank**
bone
#mill
shapeup (n., u.m.)
**share**
bone
broker
cropper
out (n., u.m.)
**sharp**
-angled (u.m.)
-cut (u.m.)
-edged (u.m.)
-freeze (u.m., v.)
-freezer
-looking (u.m.)
-set (u.m.)
shod
shooter
-tailed (u.m.)
-witted (u.m.)
shavehook
**shear**
pin
waters
shedhand
**sheep**
biter
crook
dip
faced
fold
gate
herder
hook
kill
-kneed (u.m.)
nose (apple)
pen
shank
shear (v.)
shearer (n.)
shed
sick
stealer
walk
-white (u.m.)
**sheer**
off (n., u.m.)
up (n., u.m.)

**sheet**
block
flood
rock
ways
**shell**
back
burst
fire
fishery
hole
-like
shocked
shelterbelt
shield-shaped
(u.m.)
shilly-shally
**shin**
bone
guard
plaster
shiner-up
**ship**
breaker
broken
broker
builder
lap
mast
owning
-rigged (u.m.)
shape
side
wreck
**shipping**
#master
#room
**shirt**
band
waist
**shoe**
black
brush
horn
lace
pack
scraper
shine
string
tree
shootoff
(n., u.m.)
**shop**
breaker
folk
lifter
-made (u.m.)
mark
-soiled (u.m.)
talk
walker
window
**shore**
#bird
#boat
fast
going
side
**short**
-armed (u.m.)
bread
cake
change (v.)
changer
-circuited (u.m.)
coming
cut (n., u.m., v.)
fall (n.)

-fed (u.m.)
hand (writing)
-handed (u.m.)
head (whale)
horn (n., u.m.)
-horned (u.m.)
-lasting (u.m.)
leaf (u.m.)
-lived (u.m.)
rib
run (u.m.)
sighted
staff
stop
wave (radio)
**shot**
  gun
  hole
  put
  star
shoulder-high
  (u.m.)
**shovel**
  -headed (u.m.)
  -nosed (u.m.)
**show**
  card
  case
  down (n., u.m.)
  off (n., u.m.)
  place
  through
    (printing)
    (n., u.m.)
  up (n., u.m.)
shredout (n., u.m.)
**shroud**
  -laid (u.m.)
  plate
shunt-wound
  (u.m.)
**shut**
  away (n., u.m.)
  down (n., u.m.)
  eye (n., u.m.)
  -in (n., u.m.)
  -mouthed (u.m.)
  off (n., u.m.)
  out (n., u.m.)
  up (u.m.)
shuttlecock
**sick**
  bay
  bed
  list
**side**
  arms
  band
  bone
  burns
  car
  check
  -cut (u.m.)
  dress (v.)
  flash
  head (printing)
  hill
  hook
  kick
  lap
  #light (literal)
  light
    (nonliteral)
  #line (literal)
  line (nonliteral)
  long
  note

plate
play
saddle
show
slip
splitting
step
stitch
-stitched (u.m.)
sway
swipe
track
walk
wall
-wheeler
winder
**sight**
  hole
  read
  saver
  seeing
  setter
**sign**
  off (n., u.m.)
  -on (n., u.m.)
  post
  up (n., u.m.)
**silico** (c.f.)
  *all one word*
**silk**
  -stockinged
    (u.m.)
  works
siltpan
**silver**
  -backed (u.m.)
  beater
  -bright (u.m.)
  -gray (u.m.)
  -haired (u.m.)
  -lead (u.m.)
  -leaved (u.m.)
  plate (v.)
  -plated (u.m.)
  point
    (drawing)
  print
  tip
  -tongued (u.m.)
  top
simon-pure (u.m.)
**simple**
  -headed (u.m.)
  -minded (u.m.)
  -rooted (u.m.)
  -witted (u.m.)
simulcast
**sin**
  -born (u.m.)
  -bred (u.m.)
singsong
**single**
  bar
  -breasted (u.m.)
  -decker
  -edged (u.m.)
  handed
  hood
  -loader
  -minded (u.m.)
  -phase (u.m.)
  -seater
  stick
  tree
**sink**
  head
  hole

**Sino** (c.f.)
  -Japanese, etc.
**sister**
  -german
  hood
  -in-law
**sit**
  down (n., u.m.)
  -downer
  fast (n., u.m.)
  up (n., u.m.)
**sitter**
  -by
  -out
sitting #room
sitzmark
**six**
  -cylinder
    (u.m.)
  fold
  penny (nail)
  -ply (u.m.)
  score
  -shooter
  -wheeler
sizeup (n., u.m.)
**skid**
  lift (truck)
  road
**skin**
  -clad (u.m.)
  deep
  diver
  flint
  -graft (v.)
skipjack
skirtmarker
skullcap
**skunk**
  head
  top
**sky**
  -blue (u.m.)
  gazer
  -high (u.m.)
  jacker
  lift
  look (v.)
  rocket
  sail
  scape
  scraper
  shine
  wave
slab-sided (u.m.)
**slack**
  -bake (v.)
  -filled (u.m.)
  #water
slambang
slant-eyed (u.m.)
**slap**
  bang
  dab
  dash
  down (n., u.m.)
  happy
  jack
  stick
  -up (n., u.m.)
**slate**
  -blue (u.m.)
  -colored (u.m.)
  works
**slaughter**
  pen
  -born (u.m.)

-deserted (u.m.)
holding
pen
#worker
**Slavo** (c.f.)
  -Hungarian, etc.
**sledge**
  -hammered
    (u.m.)
  meter
**sleep**
  -filled (u.m.)
  talker
  walker
**sleepy**
  -eyed (u.m.)
  head
  -looking (u.m.)
sleetstorm
sleeveband
sleuthhound
**slide**
  film
  knot
**sling**
  ball
  shot
**slip**
  along (u.m.)
  back
  band
  case
  cover
  knot
  -on (n., u.m.)
  #proof
    (printing)
  proof
  ring
  sheet
  shod
  sole
  step
  stitch
  stream
  -up (n., u.m.)
  washer
**slit**
  -eyed (u.m.)
  shell
**slop**
  -molded (u.m.)
  seller
**slope**
  -faced (u.m.)
  ways
**slow**
  belly
  down (n., u.m.)
  -footed (u.m.)
  going
  -motion (u.m.)
  mouthed
  poke
  #time
  up (n., u.m.)
  -witted (u.m.)
**slug**
  -cast (v.)
  caster
**slum**
  dweller
  gullion
  gum
  lord
slumber-bound
  (u.m.)

**small**
  #businessman
  -hipped (u.m.)
  mouthed
  pox
  -scale (u.m.)
  sword
  talk
  town (u.m.)
**smart**
  -alecky (u.m.)
  -looking (u.m.)
  -tongued (u.m.)
smashup (n., u.m.)
smearcase
**smoke**
  -blinded (u.m.)
  bomb
  chaser
  -dried (u.m.)
  -dry (v.)
  -dyed (u.m.)
  -filled (u.m.)
  jack
  jumper
  -laden (u.m.)
  pot
  screen
  stack
smoking #room
**smooth**
  bore
  -browed (u.m.)
  -cast (u.m.)
  mouthed
  -tongued (u.m.)
  -working (u.m.)
snackbar
**snail**
  -paced (u.m.)
  -slow (u.m.)
snail's #pace
**snake**
  bite
  -bitten (u.m.)
  -eater
  -eyed (u.m.)
  head
  hole
  pit
**snap**
  back
  dragon
  head
  hook
  -on (n., u.m.)
  out (n.)
  ring
  roll
  shooter
  shot
  -up (u.m.)
**snapper**
  -back
  -up
**snipe**
  bill
  -nosed (u.m.)
sniperscope
snooperscope
**snow**
  ball
  bank
  berg
  blind
  #blindness
  blink

| | | | | |
|---|---|---|---|---|
| block | tack | spade | spino (c.f.) | tide (season) |
| -blocked (u.m.) | soldier-fashion | -dug (u.m.) | -olivary | trap |
| blower | (u.m.) | foot | *rest one word* | spritsail |
| break | sole | -footed (u.m.) | spirit | spur |
| capped | cutter | -shaped (u.m.) | -born (u.m.) | -clad (u.m.) |
| -choked (u.m.) | plate | span | -broken (u.m.) | -driven (u.m.) |
| clad (u.m.) | somato (c.f.) | -long (u.m.) | #writing | gall |
| -covered (u.m.) | *all one word* | -new (u.m.) | spit | -galled (u.m.) |
| drift | some | Spanish | ball | -heeled (u.m.) |
| fall | day | -Arab | fire | spy |
| flake | how | -born (u.m.) | stick | glass |
| melt | one (anyone) | -speaking (u.m.) | splanchno (c.f.) | hole |
| -melting (u.m.) | #one | spare | *all one word* | tower |
| mobile | (distributive) | -bodied (u.m.) | splay | square |
| pack | place (adv.) | rib | footed | -bottomed (u.m.) |
| pit | time (adv., u.m.) | #room | mouthed | -built (u.m.) |
| plow | #time (some time | spark | spleen | -faced (u.m.) |
| scape | ago) | #plug (literal) | -born (u.m.) | flipper |
| shade | what | plug (nonliteral) | sick | head |
| shed | son-in-law | speakeasy (n.) | -swollen (u.m.) | -headed (u.m.) |
| shine | song | spear | spleno (c.f.) | -rigged (u.m.) |
| shoe | fest | cast | *all one word* | -set (u.m.) |
| sled | wright | head | split | shooter |
| slide | sonobuoy | -high (u.m.) | finger | squeeze |
| slip | sooth | -shaped (u.m.) | (crustacean) | -in (n., u.m.) |
| storm | fast | spectro (c.f.) | fruit | out (n., u.m.) |
| suit | sayer | *all one word* | mouth | up (n., u.m.) |
| -topped (u.m.) | sore | speech | saw | squirrel-headed |
| #water | -eyed (u.m.) | -bereft (u.m.) | -tongued (u.m.) | stackup (n., u.m.) |
| -white (u.m.) | foot (n.) | -read (v.) | up (n., u.m.) | staff-herd (v.) |
| snuff-stained | footed (u.m.) | speed | spoilsport | stag |
| (u.m.) | head (n., u.m.) | boating | spondylo (c.f.) | -handled (u.m.) |
| so | sorry-looking | letter | *all one word* | head |
| -and-so | (u.m.) | trap | sponge | -headed (u.m.) |
| beit (n., conj.) | soul | up (n., u.m.) | cake | horn |
| -called (u.m.) | -deep (u.m.) | spell | diver | -horned (u.m.) |
| -seeming (u.m.) | -searching (u.m.) | binding | -diving (u.m.) | hound |
| -so | sick | down (n., u.m.) | -shaped (u.m.) | hunter |
| soap | sound | -free (u.m.) | spongio (c.f.) | stage |
| bubble | -absorbing (u.m.) | spend | *all one word* | coach |
| dish | #field | -all (n.) | spoolwinder | hand |
| flakes | film | thrift | spoon | -struck (u.m.) |
| rock | -minded (u.m.) | spermato (c.f.) | -beaked (u.m.) | stair |
| stock | off (n., u.m.) | *all one word* | -billed (u.m.) | case |
| suds | track | spermo (c.f.) | bread | head |
| sober | soup | *all one word* | -fed (u.m.) | step |
| -minded (u.m.) | bone | spheno (c.f.) | -shaped (u.m.) | stake |
| sides | spoon | -occipital | ways | head |
| social | sour | *rest one word* | sporeformer | out (n.) |
| #work | belly | sphygmo (c.f.) | sporo (c.f.) | stale-worn (u.m.) |
| #worker | bread | *all one word* | *all one word* | stall |
| socio (c.f.) | dough (n.) | spice | spot | -fed (u.m.) |
| -official | faced | -burnt (u.m.) | -checked (u.m.) | -feed (v.) |
| economic, etc. | -natured (u.m.) | cake | -face (v.) | stand |
| sod | -sweet | -laden (u.m.) | weld (v.) | by (n., u.m.) |
| buster | south | spider | welded (u.m.) | down (n., u.m.) |
| culture | -born (u.m.) | -legged | -welding (u.m.) | fast (n., u.m.) |
| #house | -central (u.m.) | -spun (u.m.) | spray-washed | -in (n., u.m.) |
| soda | east | #web (n.) | (u.m.) | off (n., u.m.) |
| jerk | going | web (u.m., v.) | spread | offish |
| #water | lander | spike | -eagle (u.m., v.) | out (n., u.m.) |
| sofa | paw | horn | head | pat |
| #maker | -sider | -kill (v.) | out (n., u.m.) | pipe |
| -making (u.m.) | -southeast | -pitch (v.) | -set (v.) | point |
| -ridden (u.m.) | west | spin | spring | post |
| soft | soybean | back | back | still (n., u.m.) |
| ball | sow | off | (bookbinding) | up (n., u.m.) |
| -boiled (u.m.) | back | spindle | bok | standard |
| head | belly | -formed (u.m.) | -born (u.m.) | bred |
| -pedal (v.) | space | head | buck | #time |
| -shelled (u.m.) | band | -legged (u.m.) | -clean (v.) | staphylo (c.f.) |
| -soap (nonliteral) | bar | legs | finger | *all one word* |
| (v.) | -cramped | shanks | -grown (u.m.) | star |
| -soaper | (u.m.) | spine | halt | blind |
| (nonliteral) | mark | bone | head | bright |
| (n.) | ship | -broken (u.m.) | -plow (v.) | dust |
| -spoken (u.m.) | #time | -pointed (u.m.) | -plowed (u.m.) | |

gazer
-led (u.m.)
lit
lite (gem)
nose (mole)
shake
shine
shoot
-spangled (u.m.)
stroke
-studded (u.m.)
#time
starchworks
stark
-blind (u.m.)
-mad (u.m.)
-naked (u.m.)
-raving (u.m.)
starter-off
startup (n., u.m.)
stat (pref.)
*all one word*
State
-aided (u.m.)
#line
-owned (u.m.)
state
hood
quake
side
station#house
stato (c.f.)
*all one word*
statute
-barred (u.m.)
#book
stay
-at-home
(n., u.m.)
bar
bolt
boom
lace
log
pin
plow
sail
wire
steam
boating
car
-cooked (u.m.)
-driven (u.m.)
fitter
pipe
plant
power (n.)
#powerplant
-pocket (v.)
-propelled
(u.m.)
roll (v.)
roller (u.m., v.)
ship
table
tightness
steamer#line
steel
-blue (u.m.)
-bright (u.m.)
-cased (u.m.)
clad
-framed (u.m.)
-hard (u.m.)
head
plate
works

steep
-rising (u.m.)
-to (u.m.)
-up (u.m.)
-walled (u.m.)
steeple
chase
-high (u.m.)
jack
top
stem
head
post
sickness
winder
stencil-cutting
(u.m.)
steno (c.f.)
*all one word*
step
aunt
child, etc.
down (n., u.m.)
-in (n., u.m.)
ladder
off (n., u.m.)
-on (n., u.m.)
-up (n., u.m.)
stepping
-off (u.m.)
-out (u.m.)
stereo (c.f.)
*all one word*
stern
castle
-faced (u.m.)
-heavy (u.m.)
-looking (u.m.)
most
post
#wheel
-wheeler
sterno (c.f.)
*all one word*
stetho (c.f.)
*all one word*
stew
pan
pot
stick
-at-it (n., u.m.)
fast (n.)
-in-the-mud
(n., u.m.)
out (n., u.m.)
pin
-to-it-iveness
(n.)
up (n., u.m.)
sticker
-in
-on
-up
stiff
-backed (u.m.)
neck
-necked (u.m.)
still
-admired (u.m.)
birth
born
-burn (v.)
-fish (v.)
-hunt (v.)
-recurring
(u.m.)
stand

stink
ball
bomb
damp
pot
stir
about (n., u.m.)
fry
-up (n., u.m.)
stitch
down (n., u.m.)
up (n., u.m.)
stock
breeder
broker
feeder
holding
jobber
judging
list
pile
pot
raiser
rack
-still (u.m.)
taker
truck
wright
stoke
hold
hole
stomach
-filling (u.m.)
-shaped (u.m.)
-sick (u.m.)
-weary (u.m.)
stomato (c.f.)
*all one word*
stone
biter
blind
brash
breaker
broke
brood
cast
-cold (u.m.)
crusher
cutter
-dead (u.m.)
-deaf (u.m.)
-eyed (u.m.)
hand (printing)
head
layer
lifter
mason
#proof (printing)
shot
#wall (n.)
wall (u.m., v.)
#writing
stony
-eyed (u.m.)
#land
stop
back (n.)
block
clock
cock
gap
hound
list
log
-loss (u.m.)
off (n., u.m.)
watch

storage#room
store
front
ship
storm
-beaten (u.m.)
cock
flow
-laden (u.m.)
-swept (u.m.)
-tossed (u.m.)
wind
storyteller
stout
-armed (u.m.)
heartedness
-minded (u.m.)
stove
brush
-heated (u.m.)
pipe
stow
away (n., u.m.)
down (n., u.m.)
straddle
back
-face (v.)
-legged (u.m.)
straight
away
-backed (u.m.)
-cut (u.m.)
edge
-edged (u.m.)
-faced (u.m.)
forward
head
-legged (u.m.)
#line
-lined (u.m.)
-out (n., u.m.)
-spoken (u.m.)
#time
-up (u.m.)
-up-and-down
(u.m.)
strainslip
strait
-chested (u.m.)
jacket
laced
stranglehold
strap
-bolt (v.)
hanger
head
-shaped (u.m.)
watch
strato (c.f.)
*all one word*
straw
berry#field
boss
-built (u.m.)
hat
-roofed (u.m.)
splitting
stack
-stuffed (u.m.)
walker
-yellow (u.m.)
stray
away (n., u.m.)
#line
mark
stream
bank

bed
flow
head
lined
side
street
-bred (u.m.)
car
cleaner
-cleaning (u.m.)
sweeper
walker
strepto (c.f.)
*all one word*
stretchout
(n., u.m.)
strike
breaker
-in (n., u.m.)
out (n., u.m.)
striker
-in
-out
string
course
halt
#proof (density)
ways
strip
cropping
tease
strong
-arm (u.m., v.)
back (nautical)
-backed (u.m.)
hold
#man
-minded (u.m.)
point (n.)
stub
runner
-toed (u.m.)
wing
stubble
#field
-mulch (u.m.)
stubbornminded
stucco-fronted
(u.m.)
stuck
up (n., u.m.)
-upper
-uppish (u.m.)
stud
bolt
horse
mare
stupid
head
-headed (u.m.)
-looking (u.m.)
sturdy-limbed
(u.m.)
stylo (c.f.)
*all one word*
sub (pref.)
-Himalayan, etc.
machinegun
#rosa, #specie,
etc.
-subcommittee
polar, standard,
etc.
*rest one word*
subject
-object
-objectivity

| | | | | |
|---|---|---|---|---|
| **subter** (pref.) | bow | Super Bowl | **sweep** | herd |
|   *all one word* | break | **supra** (pref.) |   back (aviation) | pox |
| such-and-such | burn |   -abdominal |     (n., u.m.) | sty |
| **suck** | burst |   -acromial |   forward | **swing** |
|   -egg (n., u.m.) | -cured (u.m.) |   -aerial |     (aviation) |   back (n., u.m.) |
|   hole | dial |   anal |     (n., u.m.) |   bar |
|   -in (n., u.m.) | dog |   -angular |   stake |   dingle |
| **sugar** | down |   -arytenoid |   through |   stock |
|   cake | dress |   -auditory |     (n., u.m.) |   -swang |
|   cane | -dried (u.m.) |   -auricular |   washer |   tree |
|   -coat (v.) | -dry (v.) |   -axillary | **sweet** | **swingle** |
|   -coated (u.m.) | fall |   -Christian, etc. |   bread |   bar |
|   -cured (u.m.) | fast |   *rest one word* |   -breathed (u.m.) |   tree |
|   loaf | glade | **sur** (pref.) |   brier | **switch** |
|   plum | glare |   *all one word* |   faced |   back |
|   spoon | glass | **sure** |   heart |   blade |
|   sweet | glow |   -fire (u.m.) |   meat |   gear |
|   #water | lamp |   -footed (u.m.) |   mouthed |   plate |
|   works | lit |   -slow |   -pickle (v.) |   plug |
| **sulfa** (c.f.) | quake | **surf** |   -sour |   rail |
|   *all one word* | ray |   -battered (u.m.) |   -sweet |   tender |
| **sulfo** (c.f.) | rise |   #fish | **swell** | **swivel** |
|   *all one word* | scald |   -swept (u.m.) |   -butted (u.m.) |   eye |
| **sulfon** (c.f.) | set | **swallow** |   head |   -eyed (u.m.) |
|   *all one word* | shade |   pipe |   toad |   -hooked (u.m.) |
| **sullen** | shine |   -tailed (u.m.) | swelled-headed | **sword** |
|   hearted | -shot (u.m.) | swampside |   (u.m.) |   -armed (u.m.) |
|   -natured (u.m.) | shower | **swan** | **swept** |   bearer |
| **summer** | spot |   -bosomed (u.m.) |   back (n., u.m.) |   bill |
|   -clad (u.m.) | stricken |   dive |   forward |   fishing |
|   -dried (u.m.) | stroke |   herd |     (n., u.m.) |   play |
|   -fallow (v.) | struck |   mark |   wing (n., u.m.) |   -shaped (u.m.) |
|   -made (u.m.) | tan |   neck | **swift** |   stick |
|   tide | #time (measure) |   song |   foot | **syn** (pref.) |
|   time (season) | time (dawn) | swansdown |   -footed (u.m.) |   *all one word* |
|   #time (daylight | up | **swash** |   -handed (u.m.) | **synchro** |
|     saving) | **sunny** |   buckler |   -running (u.m.) |   cyclotron |
| **sun** |   -looking (u.m.) |   plate | **swill** |   flash |
|   -baked (u.m.) |   -natured (u.m.) | **sway** |   bowl |   mesh |
|   bath | **super** (pref.) |   back (n., u.m.) |   tub |   tron |
|   -bathed (u.m.) |   -Christian, etc. |   -backed (u.m.) | swimsuit | **Syro** (c.f.) |
|   beam |   #high frequency |   bar | **swine** |   -Arabian, etc. |
|   blind |   -superlative |   -brace (v.) |   -backed (u.m.) |   phenician |
|   #blindness |   highway, | swearer-in |   bread | |
|   bonnet |     market, etc. | sweatband |   head | |

# T

| | | | | |
|---|---|---|---|---|
| **T** | lock | **take** | **tame** |   -fashion (u.m.) |
|   -bandage | rag |   -all (n.) |   -grown (u.m.) |   -headed (u.m.) |
|   -beam | sore |   down (n., u.m.) |   -looking (u.m.) | **tapestry** |
|   -boat | **tail** |   -home (n., u.m.) | **tan** |   -covered (u.m.) |
|   -bone |   band |   in (n., u.m.) |   bark |   #maker |
|   -cloth |   -cropped |   off (n., u.m.) |   works |   -making (u.m.) |
|   -iron |     (u.m.) |   out (n., u.m.) | **tangent** |   #work |
|   -man |   -ender |   up (n., u.m.) |   -cut (v.) | tapper-out |
|   -rail |   first | **taker** |   -saw (v.) | **tar** |
|   -scale (score) |   foremost |   -down | **tangle** |   -brand (v.) |
|   -shape |   gate |   -in |   foot |   brush |
|   -shaped |   head |   -off |   -haired (u.m.) |   -coal (u.m.) |
|   -shirt |   -heavy (u.m.) |   -up | **tank** |   -dipped (u.m.) |
|   -square |   hook | **tale** |   ship |   -paved (u.m.) |
| **table** |   lamp |   bearer |   town |   pot |
|   cloth |   pin |   carrier | **tap** |   -roofed (u.m.) |
|   -cut (u.m.) |   pipe |   teller |   bolt |   works |
|   cutter |   race | talkfest |   dance | tariff-protected |
|   -cutting (u.m.) |   spin | talking-to (n.) |   hole |   (u.m.) |
|   fellow |   stock | **tall** |   net | **tarpaulin** |
|   -formed (u.m.) |   -tied (u.m.) |   -built (u.m.) |   off (n., u.m.) |   -covered (u.m.) |
|   -shaped (u.m.) |   twister |   -looking (u.m.) |   -riveted (u.m.) |   #maker |
|   spoon |   -up (n., u.m.) | **tallow** |   root |   -making (u.m.) |
|   talk |   wheel |   -faced (u.m.) |   -tap | **tarso** (c.f.) |
|   top |   wind |   -pale (u.m.) | **tape** |   *all one word* |
| **tachy** (c.f.) | **tailor** | **tally** |   string | tasksetter |
|   *all one word* |   -cut (u.m.) |   #board |   -tied (u.m.) | tattletale |
| **tag** |   made (u.m.) |   ho | **taper** | **tauro** (c.f.) |
|   -affixing (u.m.) |   -suited (u.m.) |   #room |   bearer |   *all one word* |

**tax**
-burdened (u.m.)
eater
-exempt (u.m.)
-free (u.m.)
gatherer
-laden (u.m.)
paid
payer
-supported (u.m.)
**taxi**
auto
bus
cab
meter
stand
**tea**
ball
cake
cart
-colored (u.m.)
cup
dish
kettle
pot
-scented (u.m.)
spoon
taster
**teamplay**
**tear**
bomb
-dimmed (u.m.)
down (n., u.m.)
drop
-off (n., u.m.)
-out (n., u.m.)
pit
sheet
stain
-stained (u.m.)
**teen**
age (u.m.)
ager
**teeter-totter**
**tele** (c.f.)
*all one word*
**teleo** (c.f.)
*all one word*
**tell**
tale
truth
**telo** (c.f.)
*all one word*
**tempest-rocked**
(u.m.)
**temporo** (c.f.)
-occipital
*rest one word*
**ten**
fold
penny (nail)
pins
**tender**
#boat
-faced (u.m.)
foot
-footed (u.m.)
footish
-handed (u.m.)
heart
loin
-looking (u.m.)
**tenement#house**
**tent**
-dotted (u.m.)
pole
-sheltered (u.m.)

**terneplate**
**terra**
#cotta
#firma
mara
**terrace-fashion**
(u.m.)
**test-fly** (v.)
**tetra** (c.f.)
*all one word*
**thanksgiving**
**thatch-roofed**
(u.m.)
**theater**
goer
going
**thenceforth**
**theo** (c.f.)
*all one word*
**theologico** (c.f.)
*all one word*
**there**
about(s)
above
across
after
against
among
around
at
away
before
between
by
for
fore
from
in
inafter
inbefore
into
of
on
through
to
tofore
under
until
unto
upon
with
**thermo** (c.f.)
*all one word*
**thick**
-blooded (u.m.)
head
lips
-looking (u.m.)
pated
set (n., u.m.)
skinned
skull (n.)
skulled
-tongued (u.m.)
wit
-witted (u.m.)
-wooded (u.m.)
-woven (u.m.)
**thin**
-clad (u.m.)
down (n., u.m.)
set (u.m.)
-voiced (u.m.)
**thio** (c.f.)
*all one word*
**third**
-class (u.m.)

-degree (u.m.)
hand
(adv., u.m.)
#house
-rate (u.m.)
-rater
**thistledown**
**thoraco** (c.f.)
*all one word*
**thorn**
back
bill
-covered (u.m.)
-set (u.m.)
-strewn (u.m.)
**thorough**
-bind (v.)
bred
-dried (u.m.)
fare
going
-made (u.m.)
paced
pin
**thought**
-free (u.m.)
-out (u.m.)
-provoking
(u.m.)
**thousand**
fold
-headed (u.m.)
-legged (u.m.)
legs (worm)
**thrall**
born
dom
-less
**thread**
bare
-leaved (u.m.)
worn
**three**
-bagger
-cornered (u.m.)
-dimensional
(u.m.)
fold
-in-hand
-master
penny (nail)
-piece (u.m.)
-ply (u.m.)
score
some
-spot
-square
-striper
**throat**
band
cutter
latch
strap
**thrombo** (c.f.)
*all one word*
**through**
out
put
**throw**
away (n., u.m.)
back (n., u.m.)
-in (n., u.m.)
#line
off (n., u.m.)
-on (n., u.m.)
out (n., u.m.)
-weight

**thrust-pound**
**thumb**
-made (u.m.)
mark
-marked (u.m.)
nail
print
screw
stall
string
sucker
tack
**thunder**
bearer
blast
bolt
clap
cloud
head
peal
shower
storm
struck
**thymo** (c.f.)
*all one word*
**thyro** (c.f.)
*all one word*
**tibio** (c.f.)
*all one word*
**tick**
seed
tacktoe
tick
tock
**ticket**
-selling (u.m.)
#writer
**tiddlywink**
**tide**
flat
head
mark
-marked (u.m.)
race
table
-tossed (u.m.)
waiter
-worn (u.m.)
**tie**
back (n.)
down (n., u.m.)
-in (n., u.m.)
-on (n., u.m.)
-out (n., u.m.)
pin
-plater
up (n., u.m.)
**tierlift** (truck)
**tiger**
eye
-striped (u.m.)
**tight**
-belted (u.m.)
fisted
-fitting (u.m.)
lipped
rope
-set (u.m.)
-tie (v.)
wad
wire
**tile**
-clad (u.m.)
-red (u.m.)
setter
works

**wright**
**tilt**
hammer
up (n.)
**timber**
-built (u.m.)
head
-headed (u.m.)
jack
-propped (u.m.)
wright
**time**
born
card
clerk
clock
-consuming
(u.m.)
frame
-honored (u.m.)
keep (v.)
killer
lag
lock
outs (n., u.m.)
pleaser
saver
server
sheet
slip
slot
span
-stamp (v.)
study
table
taker
waster
worn
**tin**
-bearing (u.m.)
-capped (u.m.)
-clad (u.m.)
cup
#fish
(torpedo)
foil
horn
kettle
-lined (u.m.)
pan
plate
-plated (u.m.)
pot
-roofed (u.m.)
type
-white (u.m.)
**tinsel**
-bright (u.m.)
-clad (u.m.)
-covered (u.m.)
**tintblock**
(printing)
**tip**
burn
cart
-curled (u.m.)
head
-in (n., u.m.)
most
off (n., u.m.)
staff
stock
tank
-tap
toe
top
-up (u.m.)

**tire**
changer
dresser
fitter
-mile
shaper
some
**tit**
bit
#for#tat
**titano** (c.f.)
*all one word*
**tithe**
-free (u.m.)
payer
right
**title**
-holding (u.m.)
winner
-winning (u.m.)
**to**
-and-fro
-do (n.)
**toad**
back
-bellied (u.m.)
blind
fish
-green (u.m.)
stool
**tobacco**
#grower
-growing (u.m.)
#shop
**toe**
cap
-in (n., u.m.)
-mark (v.)
nail
plate
print
**toil**
-beaten (u.m.)
some
-stained (u.m.)
-weary (u.m.)
worn
**toilet#room**
**toll**
bar
gate
gatherer
#line
payer
penny
taker
**tom**
cat
foolery
-tom
**tommy**
gun
rot
**ton**
-hour
-kilometer
-mile
-mileage
-mile-day
**tone**
-deaf (u.m.)
down (n., u.m.)
-producing (u.m.)
up (n., u.m.)
**tongue**
-baited (u.m.)
-bound (u.m.)

-free (u m.)
-lash (v )
#lashing
play
-shaped (u.m.)
shot
sore
tack
tied
tip
-twisting (u.m.)
**tool**
bag
builder
crib
dresser
fitter
-grinding (u.m.)
head
holding
kit
mark
plate
post
rack
setter
shed
slide
stock
**tooth**
ache
#and#nail
-billed (u.m.)
brush
drawer
mark
-marked (u.m.)
paste
pick
plate
powder
puller
-pulling (u.m.)
-set (u.m.)
-shaped (u.m.)
some
wash
**top**
cap (n.)
coat
cutter
-drain (v.)
dress (v.)
flight (u.m.)
full
gallant
  (n., u.m.)
-graft (v.)
hat
-hatted (u.m.)
heavy
kick
knot
liner
mark
mast
milk
most
notch
  (nonliteral)
rail
rope
sail
-secret (u.m.)
-shaped (u.m.)
side (naut.)
soil

**topo** (c.f.)
*all one word*
**topsy-turvy**
**torch**
bearer
#holder
lighted
lit
**torpedo**
#boat
#room
**torquemeter**
**toss**
pot
up (n., u.m.)
**touch**
#and#go
back (n., u.m.)
down (n., u.m.)
hole
-me-not (n., u.m.)
pan
reader
up (n., u.m.)
**tough**
-headed (u.m.)
-looking (u.m.)
-skinned (u.m.)
**tow**
away
head
mast
-netter
path
rope
**tower**
-high (u.m.)
-shaped (u.m.)
**town**
-bred (u.m.)
-dotted (u.m.)
folk
gate
going
hall
lot
ship
side
talk
-weary (u.m.)
**towns**
fellow
people
**toy**
-sized (u.m.)
town
**tracheo** (c.f.)
*all one word*
**trachy** (c.f.)
*all one word*
**track**
barrow
hound
layer
mark
-mile
side
walker
**tractor-trailer**
**trade**
#board
-in (n., u.m.)
-laden (u.m.)
-made (u.m.)
mark
off
**tradespeople**

traffic-mile
**tragico** (c.f.)
*all one word*
**trail**
blazer
breaker
-marked (u.m.)
side
sight
-weary (u.m.)
**train**
bearer
bolt
crew
-mile
shed
sick
stop
**tram**
-borne (u.m.)
car
rail
road
**trans** (pref.)
alpine
atlantic
-Canadian, etc.
pacific
uranic
*rest one word*
transit#time
**trap**
door
fall
shoot
trashrack
**travel**
-bent (u.m.)
-tired (u.m.)
-worn (u.m.)
trawlnet
treadwheel
**treasure**
-filled (u.m.)
#house
-laden (u.m.)
**treaty**
breaker
-sealed (u.m.)
**tree**
-clad (u.m.)
#line
-lined (u.m.)
nail
-ripe (u.m.)
scape
top
trellis-covered
  (u.m.)
**trench**
back
coat
foot
mouth
-plowed (u.m.)
**tri** (c.f.)
-iodide
-ply (u.m.)
state, etc.
*rest one word*
tribespeople
**tribo** (c.f.)
*all one word*
**tricho** (c.f.)
*all one word*
**trim**
-cut (u.m.)

-dressed (u.m.)
-looking (u.m.)
**trinitro** (c.f.)
*all one word*
**trip**
-free (u.m.)
hammer
wire
**triple**
-acting (u.m.)
back (sofa)
branched (u.m.)
-edged (u.m.)
fold
-tailed (u.m.)
tree (n.)
trolley#line
troopship
**tropho** (c.f.)
*all one word*
**tropo** (c.f.)
*all one word*
**trouble**
-free (u.m.)
-haunted (u.m.)
shooter
some
**truce**
breaker
-seeking (u.m.)
**truck**
driver
-mile
stop
**true**
-aimed (u.m.)
-blue (u.m.)
born
bred
-eyed (u.m.)
-false
love (n., u.m.)
penny (n.)
#time
**trunk**
back
nose
**trust**
breaking
buster
-controlled (u.m.)
-ridden (u.m.)
**truth**
-filled (u.m.)
lover
seeker
-seeking (u.m.)
teller
**try**
-on (n., u.m.)
out (n., u.m.)
square
works
**tube**
-eyed (u.m.)
-fed (u.m.)
form (u.m.)
head
-nosed (u.m.)
works
**tuberculo** (c.f.)
*all one word*
**tubo** (c.f.)
-ovarian
*rest one word*
tumbledown
  (n., u.m.)

**tune**
 out (n., u.m.)
 up (n., u.m.)
**tunnel**
 -boring (u.m.)
 -shaped (u.m.)
**turbo** (c.f.)
 -ramjet (u.m.)
 *rest one word*
**turf**
 -built (u.m.)
 -clad (u.m.)
 -covered (u.m.)
**turkey**
 back
 -red (u.m.)
**Turko** (c.f.)
 -Greek, etc.
 *rest one word*
**turn**
 about (n., u.m.)
 about-face
 again (n., u.m.)
 around
   (n., u.m.)

back (n., u.m.)
buckle
cap
coat
cock
down (n., u.m.)
gate
-in (n., u.m.)
key
off (n., u.m.)
out (n., u.m.)
pike
pin
plate
screw
sheet
sole
spit
stile
stitch
table
-to (n.)
under
   (n., u.m.)
up (n., u.m.)

**turned**
 -back (u.m.)
 -down (u.m.)
 -in (u.m.)
 -on (u.m.)
 -out (u.m.)
 -over (u.m.)
turner-off
**turtle**
 back
 -footed (u.m.)
 neck (u.m.)
**twelve**
 fold
 penny (nail)
 score
**twenty**
 -first
 fold
 -one
   penny (nail)
**twice**
 -born (u.m.)
 -reviewed (u.m.)
 -told (u.m.)

**twin**
#boat
 born
 -engined (u.m.)
 fold
 -jet (u.m.)
 -motor (u.m.)
 -screw (u.m.)
**two**
 -a-day (u.m.)
 -along (n.)
   (bookbinding)
 -decker
 -faced (u.m.)
 fold
 -handed (u.m.)
 penny (nail)
 -piece (u.m.)
 -ply (u.m.)
 score
 -seater
 some
 -spot
 -step (dance)
 -striper

-suiter
-thirder
-up (n., u.m.)
-way (u.m.)
-wheeler
**tympano** (c.f.)
 *all one word*
**type**
 case
 cast
 cutter
 face
 foundry
 -high (u.m.)
 script
 set
 write (v.)
**typho** (c.f.)
 *all one word*
**typo** (c.f.)
 *all one word*
**tyro** (c.f.)
 *all one word*

## U

**U**
-boat
-cut
-magnet
-rail
-shaped
-tube
**ultra** (pref.)
 -ambitious,
   -atomic, etc.
 -English, etc.
 high #frequency
 -high-speed
   (u.m.)
 #valorem, etc.
 *rest one word*
**un** (pref.)
 -American, etc.
 called-for (u.m.)

heard-of (u.m.)
-ionized (u.m.)
self-conscious
sent-for (u.m.)
thought-of
   (u.m.)
 *rest one word*
**under**
 age (deficit)
 age (younger)
   (n., u.m.)
#cultivation
   (tillage)
 cultivation
   (insufficient)
#secretary
 -secretaryship
   *as prefix, one
   word*

**uni** (c.f.)
 -univalent
 *rest one word*
**union**
 -made (u.m.)
#shop
 unit-set (u.m.)
**up**
 -anchor (u.m., v.)
 -and-coming
   (u.m.)
#and #up
 beat
 coast
 country
 dip
 end (v.)
 grade
 gradient

keep
lift
-over (u.m.)
rate
river
stairs
state
stream
swing
take
tight (n., u.m.)
#tight (v.)
 -to-date (u.m.)
#to #date
 town
 trend
 turn
 wind

**upper**
 case (printing)
#class
 classman
 crust (n., u.m.)
 cut
 most
**urano** (c.f.)
 *all one word*
**uretero** (c.f.)
 *all one word*
**urethro** (c.f.)
 *all one word*
**uro** (c.f.)
 *all one word*
 used-car (u.m.)
**utero** (c.f.)
 *all one word*

## V

**V**
-connection
-curve
-engine
-neck
-shaped
-type
**vacant**
 -eyed (u.m.)
 -looking (u.m.)
 -minded (u.m.)
**vagino** (c.f.)
 *all one word*
**valve**
 -grinding (u.m.)
 -in-head (u.m.)
**van**
 driver
 guard
 most
 pool
**vapor**
 -filled (u.m.)
 -heating (u.m.)
 vase-shaped
   (u.m.)

**vaso** (c.f.)
 *all one word*
**vegeto** (c.f.)
 *all one word*
**vein**
 -mining (u.m.)
 -streaked (u.m.)
**vellum**
 -bound (u.m.)
 -covered (u.m.)
**velvet**
 -crimson (u.m.)
 -draped (u.m.)
 -green (u.m.)
 -pile (u.m.)
 venthole
**ventri** (c.f.)
 *all one word*
**ventro** (c.f.)
 *all one word*
**vertebro** (c.f.)
 *all one word*
**vesico** (c.f.)
 *all one word*
**vibro** (c.f.)
 *all one word*

**vice**
#admiral
 -admiralty
#consul
 -consulate
#governor
 -governorship
#minister
 -ministry
 -presidency
#president
 -president-elect
 -presidential
#rector
 -rectorship
 regal
 -regency
#regent
 royal
#versa
#warden
 -wardenship
 Vietcong
**view**
 finder
 point

vile-natured (u.m.)
**vine**
 -clad (u.m.)
 -covered (u.m.)
 dresser
 growing
 stalk
**vinegar**
 -flavored (u.m.)
 -hearted (u.m.)
 -making (u.m.)
 -tart (u.m.)
**violet**
 -blue (u.m.)
 -colored (u.m.)
 -eared (u.m.)
 -rayed (u.m.)
#water
 violin-shaped
   (u.m.)
 virtue-armed
**viscero** (c.f.)
 *all one word*
**vitreo** (c.f.)
 *all one word*

**vitro** (c.f.)
 -clarain
 -di-trina
 *rest one word*
**vivi** (c.f.)
 *all one word*
 volleyball
**volt**
 ammeter
 -ampere
 -coulomb
 meter
 ohmmeter
 -second
**volta** (c.f.)
 *all one word*
**vote**
 -casting (u.m.)
 getter
 -getting (u.m.)
**vow**
 -bound (u.m.)
 breaker
 -pledged (u.m.)
**vulvo** (c.f.)
 *all one word*

# W

**W**
  -engine
  -shaped
  -surface
  -type
wage-earning
    (u.m.)
**waist**
  band
  belt
  cloth
  coat
  -deep (u.m.)
  -high (u.m.)
**waiting**
  #man
  #room
  #woman
**walk**
  around
    (n., u.m.)
  away (n., u.m.)
  -on (n., u.m.)
  out (n., u.m.)
  up (n., u.m.)
walkie-talkie
**wall**
  eyed
  -like
  -painting (u.m.)
  paper
  plate
  -sided (u.m.)
**walled**
  -in (u.m.)
  -up (u.m.)
**war**
  -disabled (u.m.)
  -famed (u.m.)
  fare
  head
  horse
    (nonliteral)
  -made (u.m.)
  path
  ship
  -swept (u.m.)
  #time (clock)
  time (duration)
**ward**
  heeler
  robe
  ship
**warm**
  blooded
  -clad (u.m.)
  up (n., u.m.)
warmed-over
    (u.m.)
warpsetter
**wash**
  basin
  basket
  bowl
  cloth
  -colored (u.m.)
  day
  down (n., u.m.)
  -in (n., u.m.)
  off (n., u.m.)
  out (n., u.m.)
  pot
  rag
  stand
  tray

  trough
  tub
  up (n., u.m.)
**washed**
  -out (u.m.)
  -up (u.m.)
**waste**
  basket
  leaf
    (bookbinding)
  paper
  word
**watch**
  band
  case
  cry
  dog
  -free (u.m.)
  glass
  tower
  word
**water**
  bag
  bank
  bearer
  -bearing (u.m.)
  -beaten (u.m.)
  -bind (v.)
  bloom
  buck
  color
  -colored (u.m.)
  -cool (v.)
  -cooled (u.m.)
  course
  dog
  -drinking (u.m.)
  drop
  fall
  -filled (u.m.)
  finder
  flood
  flow
  fog
  -free (u.m.)
  front
  gate
  head
  hole
  horse
  -inch
  -laden (u.m.)
  lane
  leaf
  -lined (u.m.)
  locked
  log
  mark
  melon
  meter
  plant
  pot
  proofing
  quake
  -rot (v.)
  scape
  shed
  shoot
  side
  -soak (v.)
  -soaked (u.m.)
  -soluble (u.m.)
  spout
  stain
  wall

  works
  worn
**watt**
  -hour
  meter
  -second
**wave**
  -cut (u.m.)
  form
  guide
  -lashed (u.m.)
  length
  mark
  meter
  -moist (u.m.)
  -on (n., u.m.)
  off (n., u.m.)
  -swept (u.m.)
  -worn (u.m.)
**wax**
  -billed (u.m.)
  chandler
  cloth
  -coated (u.m.)
  -headed (u.m.)
  #stone
  -yellow (u.m.)
**way**
  back (n., u.m.)
  beam
  down (n., u.m.)
  farer
  fellow
  going
  laid
  lay
  mark
  post
  side
  -sore (u.m.)
  -up (n., u.m.)
  worn
**weak**
  -backed (u.m.)
  -eyed (u.m.)
  handed
  -kneed (u.m.)
  minded
  mouthed
**weather**
  beaten
  blown
  -borne (u.m.)
  break
  cock
  glass
  going
  -hardened (u.m.)
  #house
  -marked (u.m.)
  most
  proofing
  -stain (v.)
  strip
  -stripped (u.m.)
  worn
**web**
  -fingered (u.m.)
  foot
  -footed (u.m.)
**wedge**
  -billed (u.m.)
  -shaped (u.m.)
**weed**
  -choked (u.m.)

  -hidden (u.m.)
  hook
  killer
**week**
  day
  end
  -ender
  -ending (u.m.)
  long (u.m.)
  -old (u.m.)
**weigh**
  bridge
  -in (n., u.m.)
  lock
  out (n., u.m.)
  shaft
**well**
  -being (n.)
  -beloved (u.m.)
  -born (u.m.)
  -bound (u.m.)
  -bred (u.m.)
  -clad (u.m.)
  -deserving (u.m.)
  -doer
  -doing (n., u.m.)
  -drained (u.m.)
  -drilling (u.m.)
  #field
  -grown (u.m.)
  head
  -headed (u.m.)
  hole
  -informed (u.m.)
  -known (u.m.)
  -looking (u.m.)
  -meaner
  -nigh (u.m.)
  -off (u.m.)
  -read (u.m.)
  -set-up (u.m.)
  -settled (u.m.)
  side
  -spoken (u.m.)
  spring
  stead
  -thought-of
    (u.m.)
  -thought-out
    (u.m.)
  -to-do (u.m.)
  -wisher
  -wishing (u.m.)
  -worn (u.m.)
welterweight
werewolf
**west**
  -central (u.m.)
  -faced (u.m.)
  going
  most
  -northwest
  -sider
**wet**
  back
  -cheeked (u.m.)
  -clean (v.)
  -nurse (v.)
  pack
  wash
**whale**
  back
  -backed (u.m.)
  bone
  -built (u.m.)

  -headed (u.m.)
  -mouthed (u.m.)
  ship
**wharf**
  #boat
  hand
  head
  side
**what**
  ever
  -is-it (n.)
  not (n.)
  soever
  -you-may-call-it
    (n.)
**wheat**
  cake
  -colored (u.m.)
  ear
  -fed (u.m.)
  -rich (u.m.)
  stalk
**wheel**
  band
  barrow
  base
  chair
  -cut (u.m.)
  going
  horse
    (nonliteral)
  #load
  -made (u.m.)
  plate
  race
  spin
  stitch
  -worn (u.m.)
  wright
**when**
  ever
  -issued (u.m.)
  soever
**where**
  abouts
  after
  as
  at
  by
  for
  from
  in
  insoever
  into
  of
  on
  soever
  to
  under
  upon
  with
  withal
wherever
**which**
  ever
  soever
whiffletree
**whip**
  cord
  crack
  -graft (v.)
  lash
  -marked (u.m.)
  post
  saw

**Column 1**

-shaped (u.m.)
socket
staff
stalk
stall
stick
stitch
stock
-tailed (u.m.)
**whipper**
-in
snapper
**whirl**
about (n., u.m.)
blast
pool
-shaped (u.m.)
wind
**whisk**
broom
#tail
whistlestop
**white**
back
beard (n.)
#book
(diplomatic)
cap (n.)
coat (n.)
-collar (u.m.)
comb (n.)
corn
-eared (u.m.)
-eyed (u.m.)
face
-faced (u.m.)
foot (n.)
-footed (u.m.)
handed
-hard (u.m.)
head
-headed (u.m.)
-hot (u.m.)
#line
minded
out (u.m., v.)
pot
-tailed (u.m.)
-throated (u.m.)
top (n.)
vein
wash
**who**
ever
soever
**whole**
-headed (u.m.)
-hogger
sale
some
whomsoever
wicker-woven
(u.m.)
**wicket**
keeper
keeping
**wide**
-angle (u.m.)
-awake (u.m.)
-handed (u.m.)
mouthed
-open (u.m.)
spread
-spreading (u.m.)
**widow**
#bird
hood

**Column 2**

**wife**
beater
hood
killer
-ridden (u.m.)
wigwag
**wild**
cat (n.)
-eyed (u.m.)
fire
#land
life
#man
wind
**will**
-less
-o'-the-wisp
wilt-resistant
(u.m.)
**wind** (v.)
down (n., u.m.)
up (n., u.m.)
**wind**
bag
ball
blown
brace
breaker
burn
catcher
-chapped (u.m.)
chill
fall
fast
-fertilized (u.m.)
firm
flow
gall
-galled (u.m.)
hole
-hungry (u.m.)
jammer
lass
pipe
-pollinated (u.m.)
-rode (u.m.)
row
screen
-shaken (u.m.)
-shear (u.m.)
shield
shock
side
sleeve
sock
speed
stop
storm
stream
swept
worn
**window**
breaker
-breaking (u.m.)
-cleaning (u.m.)
-dressing (u.m.)
pane
peeper
-shop (v.)
-shopping (u.m.)
sill
#work
**wine**
bag
-black (u.m.)
-drinking (u.m.)
glass

**Column 3**

growing
-hardy (u.m.)
pot
-red (u.m.)
seller
taster
tester
vat
**wing**
band
bar
beat
bolt
bone
bow
cut
-footed (u.m.)
handed
-heavy (u.m.)
-loading (u.m.)
-loose (u.m.)
nut
-shaped (u.m.)
-shot (u.m.)
span
-swift (u.m.)
tip
top
walker
wall
-weary (u.m.)
**winter**
-beaten (u.m.)
-clad (u.m.)
-fallow (v.)
-fed (u.m.)
feed
#green (color)
green (plant,
etc.)
-hardy (u.m.)
kill
-made (u.m.)
-sown (u.m.)
tide
-worn (u.m.)
**wire**
bar
-caged (u.m.)
-cut (u.m.)
cutter
dancer
draw (v.)
-edged (u.m.)
hair (dog)
-haired (u.m.)
less
#line
photo
puller
spun
stitch
-stitched (u.m.)
-tailed (u.m.)
tap
walker
works
-wound (u.m.)
**wise**
acre
crack
head (n.)
-headed (u.m.)
-spoken (u.m.)
wishbone
witch-hunting
(u.m.)

**Column 4**

**with**
draw
hold
in
out
stand
**within**
-bound (u.m.)
-named (u.m.)
**woe**
begone
worn
**wolf**
-eyed (u.m.)
#fish
hound
pack
**woman**
folk
hood
kind
womenfolk
**wonder**
strong
-struck (u.m.)
**wood**
bark (color)
bin
bined
block
-built (u.m.)
-cased (u.m.)
chipper
chopper
chuck
cut
grub
hole
horse
hung (u.m.)
-lined (u.m.)
lot
-paneled (u.m.)
pile
-planing (u.m.)
print
pulp
ranger
rock
shed
side
stock
turner
-turning (u.m.)
-walled (u.m.)
wind (music)
**wooden**
head (n.)
-hulled (u.m.)
-weary (u.m.)
**wool**
fell
gatherer
grader
growing
head
-laden (u.m.)
-lined (u.m.)
pack
press
shearer
shed
sorter
stock
washer
wheel
-white (u.m.)

**Column 5**

winder
**woolly**
-coated (u.m.)
-headed (u.m.)
-looking (u.m.)
-white (u.m.)
**word**
-blind (u.m.)
builder
catcher
-clad (u.m.)
-deaf (u.m.)
jobber
list
-perfect (u.m.)
play
seller
slinger
**work**
aday (n., u.m.)
-and-turn (u.m.)
away (n., u.m.)
bag
basket
bench
card
day
-driven (u.m.)
flow
folk
hand
-hardened (u.m.)
horse
-hour (u.m.)
housed
life
manship
out (n., u.m.)
pan
paper
people
place
saving
sheet
shoe
-shy (n., u.m.)
-shyness
slip
space
-stained (u.m.)
stand
stream
table
up (n., u.m.)
ways
-weary (u.m.)
week
worn
**working**
#load
#room
**world**
beater
-conscious (u.m.)
#consciousness
#line
#power
-self
-weary (u.m.)
**worm**
-eaten (u.m.)
-eating (u.m.)
hole
-riddled (u.m.)
-ripe (u.m.)
seed
shaft

**worn**
  down (u.m.)
  out (u.m.)
  outness
worrywart
**worth**
  while (u.m.)
  whileness (n.)
**wrap**
  around
    (n., u.m.)

  -up (n., u.m.)
wreath-crowned
    (u.m.)
wreck-free
    (u.m.)
**wring**
  bolt
  staff
**wrist**
  band
  bone

  drop
  fall
  lock
  pin
  plate
  watch
**write**
  back (n., u.m.)
  -in (n., u.m.)
  off (n., u.m.)
  up (n., u.m.)

writing # room
**wrong**
  doer
  -ended (u.m.)
  -minded (u.m.)
  -thinking (u.m.)
wrought-up
    (u.m.)

**wry**
  bill
  -billed (u.m.)
  -faced (u.m.)
  -looking (u.m.)
  -mouthed (u.m.)
  neck
  -set (u.m.)

## X

**X**
  -body
  -disease
  -virus

  -shaped
**x**
  # ray (n.)
  -ray (u.m.)

**xantho** (c.f.)
  *all one word*
**xeno** (c.f.)
  *all one word*

**xero** (c.f.)
  *all one word*
**xylo** (c.f.)
  *all one word*

## Y

**Y**
  -chromosome
  -joint
  -level
  -potential
  -shaped
  -track
  -tube
Yankee-Doodle
**yard**
  arm

  -deep (u.m.)
  -long (u.m.)
  stick
  -wide (u.m.)
**yaw**
  meter
  -sighted (u.m.)
**year**
  day
  end
  -hour (u.m.)

  long (u.m.)
  -old (u.m.)
  -round (u.m.)
**yellow**
  back
  -backed (u.m.)
  -bellied (u.m.)
  belly
  -billed (u.m.)
  -headed (u.m.)
  -tailed (u.m.)

  -throated (u.m.)
  top
**yes**
  -man
  -no
**yester**
  day
  year
**yoke**
  fellow
  mating

  -toed (u.m.)
**young**
  eyed (u.m.)
  -headed (u.m.)
  -ladylike
  -looking (u.m.)
  -manlike
  -old
  -womanhood
youthtide
yuletide

## Z

**Z**
  -bar
  -chromosome
**zero**
  axial
  -dimensional
    (u.m.)

  gravity
zigzag
**zinc**
  -coated (u.m.)
  -white (u.m.)

**zoo** (c.f.)
  *all one word*
**zoologico** (c.f.)
  *all one word*

**zygo** (c.f.)
  *all one word*
**zygomatico** (c.f.)
  -orbital
  *rest one word*

**zymo** (c.f.)
  *all one word*

# Appendix 2.
# Weights and Measures

### Avoirdupois Weight

For all articles except drugs, gold, silver, and gems

| | | |
|---|---|---|
| 27¹¹⁄₃₂ grains | = | 1 dram (dr.) |
| 16 drams | = | 1 ounce (oz.) |
| 16 ounces | = | 1 pound (lb.) |
| 100 pounds | = | 1 hundredweight (cwt.) |
| 2,000 pounds | = | 1 ton (T.) |
| 1 lb. | = | 1,000 grs. |

### Troy Weight

For gold, silver, and gems

| | |
|---|---|
| 24 grains (gr.) | = 1 pennyweight (pwt.) |
| 20 pennyweights | = 1 ounce (oz.) |
| 12 ounces | = 1 pound (lb.) |

For precious stones only

| | |
|---|---|
| 1 carat | = 3.168 Troy grains |

### Apothecaries' Weight

| | |
|---|---|
| 20 grains | = 1 scruple |
| 3 scruples | = 1 dram |
| 8 drams | = 1 ounce |
| 12 ounces | = 1 pound |

## Apothecaries' Fluid Measure

| | |
|---|---|
| 60 minims (or drops) | = 1 fluid dram |
| 8 fluid drams | = 1 fluid ounce |
| 16 fluid ounces | = 1 pint |
| 8 pints | = 1 gallon |

## U.S. Liquid Measure

| | | |
|---|---|---|
| 60 | minims | = 1 fluid dram |
| 8 | fluid drams | = 1 fluid ounce |
| 4 | fluid ounces | = 1 gill |
| 4 | gills | = 1 pint |
| 2 | pints | = 1 quart |
| 4 | quarts | = 1 gallon |
| 31½ | gallons (sometimes 32) | = 1 barrel |
| 42 | gallons (petroleum) | = 1 barrel |
| 2 | barrels | = 1 hogshead |

## U.S. Dry Measure

| | |
|---|---|
| 2 pints | = 1 quart |
| 8 quarts | = 1 peck |
| 4 pecks | = 1 bushel |

## U.S. Linear Measure

| | | |
|---|---|---|
| 12 | inches | = 1 foot |
| 3 | feet | = 1 yard |
| 5½ | yards | = 1 rod (or pole) |
| 40 | rods | = 1 furlong |
| 8 | furlongs | = 1 mile |
| 5,280 | feet | = 1 mile |

## U.S. Square Measure

| | | |
|---|---|---|
| 144 | square inches | = 1 square foot |
| 9 | square feet | = 1 square yard |
| 30¼ | square yards | = 1 square rod |
| 16 | square rods | = 1 square chain |
| 160 | square rods | = 1 acre |
| 43,560 | square feet | = 1 acre |
| 640 | acres | = 1 square mile |
| 36 | square miles | = 1 township |

## U.S. Cubic Measure

| | |
|---|---|
| 1,728 cubic inches | = 1 cubic foot |
| 27 cubic feet | = 1 cubic yard |

## Miscellaneous Measures

| | |
|---|---|
| 128 cubic feet | = 1 cord (of wood) |
| 6 feet | = 1 fathom |
| 6076.1155 feet | = 1 nautical mile |
| 1 knot | = 1 nautical mile in 1 hour |
| 12 dozen | = 1 gross |
| 500 sheets | = 1 ream |
| 500 pounds | = 1 bale (of cotton) |
| ⅕ gallon | = 1 fifth (wine measure) |
| 4 inches | = 1 hand (horse's height) |

## METRIC TABLES

### Length

| | | |
|---|---|---|
| Myriameter | 10,000 meters | 6.2137 miles |
| Kilometer | 1,000 meters | 0.62137 mile |
| Hectometer | 100 meters | 328 feet 1 inch |
| Dekameter | 10 meters | 393.7 inches |
| Meter | 1 meter | 39.37 inches |
| Decimeter | 0.1 meter | 3.937 inches |
| Centimeter | 0.01 meter | 0.3937 inch |
| Millimeter | 0.001 meter | 0.0394 inch |

### Area

| | | |
|---|---|---|
| Hectare | 10,000 square meters | 2.471 acres |
| Are | 100 square meters | 119.6 square yards |
| Centiare | 1 square meter | 1,550 square inches |

# Appendix 3.
# Signs and Symbols

## ACCENTS

- ✀ acute
- ˘ breve
- ₃ cedilla
- ∧ circumflex
- .. dieresis
- ＼ grave
- ⁻ macron
- ~ tilde

## ARROWS

- → direction
- ↖ direction
- ↦ direction
- ↱ direction
- ↷ direction
- ← bold arrow
- ▷ open arrow
- ⇌ reversible reaction

## BULLETS

- ● solid circle; bullet
- ● bold center dot
- ● movable accent

## CHEMICAL

- ⁰/₀₀ salinity
- ℳ minim
- ⊪ exchange
- ↑ gas

## CIRCLED SYMBOLS

- ⊙ angle in circle
- ⊕ circle with parallel rule
- ⊿ triangle in circle
- ⊙ dot in circle

- ⊿ dot in triangle in circle
- ⊕ cross in circle
- © copyright
- ① Ceres
- ② Pallas
- ③ Juno
- ④ Vesta

## CODE

- · No. 1 6 pt. code dot
- · No. 2 8 pt. code dot
- · No. 3 10 pt. code dot
- ● No. 4 8 pt. code dot
- ● No. 4 10 pt. code dot
- ₌ No. 1 6 pt. code dash
- ─ No. 2 8 pt. code dash
- ─ No. 3 10 pt. code dash
- ▬ No. 4 8 pt. code dash
- ▬ No. 4 10 pt. code dash

## COMPASS

- ° degree
- ⊙ degree with period
- ′ minute
- ⸴ minute with period
- ″ second
- ⸵ second with period
- ⸜ canceled second

## DECORATIVE

- ✚ bold cross
- ✛ cross patte
- ◼ cross patte
- ▨ cross patte

- ✹ (184 N)
- ⚷ key
- ⚚ (206 N)
- ¶ paragraph

## ELECTRICAL

- ℜ reluctance
- ↔ reaction goes both right and left
- ↕ reaction goes both up and down
- ↕ reversible
- → direction of flow; yields
- → direct current
- ⇄ electrical current
- ⇄ reversible reaction
- ⇌ reversible reaction
- ⇄ alternating current
- ⇌ alternating current
- ⇌ reversible reaction beginning at left
- ⇄ reversible reaction beginning at right
- Ω ohm; omega
- MΩ megohm; omega
- μΩ microohm; mu omega
- ω angular frequency, solid angle; omega
- Φ magnetic flux; phi
- Ψ dielectric flux; electrostatic flux; psi
- γ conductivity; gamma

## ELECTRICAL—Con.

$\rho$ resistivity; rho
$\Lambda$ equivalent conductivity
HP horsepower

## MATHEMATICAL

— vinculum (above letters)
$\div$ geometrical proportion
$-\colon$ difference, excess
$\parallel$ parallel
$\parallel s$ parallels
$\ne\parallel$ not parallels
$|\ |$ absolute value
$\cdot$ multiplied by
$\colon$ is to; ratio
$\div$ divided by
$\therefore$ therefore; hence
$\because$ because
$\colon\colon$ proportion; as
$\ll$ is dominated by
$>$ greater than
$\sqsubset$ greater than
$\geqq$ greater than or equal to
$\geqq$ greater than or equal to
$\gtrless$ greater than or less than
$\not>$ is not greater than
$<$ less than
$\sqsupset$ less than
$\lessgtr$ less than or greater than
$\not<$ is not less than
$\prec$ smaller than
$\leqq$ less than or equal to
$\leqq$ less than or equal to
$\geqq$ or $\geq$ greater than or equal to
$\lesssim$ equal to or less than
$\lesseqgtr$ equal to or less than
$\gtreqless$ is not greater than equal to or less than
$\gtrsim$ equal to or greater than
$\lesseqgtr$ is not less than equal to or greater than
$\perp$ equilateral
$\perp$ perpendicular to
$\vdash$ assertion sign
$\doteq$ approaches

## MATHEMATICAL—Con.

$\doteqdot$ approaches a limit
$\veebar$ equal angles
$\ne$ not equal to
$\equiv$ identical with
$\not\equiv$ not identical with
score
$\approx$ or $\doteqdot$ nearly equal to
$=$ equal to
$\sim$ difference
$\simeq$ perspective to
$\cong$ congruent to approximately equal
$\eqsim$ difference between
geometrically equivalent to
$($ included in
$)$ excluded from
$\subset$ is contained in
$\cup$ logical sum or union
$\cap$ logical product or intersection
$\sqrt{\phantom{x}}$ radical
$\sqrt{\phantom{x}}$ root
$\sqrt[2]{\phantom{x}}$ square root
$\sqrt[3]{\phantom{x}}$ cube root
$\sqrt[4]{\phantom{x}}$ fourth root
$\sqrt[5]{\phantom{x}}$ fifth root
$\sqrt[6]{\phantom{x}}$ sixth root
$\pi$ pi
$\epsilon$ base (2.718) of natural system of logarithms; epsilon
$\epsilon$ is a member of; dielectric constant; mean error; epsilon
$+$ plus
$+$ bold plus
$-$ minus
$-$ bold minus
$/$ shill(ing); slash; virgule
$\pm$ plus or minus
$\mp$ minus or plus
$\times$ multiplied by
$=$ bold equal
$\#$ number
per
$\%$ percent
$\int$ integral
$\lceil$ single bond
$\diagdown$ single bond
$\diagup$ single bond

## MATHEMATICAL—Con.

$\parallel$ double bond
$\diagdown\diagdown$ double bond
$\diagup\diagup$ double bond
$\langle\rangle$ benzene ring
$\partial$ or $\delta$ differential; variation
$\partial$ Italian differential
$\rightarrow$ approaches limit of
$\sim$ cycle sine
$\diagdown$ horizontal integral
$\oint$ contour integral
$\propto$ variation; varies as
$\Pi$ product
$\Sigma$ summation of; sum; sigma
$!$ or $\lfloor$ factorial product

## MEASURE

℔ pound
ʒ dram
fʒ fluid dram
℥ ounce
f℥ fluid ounce
O pint

## MISCELLANEOUS

§ section
† dagger
‡ double dagger
℀ account of
℅ care of
score
¶ paragraph
þ Anglo-Saxon
₵ center line
♂ conjunction
$\perp$ perpendicular to
″ or " ditto
$\propto$ variation
℞ recipe
⅃ move right
⊏ move left
○ or ⊙ or ① annual
⊙⊙ or ② biennial
∈ element of
℈ scruple
f function
! exclamation mark
⊞ plus in square
♃ perennial

## MISCELLANEOUS—Con.

- φ  diameter
- c̄  mean value of c
- U  mathmodifier
- ⊏  mathmodifier
- ⊡  dot in square
- △  dot in triangle
- ⊠  station mark
- @  at

### MONEY

- ¢  cent
- ¥  yen
- £  pound sterling
- ₥  mills

### MUSIC

- ♮  natural
- ♭  flat
- ♯  sharp

### PLANETS

- ☿  Mercury
- ♀  Venus
- ⊕  Earth
- ♂  Mars
- ♃  Jupiter
- ♄  Saturn
- ♅  Uranus
- ♆  Neptune
- ♇  Pluto
- ☊  dragon's head, ascending node
- ☋  dragon's tail, descending node
- ☌  conjunction
- ☍  opposition
- ☉ or ⊙  Sun
- ☉  Sun's lower limb
- ☉  Sun's upper limb
- ☽  solar corona
- ⊕  solar halo
- ☽  Moon
- ●  new Moon
- ☽  first quarter
- ◑  first quarter
- ◐  third quarter
- ◑  last quarter
- ☾  last quarter
- ◑  last quarter
- ○  full Moon
- ☺  full Moon

## PLANETS—Con.

- ☽  eclipse of Moon
- ♉  lunar halo
- ∪  lunar corona
- ⚳  Ceres
- ⚵  Juno

### PUNCTUATION

- { }  braces
- [ ]  brackets
- ( )  parentheses
- ⟨ ⟩  square parentheses; angle brackets
- ¡  Spanish open quote
- ¿  Spanish open quote

### SEX

- ♂ or ⚨  male
- ☐  male, in charts
- ♀  female
- ○  female, in charts
- ⚨  hermaphrodite

### SHAPES

- ◆  solid diamond
- ◇  open diamond
- ○  circle
- ▲  solid triangle
- △  triangle
- ☐  square
- ■  solid square
- ▱  parallelogram
- ▭  rectangle
- ▤  double rectangle
- ★  solid star
- ☆  open star
- ∟  right angle
- ∠  angle
- √  check
- ✓  check
- ß  German ss
- ß  italic German ss
- ☛  solid index
- ☛  solid index
- ☜  index
- ☞  index

### GEOLOGIC SYSTEMS [1]

- Q  Quaternary
- T  Tertiary
- K  Cretaceous

- J  Jurassic
- Ⅻ  Triassic
- P  Permian
- ℙ  Pennsylvanian
- M  Mississippian
- D  Devonian
- S  Silurian
- O  Ordovician
- Є  Cambrian
- pЄ  Precambrian
- C  Carboniferous

### VERTICAL

- |  5 unit vertical
- |  8 point vertical
- |  9 unit vertical

### WEATHER

- T  thunder
- ⚡  thunderstorm; sheet lightning
- ⟨  sheet lightning
- ↓  precipitate
- ⦿  rain
- ←  floating ice crystals
- ↔  ice needles
- ▲  hail
- ⊗  sleet
- ∞  glazed frost
- ⊔  hoarfrost
- V  frostwork
- ✳  snow or sextile
- ⊠  snow on ground
- ⊹  drifting snow (low)
- ≡  fog
- ∞  haze
- ⌂  Aurora

### ZODIAC

- ♈  Aries; Ram
- ♉  Taurus; Bull
- ♊  Gemini; Twins
- ♋  Cancer; Crab
- ♌  Leo; Lion
- ♍  Virgo; Virgin
- ♎  Libra; Balance
- ♏  Scorpio; Scorpion
- ♐  Sagittarius; Archer
- ♑  Capricornus; Goat
- ♒  Aquarius; Water bearer
- ♓  Pisces; Fishes

[1] Standard letter symbols used by the Geological Survey on geologic maps. Capital letter indicates the system and one or more lowercased letters designate the formation and member where used.

# Appendix 4.
# Proofreading Marks

| | | | |
|---|---|---|---|
| ⊙ | Insert period | *rom.* | Roman type |
| ⋀ | Insert comma | *caps.* | Caps—used in margin |
| : | Insert colon | ≡ | Caps—used in text |
| ; | Insert semicolon | *c+sc* | Caps & small caps—used in margin |
| ? | Insert question mark | ≡ | Caps & small caps—used in text |
| ! | Insert exclamation mark | *l.c.* | Lowercase—used in margin |
| =/ | Insert hyphen | / | Used in text to show deletion or substitution |
| ⩒ | Insert apostrophe | | |
| ⩣⩣ | Insert quotation marks | ℓ | Delete |
| $\frac{1}{N}$ | Insert 1-en dash | ℨ | Delete and close up |
| $\frac{1}{M}$ | Insert 1-em dash | *w.f.* | Wrong font |
| # | Insert space | ⌒ | Close up |
| *ld>* | Insert ( ) points of space | ⊐ | Move right |
| *shill* | Insert shilling | ⊏ | Move left |
| ∨ | Superior | ⊓ | Move up |
| ∧ | Inferior | ⊔ | Move down |
| (/) | Parentheses | ‖ | Align vertically |
| [/] | Brackets | = | Align horizontally |
| ☐ | Indent 1 em | ⊐⊏ | Center horizontally |
| ☐☐ | Indent 2 ems | ⊔⊓ | Center vertically |
| ⁋ | Paragraph | *eq.#* | Equalize space—used in margin |
| *no* ⁋ | No paragraph | ∨∨∨ | Equalize space—used in text |
| *tr* | Transpose [1]—used in margin | ........ | Let it stand—used in text |
| ∼ | Transpose [2]—used in text | *stet.* | Let it stand—used in margin |
| *sp* | Spell out | ⊗ | Letter(s) not clear |
| *ital* | Italic—used in margin | *run over* | Carry over to next line |
| ___ | Italic—used in text | *run back* | Carry back to preceding line |
| *b.f.* | Boldface—used in margin | *out, see copy* | Something omitted—see copy |
| ∿ | Boldface—used in text | *?/?* | Question to author to delete [3] |
| *s.c.* | Small caps—used in margin | ∧ | Caret—General indicator used to mark position of error. |
| ≡ | Small caps—used in text | | |

# Corrected Proof

reset 8pt. C & SC

It does not appear that the earliest printers had any method of correcting errors before the form was on the press. The learned correctors of the first two centuries of printing were not proofreaders in our sense; they were rather what we should term office editors. Their labors were chiefly to see that the proof corresponded to the copy, but that the printed page was correct in its latinity—that the words were there, and that the sense was right. They cared but little about orthography, bad letters, or purely printers' errors, and when the text seemed to them wrong they consulted fresh authorities or altered it on their own responsibility. Good proofs, in the modern sense, were impossible until professional readers were employed—men who had first a printer's education, and then spent many years in the correction of proof. The orthography of English, which for the past century has undergone little change, was very fluctuating until after the publication of Johnson's Dictionary, and capitals, which have been used with considerable regularity for the past 80 years, were previously used on the miss or hit plan. The approach to regularity, so far as we have, may be attributed to the growth of a class of professional proofreaders, and it is to them that we owe the correctness of modern printing. More errors have been found in the Bible than in any other one work. For many generations it was frequently the case that Bibles were brought out stealthily, from fear of governmental interference. They were frequently printed from imperfect texts, and were often modified to meet the views of those who publised them. The story is related that a certain woman in Germany, who was the wife of a printer, had become disgusted with the continual assertions of the superiority of man over woman which she had heard, hurried into the composing room while her husband was at supper and altered a sentence in the Bible, which he was printing, so that it read Narr instead of Herr, thus making the verse read "And he shall be thy fool" instead of "and he shall be thy lord." The word not was omitted by Barker, the king's printer in England in 1632, in printing the seventh commandment. He was fined £3,000 on this account.

# Glossary of Technological Terms

The following is a short glossary of computer and telecommunications terms. We have tried to select those words that are most appropriate for the business environment, rather than a series of technical and programming terms. Most of these words have appeared in some form in the text, and they are terms that will be important if you now use, or plan to use, computers and software. Use this handy guide to help you read through manuals and sales literature, and to make intelligent decisions based on understanding these terms.

*abort:* To cancel an operation in progress.

*acoustic coupler:* A type of modem using rubber cups that connect to a telephone handset. Used for telecommunications.

*Ada:* A structured, high-level programming language, developed by the U.S. Department of Defense.

*address:* A location in a computer's memory, identified by a number or a name.

*AI:* Artificial Intelligence, the area of computer science that attempts to create computer systems that can approximate human thinking.

*ALGOL:* Acronym for ALGOrithmic Language, an older, high-level computer language used for scientific programming.

*algorithm:* A step-by-step process used to solve a problem. In computer programming, code is developed to help solve each step in an algorithm.

*alphanumeric:* Data that contains both letters and numbers.

*analog computer:* A computer that deals with variable data, used primarily in scientific and engineering applications.

*append:* To link or add files or sections of computer code to the end of another file or section.

*applications program:* A program written to perform specific tasks for the computer user, such as accounting or word processing.

*architecture:* The computer's components and the way they interrelate.

*ascending sort:* A program routine, often used in data processing, that orders information from lowest to highest (A to Z, 26 to 55).

*ASCII:* Acronym for American Standard Code for Information Interchange (pronounced as-key), which assigns a seven-bit code to every letter, number, punctuation symbol, and output command (128 in all).

*asynchronous:* Indicating in code the beginning or end of a segment of data.

*backup:* An exact copy of a program or data file stored on another disk.

*bar code:* Vertical stripes or bars, each corresponding to a specific number, used for product marking and designed to be read by a computer.

*BASIC:* Acronym for Beginners All-purpose Symbolic Instruction Code, a relatively easy programming language.

*baud rate:* The speed of data transmission between computers. It is a measure of the number of signal elements that can be transmitted per second.

*BBS:* Bulletin Board System, used to provide information exchange, electronic mail, free programs, etc., accessed by computers.

*binary system:* Base 2, the mathematics system used by computers. It uses only the numbers 0 and 1, which represent on and off, yes and no, or true and false.

*bit:* The smallest unit (0 or 1) of information in a computer, standing for BInary digiT.

*boot:* To load a program into a computer.

*bubble memory:* A form of memory, coded on a chip, that retains information whether the computer's power is on or off.

*buffer:* The area in the computer's main memory used for temporary storage.

*bug:* An error in a computer program or hardware, that interferes with the computer's operation.

*bundled software:* Software programs that are packaged and sold together with hardware.

*byte:* The number of bits needed to define a character. Usually 8 bits make up a byte.

*CAD:* Acronym for Computer Aided Design, the use of computers for designing and drafting.

*CAI:* Acronym for Computer Assisted Instruction, the use of computers in education.

*card reader:* An electromechanical or photoelectric device used to read data encoded by holes punched in data cards.

*card sorter:* Equipment used to sort punched cards.

*central office:* A telephone company location where telephone lines are joined to the company's switching equipment.

*character:* A set of bits (a byte) that represents a number, letter, punctuation mark, or another symbol used on computers.

*chip:* A wafer of silicon with an integrated circuit etched onto its surface.

*command:* An instruction given to a computer, either by a program or directly from the keyboard.

*compatible:* Used in describing computers and peripherals, and meaning able to interact with other equipment, share information, and read files generated by other machines.

*computer:* A device that stores and processes information and instructions.

*computer graphics:* The broad category of images produced on or with the assistance of a computer, including charts, graphs, animation, illustration, etc.

*computer literacy:* The understanding of computers and their use.

*connect time:* The length of time a terminal or computer is connected to a mainframe computer or information network.

*control character:* A keyboard character that passes commands to the computer or an output device.

*CPU:* Central Processing Unit, the part of a computer that performs the work.

*crash:* A situation in which the computer system becomes inoperable because of a hardware or software problem.

*CRT:* Cathode-Ray Tube, the monitor or television screen used to display data. Also called VDT.

*cursor:* An illuminated block or other symbol that indicates on the video screen where the next character will appear.

*daisy wheel printer:* An impact-type printer much like a typewriter.

*data:* Information input into a computer.

*data base:* A file used to organize a collection of information stored on disk or tape.

*data processing:* The activity of a computer and a program to manipulate data.

*dedicated:* Used in describing a computer or other equipment and meaning designed for one specific task—such as dedicated word processing.

*demodulate:* To convert incoming analog signals into digital elements the computer can read.

*digital computer:* A computer that converts information into binary digits.

*direct connect modem:* A modem that plugs directly into the telephone line.

*disk:* A form of magnetic storage for computer files and programs. Disks may be hard or floppy.

*disk drive:* Much like a record turntable, this device is used to transfer data between a disk and the computer's internal memory.

*diskette:* A floppy disk.

*documentation:* The printed instructions, etc., that help explain a computer system or program. Also, comments in a program intended to help you understand the code.

*DOS:* Disk Operating System, software that controls the transfer of data between a computer and disk drives. Incompatibility arises when computers have a different DOS.

*dot matrix printer:* A printer that creates characters and other images composed of little dots in what is normally called computer printing.

*double-density disk:* A disk with quality magnetic coating that has greater information storage capacity than a regular disk.

*double-sided disk:* A disk that stores information on both sides or surfaces.

*download:* To receive information from another computer via modem.

*Dvorak keyboard:* A keyboard on a typewriter or computer whose arrangement of keys is reputed to be faster and easier to use than the standard QWERTY arrangement.

*edit:* To make corrections, additions, deletions, or other changes to a program, text, or other type of data.

*emulation:* The process in which one system or device mimics another; often used in communications software to permit a microcomputer to talk to a mainframe.

*encrypted disk:* A programmed disk that permits only authorized users to access the disk's files.

*ENIAC:* Electronic Numerical Integrator And Calculator, one of the earliest computers.

*ergonomics:* The field of study of the problems of people in relation to equipment and procedures.

*executive workstation:* This term has two meanings: first, a desk that is designed to be ergonomically compatible with computers—an electronic desk; second, a telephone/computer combination.

*facsimile machine:* Equipment that transmits and receives text over telephone lines and creates an exact copy of the information that was sent. Especially valuable in transmitting illustrations.

*field:* The smallest unit of information stored in a data file.

*FIFO:* First In, First Out, a method in which data is processed by a computer.

*file:* Information stored under a single heading.

*floating point:* A mathematical system that can handle decimal numbers, allowing for greater storage capabilities.

*floppy disk:* A thin, flexible plastic storage medium. See *disk.*

*form letter:* A document meant to be sent to many people; multiple copies are printed with small changes in each, usually name, address, and other personal items. Most word processing programs can be used to produce these letters and make them appear completely personalized.

*full duplex:* Used in describing communication between computers in which each can receive *and* transmit in two directions at the same time.

*function keys:* Keys used to perform specific tasks other than printing a letter, number, or punctuation mark; often used to change margins, type repetitive phrases, etc.

*GIGO:* Garbage In, Garbage Out; if inaccurate information is input into the computer, inaccurate information will be generated.

*global:* Occurring everywhere in the system or program. In word processing, it often describes the process of locating every mention of a letter or word and then replacing or changing that item.

*graphics:* Pictorial representation of data, whether graphs, charts, diagrams.

*half duplex:* Used in describing communication between computers in which each system can either receive or transmit data but cannot do both at once.

*hard copy:* Usually a printout, but may be a photograph of a computer screen.

*hard disk:* A magnetic storage medium, with greater storage capacity than a floppy disk. See *disk.*

*hardware:* The mechanical and electric parts of a computer system.

*high resolution:* Used in describing the clarity and number of pixels on a computer monitor: the higher the resolution, the clearer the picture.

*information utility:* A commercial data base, such as CompuServe or The Source, available for access by computer users.

*ink-jet printer:* A nonimpact dot matrix printer, whose printhead sprays tiny jets of ink onto the paper. It is extremely quiet and very fast.

*input:* To enter data into a computer, via keyboard, storage medium, or punch card.

*interactive:* Used in describing a system or program that can work with other programs, or a program that prompts the user for a response before executing the next phase of an operation.

*I/O:* Input/Output, the process of moving data in and out of computers.

*joystick:* A device used to control the cursor on a computer. Usually used with games.

*justify:* In a text formatting mode, to add extra space between words in a line of type in order to produce margins that are flush either on the right or the left or on both sides.

*K, or Kb:* Kilobyte: A measure of the number of bytes in a computer. Although "kilo" usually equals 1,000, in the computer it is 1,024. Thus a computer with 64K of RAM actually has 65,536 bytes.

*keypunch:* The operation of encoding cards by punching holes into them for computer use.

*LAN:* Local Area Network, used to connect computers to each other in order to permit the sharing of software and peripherals.

*laser printing:* A high-speed, nonimpact type of printing that uses concentrated light beams to produce an extremely high-quality image.

*letter quality:* Used to describe a standard for computer printer type that looks like the type produced by a standard office typewriter. Normally produced by daisywheel printers.

*LIFO:* Last In, First Out, the usual order in which data are taken from a stack in a computer program.

*log on:* To enter the required password or identification number in order to begin a session at the terminal. Usually required in information networks and bulletin boards.

*loop:* The copper wires that connect your telephone system to the central telephone office.

*magnetic media:* Electromagnetic devices that can store data, such as hard and floppy disks, tape, etc.

*mainframe:* A large computer with storage and processing capacities far beyond those of the smaller mini- and microcomputers.

*memory:* The general term for devices that store data in a computer system. See *RAM* and *ROM*.

*menu:* A list of choices displayed on the CRT from which you instruct the program and machine what you wish to do next.

*merge:* To combine program or data files in the computer.

*microcomputer:* Any computer built on a microprocessor, the circuits of which are etched onto a silicon chip. The processing and speeds of microcomputers are based on their bit sizes, many machines using 8-bit, 16-bit, or 32-bit words.

*minicomputer:* Term for a small computer, used in business and science before "microcomputer" took over. Actually, there is little distinction between small computer types.

*modem:* Acronym for MOdulator/DEModulator, a device that modulates digital computer data into pulses that can be transmitted over telephone lines and then demodulated at the other end for the receiving computer.

*mouse:* A small, portable device that plugs into a computer and is used with specific software to control the cursor as well as other portions of a computer display screen. The mouse is rolled along the table to move the cursor, and a button is pushed to make selections from the screen.

*multiprocessing:* The use of two or more connected computers.

*network:* A linked computer system, not necessarily physically connected (hard wired).

*nonimpact printer:* A computer printer that forms characters on paper without striking it, such as a laser or ink-jet printer.

*nonvolatile:* Used to describe computer memory that is retained even after the power is turned off.

*numeric keypad:* A separate set of number keys on many computer keyboards, like those on a calculator, that can be used for faster numeric data entry.

*OCR:* Optical Character Recognition, a process that can scan printed characters on a page and translate them into the computer without manual entry.

*OEM:* Original Equipment Manufacturer, usually a company that does not manufacture computers but, rather, assembles them from other elements for sale to users.

*operating system:* Programming that drives the computer and its activities, including arithmetic, logical and relational operations, data transfer, etc.

*output:* The data produced by the computer.

*paper tape:* A paper strip into which a coded pattern of holes is punched to be read by computers, teletypes, and other machines. The original ticker tape from the stock exchange was coded paper tape.

*parallel transmission:* A system or device that transmits data several bits at a time. It is faster than serial transmission.

*password:* A group of characters that a user inputs into a program or operating system to restrict access to specified individuals. It prevents unauthorized entry into private programs or data, such as accounting or personnel records.

*PBX:* Private Branch Exchange, an electronic switch that acts as a computerized switchboard.

*peripheral:* A device connected to and controlled by a computer, such as a printer.

*PERT:* Acronym for Program Evaluation and Review Technique, a method of tracking work flow.

*pin feed:* A device that guides continuous feed paper through a computer printer. The paper has a series of holes along the edges that fit onto sprockets on the pin feeder, controlling the even flow of the paper.

*pixel:* Usually a tiny dot representing a single position on a computer display.

*portables:* A category of computers that are usually small in size and easily transported, including lap-sized machines, as well as briefcase and handheld computers.

*printer:* A device that receives data from a computer in digital code and translates it into symbols on paper. There are two basic types: impact and nonimpact.

*printout:* The hard copy produced by the printer.

*program:* An ordered set of instructions written in a structured language that passes operating commands to the computer.

*punch card:* A paper card encoded with punched holes that is read by a computer.

*QWERTY:* The standard arrangement of keys on a computer or typewriter keyboard, named for the six keys on the left side of the top row of letters.

*RAM:* Random Access Memory, the active memory of the computer, which can be written to or read from. If you turn off the computer without storing the data, the RAM is erased.

*random access:* The method of reaching a position in an array or group of data without following all of the data sequentially. For example, random access permits the computer to locate any information beginning with the letter L without going through all of the letters of the alphabet to reach L.

*record:* A collection of related data.

*ROM:* Read Only Memory, the permanently installed memory encoded on chips in the computer, which holds programming language, operation systems, or other data that usually cannot be changed by the user. The ROM is not lost when the machine is turned off.

*scrolling:* The movement of the lines on the screen, through the use of the cursor, as additional data or words are input.

*search:* To locate an entry in a data file.

*sequential access:* The method of searching in sequential order through an entire file to find the desired material, the opposite of random access.

*serial transmission:* A method of handling data in which bits are transmitted one at a time.

*software:* Computer programs that instruct the computer in its operations.

*spreadsheet:* A financial program that permits manipulation of rows and columns of numbers and automatic recalculations, to increase the speed and productivity of financial modeling.

*storage:* Data retained on disk or tape.

*synchronous:* Used to describe a method of data transmission in which the signals are precisely timed.

*system:* The computer and its peripherals, such as disk drives, printers, modems, etc.

*telecommunications:* Any communication over telephone lines, including voice, data, or videotex.

*thermal printer:* A dot matrix printer that creates an impression on paper using heated wires on heat-sensitive paper.

*transmit:* To send data from computer to computer or over telephone lines.

*turnkey system:* A computer system that is complete and ready to use.

*user:* Any person other than a programmer who operates a computer system.

*user friendly:* A term, now a cliché, that indicates that a program or computer is easy to use.

*VDT:* Visual Display Terminal. See *CRT.*

*video monitor:* A computer display or CRT, similar to a television set but without sound controls. A video monitor is sharper than a TV screen and is available in monochrome or color.

*videotex:* An interactive information retrieval system through which data is transmitted by telephone wires between a distant computer and TV screen.

*voice recognition:* The ability of a computer to recognize sounds of individuals and determine differences among people.

*volatile:* Used to describe a type of computer memory that retains data only as long as the power is on.

*wafer:* The base on which a chip is created, usually a piece of silicon or germanium.

*Winchester disk drive:* The most common form of hard disk drive designed for home and business computers, which can store more than ten times as much data as a floppy disk and is much faster to use.

*window:* A separate frame on the computer display that allows a different part of a file or program to be viewed along with other material.

*word processing:* Composing words and text on a computer using the computer-assisted commands provided by a program. These commands enable the user to enter and edit text, move and delete words or paragraphs, and print out the final documents.

*word wrap:* The system by which the portion of a line exceeding the width of the screen wraps around to the start of the next line so that it can be seen.

*XON, XOFF:* Abbreviation for transmitter on, transmitter off, which informs other computers or transmitters that your machine is either ready or not ready to receive information.